The politics of the welfare state

The Politics of
the Welfare State

Edited by

Ann Oakley &
A. Susan Williams

University of London
Institute of Education

First published in 1994 by UCL Press
UCL Press Limited
University College London
Gower Street
London WC1E 6BT

The name of University College London (UCL) is a registered
trade mark used by UCL Press with the consent of the owner.

British Library Cataloguing-in-Publication Data
A CIP catalogue record for this book is available from the British Library.

ISBN: 1-85728-205-1   HB
          1-85728-206-X   PB

Library of Congress Cataloging-in-Publication Data
The Politics of the welfare state/edited by Ann Oakley & A. Susan
Williams.
         p.   cm.
    Includes bibliographical references and index.
    ISBN 1-85728-205-1 : $75.00. — ISBN 1-85728-206-X (pbk.) : $27.00
    1. Great Britain—Social policy.   2. Human services—Great
Britain.   3. Welfare state.   I. Oakley, Ann.   II. Williams, A.
Susan.
HN385.5.P395   1994
361.6'1'0941—dc20   94-12566
                                                             CIP

Typeset in Baskerville.
Printed and bound by
Biddles Ltd, Guildford and King's Lynn, England.

Contents

Notes on contributors

Mel Bartley is a researcher in Public Health Policy at Nuffield College, University of Oxford. Her main interests are in health inequality and the relationship between health and unemployment.

Nick Black is a Reader in Public Health Medicine and Head of the Health Services Research Unit at the London School of Hygiene and Tropical Medicine. His principal research interests are the assessment of the effectiveness and appropriateness of health care interventions, and the implementation of research findings in health policy and services.

Tony Edwards is Professor of Education and Dean of the Faculty of Education at the University of Newcastle upon Tyne. His recent research has been on the government's promotion of parental choice in education.

Sharon Gewirtz is a researcher at the Centre for Educational Studies, University of London King's College. She is researching the rôle of market forces in secondary education and has published mainly in the field of education policy.

Chris Ham is Director and Professor of Health Policy Management at the Health Services Management Centre, University of Birmingham. His research activities include the financing and delivery of health services both within and outside the United Kingdom.

Frank Honigsbaum is an historian who has written major works on the development and present operation of the National Health Service. He is currently concentrating on the allocation of health resources.

Jane Lewis is Professor of Social Policy at the London School of Economics. She has published extensively on the history of social policy and on current social policies relating to gender, the family, voluntary organizations, community care and health.

Rodney Lowe is Reader in Economic and Social History in the Department of Historical Studies at the University of Bristol. He has published widely on the history of British welfare policy and is now working on the replanning of the welfare state between 1957 and 1964.

Ann Oakley is Professor of Sociology and Social Policy at the University of London Institute of Education, where she is Director of the Social Science Research

Unit. She has researched and published extensively in the areas of health, education and gender studies.

Jennie Popay is Professor of Community Health Studies at the University of Salford and Director of the Public Health Research and Resource Centre, Bolton, Salford/Trafford and Wigan Health Authorities. Her research interests include gender and social class inequalities in health, and the nature of relationships between lay and professional knowledge of health, illness and health care.

Sheila Rowbotham is the author of several books on women's history and is a Simon Senior Research Fellow in the Sociology Department at Manchester University. She is currently writing a history of British and American women in the 20th century.

David Thompson is a Lecturer at the Health Services Management Centre, University of Birmingham. He has researched and published extensively in the field of management development, organization behaviour and human resource management.

Elizabeth Thompson is a researcher in the Health Services Research Unit within the Department of Public Health and Policy at the London School of Hygiene and Tropical Medicine. She is interested in the policy implications of medical audit.

Charles Webster is a Fellow of All Souls College, University of Oxford. His main activities and publications relate to medicine and science in early modern Europe and welfare in the 20th century.

Geoff Whitty is the Karl Mannheim Professor of Sociology of Education and Chair of the Department of Policy Studies at the University of London Institute of Education. His present research interests are in teacher education, health education, and the impact of recent educational reforms.

A. Susan Williams is a researcher at the Social Science Research Unit, University of London Institute of Education. Her interests include the development of the state and voluntary sectors in the provision of maternity services in 20th century Britain.

Gareth Williams is Reader in the Sociology of Health and Illness, Department of Sociology, University of Salford. He is currently working on a number of studies relating to the organization of health services and lay perspectives on health.

Introduction

Ann Oakley

This book originates from a series of seminars given at the Social Science Research Unit, the University of London Institute of Education, in the spring of 1993. As members of a relatively new research unit committed to policy-relevant work in the fields of education, health and welfare, unit staff wanted to promote an open debate of some of the key issues confronting them in their work. These issues include the implications in Britain of: the market-oriented reforms of health, education and welfare services; the shifting balance between central and local control; the changing social demography of user populations and the rôles of users in shaping service provision; and the ways in which "needs" for services are subject to particular forms of interpretation as a result of their inclusion in the political agendas of government. Underlying these questions are two broader ones, which concern the social construction of knowledge, and the philosophies and value systems that shape different meanings of "welfare", both now and in the past.

To frame and debate these questions is to engage in a pretty hefty confrontation with some of the crucial issues of our time. The debate at the seminars was wide-ranging and marked by both conflict and consensus. The intention was not to discover answers but, rather, to return to the foreground the concept of "the welfare state" in social policy analysis and research, both as a conceptual tool and as an historical/political reality. After 14 years of consecutive Conservative government in Britain, certain government policies were seen to be dismantling or undermining those established forms of welfare through which the national state had assumed centralized responsibility for the equal welfare of all its citizens.

And in that slippage which occurs between the policy formulations of government and the views of "ordinary" people, a different set of values was claimed to be emerging about the rights of different sectors of the population to have their particular needs met in particular ways.

The presentations in the seminar series provided raw material for this book. This brief introduction attempts to reflect some characteristics of the discussions that took place during the seminars, by identifying a number of basic themes running through the different contributions, and by locating these within the framework of the meanings and practice of welfare in the broadest sense.

"The welfare state": origins

The term "welfare state" is a recent one. It was invented in 1934 by Alfred Zimmern, Professor of International Relations at Oxford, then used three years later by another British academic, the economist George Schuster; they may have been picking up a usage in 1920s Germany describing the Weimar Republic (Hennessy 1992, 121). The term was popularized by the Archbishop of Canterbury in 1941 in his book *Citizen and churchman*, where he contrasted the notion of a "welfare state" with that of a "power state", which lacked a spiritual and moral commitment to the welfare of the people (Titmuss 1963, 2). The phrase assumed both political and historical power. Indeed, the historian Asa Briggs has noted the tendency for the history of the 19th and early 20th centuries to be reinterpreted in its light, so as to constitute the "origins" of the welfare state, rather than whatever other developments might have been proceeding at the same time (Briggs 1965). As was noted by both Briggs and Richard Titmuss, one of the chief analysts and defenders of the welfare state, the term was usually deployed with extraordinary vagueness. It was used loosely to denote both social and economic changes and to link the idea of comprehensive social security – "freedom from want" – with the notion of equality of opportunity through educational reform. It was used to talk about developments as diverse as the introduction of free school meals and the redefinition of citizenship to include marginal groups. It was used to contrast the 20th-century state with the *laissez-faire* state of the 19th century, and to highlight the demand for "social", as opposed to purely "political", rights. It was used to suggest a teleological notion of the evolution of the modern state, whereby the mistakes of the 19th century were replaced by the solutions of the 20th; the point about the welfare state was that things got – and had got – better and better all the time. As the phrase meant many things, so the welfare state was some kind of chameleon, changing its shape to suit a variety of purposes. In time, it generated its own myths: the myth that the welfare state existed, and the myth that the welfare state did not exist; the myths of efficiency and inefficiency; the myth of equality and sameness; and the myth of equal opportunity.

Yet the welfare state was, and is, something more than an abstraction. In Britain, as Rodney Lowe observes in his chapter in this book, the welfare state can be understood to consist of five core services: social security, education, housing, the personal social services, and the National Health Service (NHS). It was the foundation of the NHS in 1948 that heralded what is often called the "classic" phase (until 1976, when the commitment to full employment was abandoned) of the British welfare state. Although the welfare state had its key architects, notably William Beveridge and Aneurin Bevan, the pathways to planned state provision were being laid down over a long period of time. During the 19th and early 20th centuries, as Sheila Rowbotham argues in her contribution to this book, an increasing political consensus – between not only socialists and trade unionists, but also some liberals and Tories – developed about the propriety and efficiency of state intervention in promoting individual welfare. The practical experience of individuals and groups in various social reform movements added a grassroots pressure for wider state involvement in welfare. The eventual combination of a capitalist mixed economy and centralized state welfare represented a compromise between various political forces: it did not, shows Rowbotham, correspond much to the visions of many early radical socialists. The experiences of the Second World War were especially formative in creating a degree of political party consensus on the need for a post-war programme of social reconstruction and reform in response to the revealed depth and extent of social inequalities. Reports in 1939 about the dire, poverty-stricken and lice-ridden condition of many evacuated mothers and children "aroused the conscience of the nation", stimulating proposals for reform which, over the ensuing five years of war, resulted in sustained pressure for a higher standard of welfare and a deeper comprehension of social justice (Titmuss 1950, 507–8).

During the early 1940s, there was a call from voices over a broad political spectrum for economic planning, political equality and the equitable distribution of resources (Titmuss 1963). By the end of the war, the National Government had assumed a degree of responsibility for people's health and welfare which, compared to the rôle of government in the 1930s, was "little short of remarkable" (Titmuss 1950, 506). Furthermore, it had produced the Beveridge Report (1942), which stated a commitment to the abolition of want, ignorance, disease, squalor and idleness. Central to the broadening of government responsibility was the notion that central government should properly concern itself with the prevention of distress and strain among *all* sectors of society. Popular support for this notion was exemplified by the sweeping to power of the Labour Party in the 1945 General Election on a platform of social change to implement the proposals of the Beveridge Report.

A British invention?

The term "the welfare state" is usually seen as a peculiarly British invention. It did not feature much in social policy discourse in Britain, however, until its use on the other side of the Atlantic in the 1950 congressional campaign, where President Hoover declared it "a disguise for the totalitarian state" (Titmuss 1963). It was a major issue in the British 1951 election campaign. Some of the trends and tendencies that produced the term "the welfare state" in Britain can be noted in other modern industrialized societies. In 1950, the International Labour Office observed that a "new conception" was transforming pre-war systems of social insurance in many countries. Intrinsic to this conception was a broader view of the population to be covered, a closer link between benefit and need, a loosening of the tie between benefit and contribution payment, and an integration of social and economic policies, at least on the administrative level (International Labour Office 1950). The eminent Swedish economist and political scientist, Gunnar Myrdal, saw the welfare state as a feature of all "rich" Western countries, reflected in their "fairly explicit commitments to the broad goals of economic development, full employment, equality of opportunity . . . social security, and protected minimum standards as regards not only income, but nutrition, housing, health, and education for people of all regions and social groups" (Myrdal 1958, 45).

While most of the chapters in this volume address aspects of welfare within the British context, links with the international scene are made in two of them. Sheila Rowbotham considers the development of attitudes

A BRITISH INVENTION?

Collecting Family Allowance for the first time, 6 August 1946 (Hulton Deutsch Collection Limited).

to the state and welfare within the context of the international trade union movement and other European and North American influences in the late 19th and early 20th centuries (Ch. 1). In their chapter on the new politics of education (Ch. 8), Geoff Whitty and colleagues document the rise of City Technology Colleges (CTCs) against a backdrop of a general "depoliticization" process applied across the education, health and welfare domains; they claim that the British government's rhetoric of quality, diversity, parental choice, school autonomy and accountability (DFE 1992) has been echoed in some other countries (Whitty and Edwards 1992), where policies similar to those which generated CTCs have developed. Whitty and colleagues argue persuasively that some recent developments in educational policy and practice in Britain can only be understood as a reflection of deep-seated changes in the nature of modern industrialized societies. Instead of mass production and mass consumption, there is an emphasis on more differentiated and specialized production and distribution. Thus, similar changes have developed as a result of British government policy in all three spheres of education, health and welfare; for example, the devolved, local management of schools instituted by the 1988 Education Reform Act is paralleled by the move towards local fund-holding and devolved management in the health service, and by the emphasis on local needs assessment and the development of tailored care packages in the community care and social service sectors. On one level, the policy parallels across the different services can be seen to be reflecting a consistency in government philosophy. But on another level, the move away from older meanings and practices of welfare must be seen in the light of new understandings of the relationship between individuals and the state, and of their respective rights and responsibilities.

Defining welfare

The British welfare state (and, indeed, all welfare societies in the sense used by Myrdal) rests on the paradox that some people's access to health, education and personal welfare depends on the intervention of the state in other people's freedom to arrange these as they choose. This tension between constraint and opportunity, between freedom from and freedom to, between individual liberty and the principle of equal rights, runs through much discourse about welfare. How the tension is balanced is a matter of political and moral value; but its wider ideological framing in different historical periods is also important in explaining the evolution of welfare policies and practices.

In a review of structural inequalities and personal welfare for the Economic and Social Research Council's Management of Personal Welfare Initiative, Fiona Williams (1992) has identified two paradigms of welfare that offer different explanations of how and where the individual is located in relation to theories of welfare. Broadly speaking, the classic phase of the welfare state (1945–76) described by Rodney Lowe (Ch. 2) was accompanied by an understanding of welfare that emphasized the rôle of material and other structural factors in determining individual welfare. People do well or badly, depending on the social circumstances in which they find themselves. Class divisions, seen in a unidimensional light, provided the raw material for welfare intervention: in this sense, both the existence of class inequalities and the motive of eradicating these were intrinsic to post-war conceptions of welfare. The policy implications of this formulation centred on attention being paid to improving the disadvantages inherent in poor social circumstances – bad housing, inadequate education, low income, lack of employment, poor access to (poor) health care, and so on.

But, while this perspective provided a clear rationale for state intervention on all these levels, it posed a problem for the conceptualization of human agency: people were defined as reacting to their individual circumstances, rather than as seeking to shape these in creative ways. The necessary dependence of human beings on their social circumstances, it was argued, turned them too easily into victims. Over the period since the 1970s, the traditional structural paradigm of welfare came to be seen to be providing an inadequate explanation of the origins of differences between people in health and welfare outcomes. For example, why do some working-class children do better than others, given similar family settings and educational opportunities? When exposed to similar stressful life events and conditions of material disadvantage, why do some people become ill and others not? It was argued that the search for the explanation of these differences had to include some notion of individual coping strategies – some idea of humans as being capable of constructing their own lives creatively, even in "objectively" difficult conditions. Contributing to this reformulation were the objections made by feminists, by ethnic minorities and other marginalized groups, to the unidimensional notion of class intrinsic to the "old" welfare state. Men and women, and black people and white people, constitute other kinds of classes with their own distinct locations in the relations of production and reproduction. A welfare state based simply on notions of economic class will provide an inadequate challenge to gender and ethnic discrimination; moreover, forms of institutionalized welfare provision may be inappropriate to the needs of women, black people and other social minorities, who will need to create their own in "self-help" movements of various kinds (for example, women's refuges, and "Saturday schools" for black children). In the USA, as Geoff Whitty and colleagues show in Chapter 8, some educational reforms have resulted from an alliance between black groups wanting community control of schools and "new right" advocates of school choice. Similarly, in Britain, some black parents have welcomed local management of schools as a real opportunity to create more culturally appropriate forms of schooling for their children.

This "individualization" of welfare is helped by the shift from the old "politics of liberation" to a new "politics of identity". Following the black, women's and gay movements of the 1960s and 1970s, which emphasized the "sameness" of people caught in the same social structural traps, there was a new desire to celebrate diversity and difference. These challenges to the welfare state were accompanied by others. A critique developed of the hierarchical relationship suggested by the idea that some people provide welfare while others consume it, and of the notion that all relevant knowledge is held by "experts", rather than by people themselves. The substance of these challenges is explored by Jennie Popay and Gareth Williams in Chapter 4, which looks at the kinds of input provided by local communities in current NHS needs-assessment exercises, and at the rise of a "lay" epidemiology of health. This stresses the sometimes different understandings about the causes of ill-health that are derived from people's experiences, as compared with the theories of medical and epidemiological "experts". Although some of the insights offered by a community-based and needs-led approach to health care stress the old structural paradigm of the social production of health and ill-health, other findings do not pose the same challenge. In the priority setting exercises of the District Health Authorities (DHAs) explored by Chris Ham, Frank Honigsbaum and David Thompson in Chapter 5, a preference for expensive, unevaluated technological solutions is sometimes more likely to be declared by ordinary people than by care providers. But as Popay and Williams note, there is no guarantee that the voices of local people will carry as much weight in any rationing process as those of managers and clinicians: consultation is not the same thing as effective power in the priority setting process.

Buying and selling welfare

A major theme running through most of the chapters in this book is the "marketization" of welfare – the reframing of welfare policies and practices within an economic model of supply, demand, cost-efficiency and profit motives. The language used to describe this is that of "quasi-markets". Quasi-markets differ from "true" markets on both demand and supply sides: for example, the supplier is not usually out to maximize profits, and on the demand side, purchasing is financed by taxes rather than by the consumer, who may not in any case be in a position to exercise choice in purchasing. This economic model, which attempts to divide purchasing from providing, and providing from using, is characteristic of changes throughout the health, education and welfare domains. In Chapter 7, Jane Lewis explores the implications of the development of quasi-markets for the "new" community care, while Ham and colleagues look at the way the new rôle of DHAs as purchasers of health services involves complex and politically tricky decisions about the prioritization of services (Ch. 5). As both of these chapters show, a key characteristic of the "new" health and welfare services is the uneven nature of local response to devolved decision-making. The implications of this pattern for service-users are that disparities and inequalities are likely to be greater today than they were under the "old" welfare state.

Away from universalism?

The classic welfare state rested on the principle of comprehensive provision; welfare was for everyone, not just for those calculated to need it according to some formula or other. The preservation of individual freedom was regarded as being guaranteed by state intervention, rather than obstructed by it. It is difficult now to look back and to understand how promising and beneficial these principles were at the time they were introduced. For example, the NHS in 1948 meant that access to health care – which had previously been limited to men in paid employment – was established as the right of every woman, man and child in Britain.

Changes in education, health and welfare since the early 1980s in Britain represent a series of incremental moves away from universalism and towards selectivity. However, this ideological and practical shift started much earlier. In Chapter 3 Charles Webster argues that the NHS was subjected to sustained attack by the Conservatives from the 1950s onwards, and that the scale of the changes made between 1951 and 1964 represented a very significant departure from the original conception. The Conservatives' lack of commitment to the NHS prevented several key elements, according to the original blueprint, of the new service getting off the ground. A system of universal health centres, for instance, envisaged as central to the development of a comprehensive network of primary preventive services and to successful co-operation between doctors and local authorities, was held back by Conservative opposition. Only 10 centres were established in the first 12 years of the NHS, and by 1960 the health centre policy had effectively been abandoned. The Conservatives inherited the NHS at a point, in 1951, when much basic building remained to be done. During the first eight years of Conservative rule, the share of the gross national product (GNP) absorbed by the health services in fact fell.

During the 1950s and 1960s, the Conservatives attacked the NHS for two reasons: first, the provision of a universalist service, free at point of use, was not seen as a priority; and secondly, there were fears of the NHS swallowing larger and larger amounts of expenditure. This spectre of health becoming an increasingly expensive good is still around today; indeed, it is a prominent reason cited for the move towards "quasi-markets". It has also led to the explicit rationing of NHS provision. Ham and colleagues argue in Chapter 5 that this kind of priority setting has the potential to produce overall "health gain"; however, as Jane Lewis, and Popay and Williams warn (Chs 7 & 4), the current process of prioritization will not necessarily lead to a more democratic distribution of health care resources.

Some critics of the welfare state claim that spending on welfare will mushroom out of control; in the case of social security spending, for example, they warn that an ageing population will produce a monstrous tax burden. A recent analysis by John Hills and the LSE Welfare State Programme, however, shows that Britain's welfare spending has been stable as a share of the gross domestic product (GDP) for 20 years, and is notably smaller than in most other European countries (Hills 1993). It argues that there is no evidence, based on built-in trends, to support the prediction of a crisis generated by excessive spending.

Charles Webster, in Chapter 3, hangs a large question mark over the common assumption of broad political consensus about welfare provision which is said to have developed during the Second World War, remaining intact until it was fractured by the policies of Margaret Thatcher's government. In any case, it would appear that the welfare state never existed in the pure and protected form cherished in some people's memories. Jane Lewis quotes Titmuss's horticultural metaphors about the conversion of "wild and unlovely weeds" into "the most attractive flowers" that bloom all year round, by hopeful – but confused – public opinion. His target here was the fiction that community care is an easy and cheap option for securing welfare: there was a danger, he argued, of being misled by the assumptions of warmth and human kindness implied by terms such as community care, into a blindness about the human implications of moving the care of seriously ill people out of institutions (Titmuss 1968). As Lewis shows, the real social and economic costs of community care do not figure in the government's community care policy. Key principles for community care were advanced in the 1989 White Paper *Caring for people*: the promotion of independent living at home by means of domiciliary, day and respite services, encouraging the development of a flourishing private sector and securing better value for tight resources. In this schema of principles, no account was taken of whether people actually *want* community care. Nor was there consideration of the possible clash between the views of formal and informal carers, or between carers and the cared-for, or of the consequences stemming from the imperative of referring every aspect of any proposed service to the limited cash constraints.

By 1962, "the welfare state" had already become "a term of abuse" (Titmuss 1963, 3). In 1968, when Titmuss's *Commitment to welfare* was published, the merits of universalist *vis-à-vis* selective welfare services were being debated actively. Surveys of the operation of welfare services demonstrated that these depended significantly on local interpretation; thus, local authorities employed 3,000 means tests, of which 50 per cent were different from one another (Titmuss 1968, 132). Behind an apparently uniform welfare state lay, on a local level, 1,500 different operational definitions of poverty, financial hardship and ability to pay. This reality of differential, and socially differentiating, provision stretched across welfare, education and health. Class discriminated access to services and health outcomes in the old NHS as it does in the new; but strategies for tackling class, gender and ethnicity as axes of discrimination in the health sector were never developed (King's Fund Institute 1988). In the education sector, as Whitty and colleagues point out, comprehensive schooling was never as homogeneous as the notion of mass-produced welfare suggested.

Welfare gains?

Recent changes in the allocation of services contain the seeds of several interesting paradoxes. In theory, the shift from a service-led to a needs-led approach to provision places people's needs for health care more at the centre of scripts determining its shape: the vocabulary of need and needs assessment plays down the power of the medical and allied professions to provide the services they prefer to give. In this sense, the new NHS promises some containment of the "technological imperative" within medicine – the tendency for medical care to become more and more technological (and more and more expensive) (Boyle et al. 1977; Reiser 1978). It also creates the possibility of a more scientific service, as monitoring, evaluation and accountability become bywords of the new service. Yet, as Nick Black and Elizabeth Thompson show (Ch. 6), British doctors are not particularly willing to have their professional competencies evaluated. Medical audit is either seen to be what doctors already do, or is viewed as a ritualistic, time-wasting exercise that has more to do with the cost-cutting motives of central government than with the desire to rest medical practice securely on scientific evidence as to effectiveness, appropriateness and safety. While some doctors in Black and Thompson's survey were willing to have administrative aspects of their work audited, far fewer regarded their clinical activities as proper audit material; doctors described as paramount their need to retain autonomy in clinical decision-making, an autonomy that allows for medicine being an art, in which intuition plays a big rôle, rather than a "routinized" science.

"Need" is a term that can mean all things to all people. In the new jargon of the NHS, as Popay and Williams show, it has the restricted meaning of "the ability to benefit" from health care (NHSME 1991). In the assessment of need, the views of local people are to be subordinated ultimately to the doctrines of clinical epidemiology and health economics, and shackled by broad resource constraints. The point of the new NHS is not, therefore, to ensure that the people have the health service they want, but rather to persuade them that the health service they are given is the one they have chosen. In this sense, the very concept of "need" can be argued as being a paternalistic one.

Changes in the organization and administration of health, education and welfare services may, or may not, be related to changes in people's wellbeing. The nature of such links is hard to establish. During the Second World War, a more even distribution of the material resources relevant to health was associated with significant health gain; although the former is the more *likely* explanation of the latter, other factors cannot be ruled out (Titmuss 1950). Similarly, the impact on wellbeing of access to health and welfare service use has been much debated; while those with the greatest "need" use the services less (Tudor Hart 1971; Oakley 1991), some aspects of service provision may be rejected because they are culturally inappropriate (Scott-Samuel 1980). In the health sector, paternalistic and socially divisive services stressing high technology rather than primary "care" may not predict good health outcomes (Sagan 1987; Oakley et al. 1993).

However, there is no doubt that in the period of significant Conservative "dismantling" of the welfare state, social inequalities have increased
significantly. For example, although average income rose by 20 per cent
between 1981 and 1987, the lowest 10 per cent experienced a rise in
income of only half the average (DSS 1990). Against the backdrop of
overall falls in mortality, as Marmot and McDowall (1986) have shown,
the relative disadvantage of manual, compared to nonmanual, social
groups increased over the period 1970 to 1983. The systematic nature of
the links between social structure on the one hand, and health and ill-
health on the other, are well-established (Black 1980; Blaxter 1987); it
has also been shown that life expectancy is highest in those countries
with the most egalitarian income distributions (Wilkinson 1990). What
this means for the population of the UK is that the poor as a category
have increased; half of all British children, for example, live in poverty,
and this figure represents a two-and-a-half-fold increase over ten years
(Smith 1990; Children's Rights Development Unit 1993). This is a bigger increase than in any other European country (Children's Rights
Development Unit 1993).

Power and the irresponsible society

Changes in social policy take place in a context of established power relations. It is thus, paradoxically, the entrenched power of the education,
social work and medical professions that is likely to provide important
brakes to the pace and extent of change. Furthermore, the ways in which
popular thinking about health and health care has been influenced by
the professional ideology of medicine over a long period of time can
provide an important impediment to any "democratization" of health
care. As Ham and colleagues demonstrate, population-based needs
assessment may uncover a popular preference for expensive, ineffective
high-technology care, such as liver transplantation, above such lower-
cost strategies for health promotion as increased access to basic services.

Black and Thompson's study of medical audit raises another critical
issue – the implications of new knowledge for existing practice. Doctors'
activities may be audited, but how are the results of this process to be
translated into more effective future practice? This issue of the social
construction of knowledge and the uses to which it is put is addressed in
Mel Bartley's contribution to this volume (Ch. 9). Bartley takes a detailed

13

look at the debate about the links between unemployment and health over the period 1979 to 1987. She shows that whether or not something is considered to be known in an active, policy-relevant, sense does not depend on the strength of the established "facts". Rather, the moving of research findings out of the domain of academic knowledge and into the policy field depends on an entrepreneurial process that determines the status of research findings as knowledge claims; it also depends on the ways in which these claims attract the support of social groups and networks with sufficient power to impose these claims on the policy decision-making process. Substantial academic evidence of a causal link between joblessness and ill-health has effectively been dismissed by a policy context that is reluctant to return to the structural paradigm of the old welfare state. This is one factor. The other is the social and power relations of medicine itself. The major proponents of the "unemployment is bad for health" argument, community medicine doctors, were themselves responding to changes in their own function which threatened to strip them of their traditional rôle as guardians of public health. In stressing the impact of social disadvantage on health, the community medicine doctors were thus both re-emphasizing their traditional function, and speaking with a voice that was not listened to in policy circles.

One conclusion is that in the new model of welfare provision, the devolution of decision-making within an economic model of quasi-markets hides the continuing power of central government to enforce policy decisions. How, for example, are the needs expressed by local communities as a result of needs-assessment exercises to be squared with the *Health of the nation* targets selected by central government? How is it, as Lewis asks, that the policy of community care for the elderly has been developed without any consultation with elderly people themselves? Whitty and colleagues suggest that the effect of recent policy changes may be primarily to give the *appearance* of removing welfare from the political arena. In a process of "decentralizing" blame, responsibility for decision-making appears to be shifted conveniently from central government to local corporations of managers and users; the result is that central government is exonerated from errors, either of commission or omission. Similarly, behind the rhetoric of "consumer choice" lies the division between those who are in a position to choose and those who are not, and between those who determine the shape of those choices and those who have choice determined for them. This division is likely to be as inequitable now as it was when analysts of the "old" welfare state revealed the abuses of power that resulted from the privatization of choice by the market in fields as apparently diverse as occupational pensions (Titmuss 1962) and the availability of blood for transfusion (Titmuss 1970).

Among the many myths of the welfare state is the one that ties the classic welfare state to inevitable economic inefficiency. Lowe's study of the classic phase shows the extent to which the linking of economic and social policies resulted in a system that functioned well to secure collective welfare on a low-cost basis. The old welfare state represented value for money which, under the new system's equation of value *with* money, is unlikely to be the case. Indeed, many of the contributions in this volume detail the inefficiencies that result from the current marketization of welfare.

Conclusion

While both government rhetoric and welfare practice enforce the view that individualized and marketized welfare is ensuring significant gains in terms of choice and cost-containment, the evidence of the contributors to this volume points in the opposite direction. Changes in health, education and welfare provision have introduced more choice for a few, at the expense of a lower quality of service for many. This is one of the hidden costs of a quasi-market system. Part of the economic efficiency of the old welfare state lay in the equitable distribution of a wide range of social costs and benefits.

Whereas the old paradigm of welfare, which stressed the dependence of individual welfare on material circumstances, is not promoted by the new language of choice and enablement, a powerful groundswell of opinion remains in the community on the need for health promotion to attend first and foremost to material disadvantage and inequity. Without decent living circumstances – and the full employment which accompanied, not coincidentally, the classic phase of the welfare state in Britain – the rhetoric of choice remains an empty and meaningless one.

There are questions, too, about the real extent of change underlying the apparent upheaval in welfare policies and the swings of rhetoric from "rights", "equity" and "entitlement", to the individualized language of choice and quantitatively-assessed need. As Whitty and colleagues put it in Chapter 8 of this volume: "To regard the current espousal of hetero-

15

geneity, pluralism and local narratives as indicative of a new social order may be to mistake phenomenal forms for structural relations." While some things may seem to have changed a lot, others have stayed exactly the same. The future may well see a return to the old questions about welfare, and the framing of a revitalized language of people's rights to a collective and comprehensive welfare system. As Titmuss put it in 1968 (122): "The challenge that faces us is not the choice between universalist and selective services. The real challenge resides in the question: what particular infrastructure of universalist services is needed in order to provide a framework of values and opportunity bases within and around which can be developed acceptable selective services provided, as social rights, on criteria of the *needs* of specific categories, groups and territorial areas, and not dependent on *individual tests of means?*"

References

Black, D. 1980. *Inequalities in health: report of a research working group.* London: Department of Health and Social Security.

Blaxter, M. 1987. Evidence on inequality in health from a national survey. *Lancet* 4 July, 30–3.

Boyle, G., D. Elliot, R. Roy, 1977. *The politics of technology.* New York: Longman.

Briggs, A. 1965. The Welfare State in historical perspective. In *Social welfare institutions: a sociological reader,* M. N. Zald (ed.). New York: John Wiley.

Children's Rights Development Unit 1993. *Children's right to an adequate standard of living: a consultation document.* London: Children's Rights Development Unit.

DFE (Department for Education) 1992. *Choice and diversity: a new framework for schools.* London: HMSO.

DSS (Department of Social Security) 1990. *Households below average income: a statistical analysis 1981–7.* London: Government Statistical Service.

Hennessy, Peter 1992 (rpt. 1993) *Never again.* London: Vintage.

Hills, J. 1993 *The future of welfare: a guide to the debate.* York: Joseph Rowntree Foundation.

International Labour Office 1950. *Objectives and minimum standards of social security.* International Labour Conference, 34th Session.

King's Fund Institute 1988. *Health and health services in Britain, 1948–88: a background paper for a King's Fund Conference to celebrate the 40th anniversary of the National Health Service.* London: King's Fund Institute.

Marmot, M. G., & M. E. McDowall, 1986. Mortality decline and widening social inequalities. *Lancet* (2 August), 274–6.

Myrdal, G. 1958. *Beyond the Welfare State.* London: Duckworth.

REFERENCES

NHSME (National Health Service Management Executive) 1991. *Assessing health care needs: a NHS project discussion paper.* London: NHSME.

Oakley, A. 1991. Using medical care – the views of high risk mothers. *Health Services Research* **26**(5), 651–69.

Oakley, A., A. S. Rigby, D. Hickey 1993. Women and children last? Class, health and the maternal and child health services. *European Journal of Public Health* **3**, 220–6.

Reiser, S. J. 1978. *Medicine and the reign of technology.* Cambridge: Cambridge University Press.

Scott-Samuel, A. 1980. Why don't they want our health services? *Lancet* (23 February), 412–3.

Sagan, L. A. 1987. *The health of nations.* New York: Basic Books.

Smith, T. 1990. Poverty and health in the 1990s. *British Medical Journal* **301**, 349–50.

Titmuss, R. M. 1950. *Problems of social policy.* London: HMSO.

Titmuss, R. M. 1962. *Income distribution and social change.* London: Allen & Unwin.

Titmuss, R. M. 1963. The welfare state: images and realities. *Social Service Review* **37**(1), 1–11.

Titmuss, R. M. 1968. *Commitment to welfare.* London: Allen & Unwin.

Titmuss, R. M. 1970. *The gift relationship.* London: Allen & Unwin.

Tudor Hart, J. 1971. The inverse care law. *Lancet* (27 February), 405–12.

Whitty, G. & T. Edwards. 1992. School choices in Britain and the USA: their origins and significance. Paper presented at the American Educational Research Association annual meeting, San Francisco, 20–24 April.

Wilkinson, R. G. 1990. Income distribution and mortality: a "natural" experiment. *Sociology of Health and Illness* **12**(4), 391–412.

Williams, F. 1992. Structural inequalities and the management of personal welfare: a selective literature review and assessment. Unpublished manuscript.

1

Interpretations of welfare and approaches to the state, 1870–1920

Sheila Rowbotham

Introduction

Today in Britain, as many of the welfare gains of the late 19th and early 20th centuries are being whittled away, new questions need to emerge about the origins and early forms of welfare. In particular, a critical assessment is required of the ways in which policies on reproduction and economic production have converged in the context of the development of state intervention. Such an assessment requires an examination of attitudes towards the rôle of the state and of earlier interpretations of the meaning of welfare.

Attitudes towards the rôle of the state have changed over time, and have caused conflict not only between those on the political right wing, and those on the left, but also *within* both political camps. This is partly because the intervention of the state in people's affairs and individual liberty are difficult to balance; and partly because an unresolved dilemma of democracy is to what extent should the powers of a government accord with the interests of a majority, or give protection to specific groups of underprivileged citizens? Currently, there is considerable scepticism about the state's contribution in democratizing society. It is true that in modern welfare states class, gender and race have all created obstacles preventing equal access to policy-making and resources. It is also the case that there have been differing interpretations of the welfare needs of various groups, within which are implicit class and gender prejudices. Racism and imperialism have similarly structured the way that welfare policies have developed. On the other hand, the power of the state has been a significant means of checking the influence of the short-term goals and narrow aspirations of a market-oriented capitalism; as a result, subordinated groups have benefited from the state's authority, as well as from the resources it controls.

This chapter offers a critical assessment of attitudes towards the rôle of the state between 1870 and 1920 in the UK, when various intellectual and social factors combined to present a new approach to economic and social welfare. A set of ideological attitudes took shape, which were to have a significant impact on the social organization of both production and reproduction. In this period there was a shift in emphasis away from the freedom of the individual, towards the collective responsibility of the state for the "welfare" of its citizens. A view developed of society as organic, supplanting the image of society as a collection of freely competing atoms that had prevailed in the middle of the 19th century. The impetus for this shift came partly from the economic and social problems that had accumulated in the process of industrialization, and partly from the new reality of a limited working-class franchise from the late 1860s. It was a shift that had wide-ranging implications for economic theory, for approaches to industrial relations, and for social policies.

The new economics

In the 1870s, a crisis arose in the authority of the *laissez-faire* free-market economic concepts, which had coasted along through the middle years of the century. The liberal author of *Principles of political economy*, John Stuart Mill, had recanted on the wages fund – the economic "law" which held that a fixed amount could go to wage earners, making futile any efforts to raise wages. There was uncertainty about the laws of supply and demand, and there seemed to be no authoritative reply available to give to workers who demanded a larger share of the wealth of the nation. At the same time, schemes involving nationalization of land, which were being proposed by an American called Henry George, became increasingly popular with British workers. In addition, the economic writings of John Ruskin, the art critic with a social message, now seemed important rather than quaint: they were finding a resonance among many thoughtful workers and anxious, upper-middle-class intellectuals.

Ruskin was never a radical. He was an autocratic and conservative thinker who did not accept the concept of individual liberty and was anxious to promote a harmony among the classes that was based on duties, rather than rights. In the process of advocating such a society, however, he overturned the prevailing consensus about the proper relations of state and economy, and state and society. In the Preface to *The political economy of art*, first published in 1857, he wrote:

> Political economy means, in plain English, nothing more than citizens' economy; and its first principles ought therefore to be understood by all those who mean to take the responsibility of citizens, as those of household economy, economy by all who take the responsibility of householders (Ruskin 1857, xvii).

Economy, he argued, should not be assumed to mean the saving, but rather the administration or "stewardship", of money or time (Ruskin 1857, 4–5). He suggested that human capacity was a form of wealth, and that the consummation and outcome of economic wealth should result in the production "of as many as possible, full-breathed, bright-eyed and happy hearted human creatures"; in this way, he said, "multitudes of human creatures" would not have to remain in a "dim-eyed and narrow chested state of being" (Ruskin 1862, 152). Ruskin's criticism of *laissez-faire* was to be important in the development of the view that the state was responsible for welfare: it inspired liberal men and women reformers in the 1870s and also influenced the socialist movement emerging in Britain from the 1880s. Several separate strands of collectivism thus developed simultaneously, and were often confused by contemporaries.

As a response to these ideas, attempts were made from the 1870s to revise economic theory in order to establish the old orthodoxies as hegemonic imperatives. Alfred Marshall, an economist in Cambridge, advocated that economics should be reinstated as a science, capable of explaining the economic mechanisms at work in capitalist society as an ethical and just distribution of wealth. One of the originators of the "marginal utility" school, which refuted theories of value based on labour, emphasizing individual consumer choices and advocating increased productivity rather than redistribution, Marshall believed economists should leave the ivory tower. Only by becoming evangelical could they combat arguments for land nationalization and socialist ideas. Economists had "to go out into the market place", he said, "to slay the old fallacies again and again before their [the people's] eyes" (Pigou 1925, 361); by "old fallacies", he meant ideas such as those put forward in the popular writings against the political economists by the socialist

Robert Blatchford, whose campaigning pamphlets and newspaper, *The Clarion*, were reaching a mass audience from the 1890s.

Convinced that economic principles were objective and transcended class interests, Marshall was intent on showing that working-class needs could be met within capitalism. His new theory for the distribution of wealth was influenced by F. A. Walker, a forgotten American economist whose writings were influential in the 1870s and 1880s. Walker regretted the unfortunate tendency of the worker, "the residual claimant", who got what was left over after profit had been secured, to go against his own best interests through "excessive reproduction sexually" and "weak, spasmodic or unintelligent competition with the employing class" (Walker 1886, 220–4). Marshall maintained it was in the interest of the working class to support continuing economic progress and increased productivity, rather than to contest the division of wealth. He advocated a new social model, with small families and industrial harmony. In this way, his approach to economics connected efficiency in *reproduction* with efficiency in *economic production*, and allowed for a mixture of private enterprise and state intervention. The rôle of the state, he said, was to prod the market, in order to maximize utility. This could be interpreted to mean either a limited development of welfare, or the more extensive intervention as proposed by Fabian socialists such as Philip H. Wicksteed. Influenced by Ruskin and the Italian poet Dante, Wicksteed convinced Fabians such as George Bernard Shaw and Sidney Webb that "marginal utility" was the ideal basis for welfare economics (Hobsbawm 1964).

Walker's preference for long-term planning and the creation of large firms influenced Arnold Toynbee, another Ruskinite and an economic historian with a social mission; it was Toynbee who inspired the University Settlement movement which brought young intellectuals to live and work in working-class slums, doing community service. He argued in the 1870s for the legalization of trade unions, on the grounds that the integration of official structures was greatly preferable to the anarchy of wild-cat eruptions, which made it impossible for business to make plans for the future.

Changing approaches to the state

The attempt to reconstitute economic theory thus fed into a new social liberalism which accepted the idea of a strong state, a conservative populism based on organic social theories, and also Fabian socialism, which from the late 19th century presented social reform from above as an alternative to class struggle from below. All these were to become a powerful ideological lobby for a new kind of state. The extension of the power of the state into industrial disputes, the recognition of trade unions, and large-scale production, along with high wages, were presented as a modernization project that would make industry more efficient and reduce labour unrest. Investments in social welfare were therefore advocated not simply on humanitarian grounds, but also in order to serve the long-term interests of the economy. By the early 20th century, advocates for this kind of wider rôle of the state were having a profound influence on policy, and they had supporters within the state machinery. This support was particularly evident at the Board of Trade – where Winston Churchill, at that time still a Liberal Party politician, was ready to back limited intervention in both industry and society, and where a junior post was occupied by the young William Beveridge, who was later to shape the welfare state after the Second World War.

From a differing perspective, some working-class radicals during the 1870s came to accept the idea of state intervention in education and training. From the 1880s, this idea was strengthened by the growth of new unionism, which demanded legislation for the eight-hour day, and also by the rise of socialism, although socialists were to divide by the early 1890s over the question of using the state. A similar split can be observed among feminists: whereas the traditional liberal wing led by Millicent Fawcett was anti-statist, Lady Dilke and the Women's Trade Union League argued for protective legislation for women workers, and socialist women concurred with social liberals on the need for state intervention.

Another element in the arguments for welfare, and against *laissez-faire*, was the social imperialist concern about a supposed decline in the physical stock of the white races. It was feared that without social reform at home in Britain, the empire would lose its vigour. In the early 20th century this fear informed the thinking not only of those on the political right wing, but also of some of the Fabian socialists. It was also taken on board by some feminists, in so far as it was seen to contribute to concern about the conditions of motherhood.

The state and "sweated" women workers

From the 1870s onwards, concern was growing about the concentration of male casual workers in big cities, especially London, on the grounds that they constituted a threat to public order. There were even proposals to control them in camps and to prevent them from breeding any more of the "feckless poor". There was anxiety, too, about the conditions of "sweated" women workers who, poorly paid and subcontracted, toiled in small workshops or slum dwellings. By the end of the 19th century, "sweated" women workers were the subject of many reports, journalistic exposures and earnest debates among middle-class social investigators; in 1906, their conditions were dramatically brought to the public's attention in the Sweated Industries Exhibition, which was extensively publicized. Again, the need to extend state control over *reproduction* and *production* converged: the low-paid married woman worker was regarded as bringing down wage rates *and* as neglecting her rôle as a mother. Reformers disagreed, however, on whether improved pay for women, or a better family wage paid to the man, combined with welfare benefits to the mother, might be the solution.

Although subcontracted homework in poor areas of the inner cities – especially London, where the flexible demand of the fashion market and

Weavers at work in the early 20th century (Local Studies Collection, Rochdale Library).

23

low rents caused it to proliferate – became the focus of the campaign against "sweating" in the 1900s, contemporaries had been well aware from the 1880s that the problem of "sweated" work was not confined to homeworkers. Beatrice Potter (later Webb) said in 1888 that it was: "all labour employed in manufacture which has escaped the regulation of the Factory Acts and the trade unions" (House of Lords Select Committee 1888, 20). A leaflet published in about 1907 by the National Anti-Sweating League, a campaigning organization, linked "sweating" to health and housing, as well as to moral decline. It led, they said, to "acute under-payment. It entails overwork, under-feeding, bad housing conditions, and a poverty and debasement which lie at the roots of many other social evils" (National Anti-Sweating League n. d.).

In practice, it was hard to develop and to push policies which challenged low pay, poor nutrition and inadequate housing as a whole. Anti-sweating campaigners therefore isolated what they saw as infected spots within the social structure and recommended that the regulation of homework – and preferably its abolition – was the solution. This ignored the evidence available, which showed that homework was only *one* aspect of women's working situation, which in turn was part of a submerged economic sector. For example, in 1894 Ada Nield Chew, who worked in a clothing factory in Crewe that took in contract work from the government (the lowest grade of clothing), pointed out that because her pay was so low, she had to do homework as well. In a letter to the *Crewe Chronicle* in May 1894, she described homework as: "the only resource of the poor slave who has the misfortune to adopt 'finishing' as a means of earning a livelihood. I have myself, repeatedly, five nights a week besides Saturday afternoon for weeks at a time, regularly taken four hours, at least, work home with me and have done it" (Chew 1982, 80). She asked in a subsequent letter:

> Now I wonder if the Government of this country know (or care) that those on whom the real business of executing their orders fall are "sweated" thereby. And is the Government so frightfully poor that it cannot afford to pay a living wage to those who made the clothing of our soldiers and policemen? (Chew 1982, 104)

Low pay was not the only grievance which led Chew to describe this kind of factory work as "sweated". Just like homeworkers, the women had to pay for materials. They also had to scrabble and fight for work: there was no fair allocation of tasks, but a system of favouritism which decided who got the best jobs. When work was slack they had to wait around and lost money. Unlike the homeworker, though, they were subject to direct control, and there were fines if they were late. A final resentment was that tea money was automatically extracted from a woman's wages, even if she had not drunk any tea (Chew 1982, 75–134).

"Sweating", then, could be a feature of large factories – Messrs Compton of Crewe, after all, employed 400 workers. It could also draw on workers with a high degree of skill, as Clementina Black, a social investigator concerned about women's conditions, discovered in the course of her survey into Married Women's Work, which was conducted during 1908–10. She interviewed a waistcoat maker from London, who had worked on high-quality waistcoats in a West End firm, earning 18 shillings (80p) a week. Thirteen pregnancies and five children later, with her husband unemployed and helping her with the housework, she had to support the whole family on the 14 shillings (60p) she earned every week as a homeworker (Black 1983, 90–92).

The consequence of married homeworkers allegedly neglecting their children was an emotive theme within a broader argument for state intervention. Protection of mothers and children was frequently linked to the demand for a living wage. Reformers advocated better pay for the workforce, as well as welfare benefits for those unable to labour. From the early 1890s, Clementina Black had argued for a living wage, sufficient to meet workers' basic needs, and for the state's responsibility to secure welfare at work. This position challenged the idea that wages were an individual bargain between employer and employee. Throughout the 1890s the idea of state intervention on these lines remained marginal, although the anti-sweating lobby did achieve the fixing of rates in certain low-paid trades, through the passing of the Trades Boards Act in 1909. The specific needs of women as mothers were invoked to justify this break with market forces. The concept of welfare thus came to span both economic *and* social needs, work *and* daily life in the household and community.

Class, gender and international state regulation

These developments in Britain took place in a wider international context of pressure for state intervention, in which policies on reproduction and production developed together. Sheila Lewenhak shows in *Women and trade unions* that international links between trade unionists were greatly influenced by efforts to establish an international code of standards for conditions of work for women and children (Lewenhak 1977, 93). In 1890, various resolutions were agreed by an international trade union conference: the banning of women in mines and on nightwork; the reduction of hours to an 11-hour day, with a rest period of at least one and a half hours; restrictions on unhealthy and dangerous occupations; and four weeks maternity leave (International Labour Office 1921, 97–8). There was no means, however, of making these resolutions binding. Some of the German socialists and feminists advocated protection: commenting on the German socialist Erfurt programme in 1891, Eduard Bernstein wrote that women needed special protection because they were in a socially weaker position. Since this was especially true in the case of homework, in 1895 the German Social Democrats broadened their demand for workers' protection to include domestic industry (Thönnessen 1969, 47–53).

In 1897 the International Labour Congress, which was initiated by the Swiss Workers League, demanded an 8-hour day, a 44-hour week, equal pay for equal work, eight weeks maternity leave, and the protection for pregnant women against work that was dangerous for them. British representatives included Miss Sullivan from the West End Tailoresses, and Herbert Burrows, a middle-class socialist from the Match Makers Union and the Women's Trade Union League, who had helped in the organization of the match girls. Assisted by the German feminist and socialist Lily Braun, Miss Sullivan almost got a resolution passed demanding the abolition of homework. German feminists had become more involved in welfare work from the late 1880s and some, like Lily Braun, were also beginning to place great emphasis upon social reforms around motherhood. A German Social Democrat, Georg Heinrich Von Vollmar, managed to block their resolutions because large districts in Germany depended on homework (Lewenhak 1977, 98)

The International Association for Labour Legislation was founded in 1897, with its headquarters in Basle, Switzerland. This was an association of academics, church people, social reformers and trade unionists, and it became known as the laboratory in which international treaties were made. It had two sides: an International Labour Bureau, which collected and classified information on international law and published its findings; and the Federation of National Sections. This association was responsible for getting night work for women banned and preventing the manufacture and importation of white phosphorus matches (which had given the match girls the fatal condition known as "phossy jaw", because the phosphorus ate away at the worker's jaw).

In 1906, homework was on the agenda for discussion and there were proposals to improve working conditions and to exclude dangerous trades. Wages Boards were suggested, but only tentatively (Smith 1914, 158–9). In a lecture to an interdenominational church conference in 1912, Constance Smith said that by 1908 there had been a dramatic change: "the question of a minimum wage for sweated workers occupied the greater part of the time of one of the five committees" (Smith 1914, 159). A minimum wage came to be seen as the wage that a particular trade would bear, rather than a wage that was based on the concept of social need. At the same conference, Mary Theresa Rankin opposed the idea of a living wage. Drawing on the Australian and New Zealand experience of fixing minimum rates in certain trades, which had resulted in a loss of wages for homeworkers in some cases where rates were fixed too high, Rankin argued that a living wage would be a two-edged sword and actually harm the vulnerable workers, driving them out of a trade. The minimum rate, she said, should "not exclude the older and slower workers who have as much a right to work as any other" (Rankin 1914, 141).

The state regulation of wages was thus being urged in many countries in the late 19th and early 20th centuries, for various social, economic and political reasons. The motives for internationalism were not simply altruistic: international investigations into wages and conditions of production were started in the early 20th century, because once wages had been raised in one country, employers faced undercutting from foreign rivals.

While some socialists and trade unionists wanted state intervention to improve working-class conditions, some liberals and even conservatives hoped that the state could act as a mediator. It was seen as a means of protecting the weak, especially mothers, securing the eugenic stock, regulating casual trades, improving production methods, and raising standards of industrial efficiency. It was also perceived as having the potential to diminish workers' anger about their conditions: state regulation was seen as an option that was more attractive than the threat of rebellion. The urgency of the debates between 1908 and 1913, and the legislative measures which ensued, arose partly because of the increasing cost of living, which meant that low-paid workers were suffering, and partly because of the threat of syndicalist-led strikes (Smith 1914, 165–6).

Reformers presented their case not only in ethical terms, but also as a means of modernizing economic organization. The organic theoretical models presumed interactions: concepts of welfare and of social need were entangled with biological metaphors of eradicating "infected spots" within the "body politic". Reproduction was linked to production, and welfare in the community was seen to have an impact upon the workplace.

Social missionaries and community projects

Viewed through a long-distance lens, these economic and social concerns of the reforming intelligentsia take on a somewhat Machiavellian cast. However, it was not merely an effort at social engineering. A closer focus also shows considerable subjective angst about the ethics of the capitalist economy and the scope of social action. The pioneers who had established settlements, which – as will be shown – laid the basis for the introduction of state services through the creation of alternative models, did not blandly support the system from which they benefited. Instead, many of them, like Arnold Toynbee, had a populist desire to cast off privilege. These pioneers equated the system which they defended, albeit with a few modifications, with civilization. They feared that the workers, "the democracy" as they were called, were likely to use their franchise to create some kind of barbarism. The young men and women who went to live in the University Settlements in the 1870s, 1880s and 1890s among working-class people saw themselves as colonisers bringing civilization. It was a secularized form of evangelism, which was made more attractive by a desire for personal communion between classes and a certain unease with the relationships that were characteristic of upper-middle-class life.

Leonard Montefiore, for instance, who started the settlement called Toynbee Hall, was influenced by visits to American utopian communities. The spirit of the transcendentalists' search for inward growth and of Walt Whitman's poetic vision of a simplified life also found their English advocates. In the 1880s, Charles Ashbee, who was to break away from Toynbee Hall because it was too stuffy, and form a Guild and School of Handicraft (which became part of the arts and crafts movement in design), said he longed to "shake off this churlish gentility" (Ashbee 1886). Martha Vicinus, in *Independent women*, notes the connection between service and simplification of style in the women's settlements: "Dedicated to

28

service," she observes, "they held the showiness of their less high minded contemporaries in contempt" (Vicinus 1985, 230). These late-Victorian women felt immensely liberated by their release from hats, gloves and parasols. Vicinus quotes Mary Simmons of the Bermondsey Settlement as saying that she and the other women residents revelled "in a picturesque lack of respectability" (Vicinus 1985, 230).

The settlements not only provided an alternative to the confines of the Victorian middle-class world, but they also confronted the settlers with the wants and needs of working-class people. In the process of developing practical solutions, the settlers began to formulate social policies. "The settlement paved the way," argues Vicinus, "for a state system of social services both in the training of social workers and in special services for the handicapped and for children" (Vicinus 1985, 234). For example, the Passmore Edwards Settlement set up a model school for the physically handicapped, including meals and physical therapy. The results of the school were then used to pressurize the London County Council to establish similar schools. Margaret McMillan, a socialist involved in settlement work, first pioneered summer camps for children, and later pressed for school meals, medical inspection and nurseries based on learning through play. Grace Kimmins, at the Bermondsey settlement, founded the Guild of Play to teach folk dances and songs, which eventually entered the education system. Women settlers also offered classes in baby care, nutrition and housewifery. These formed a basis for the maternity welfare centres which were established on a self-help basis and later by local councils, in the early 20th century.

The settlements were not the only places where innovatory self-help projects were initiated. Middle-class and upper-class women were also involved in the administration of the Poor Law and the School Board, which was responsible for education locally. State education in 1870 had revealed the social problems of many of the pupils, who often went to school too hungry to learn. In 1899 Charlotte Despard, who was later to become an active suffragette and socialist, was elected manager of two elementary schools in Nine Elms in South London. She proposed to the rather startled board that some spare rooms should be made into a dining room and kitchen. The School Board members, who usually discussed blocked lavatories or the problem of children throwing stones over the wall on to the Conservative Club's bowling green, replied that money could not legally be spent on this venture. Undeterred, Charlotte Despard provided saucepans, a stove, tables and benches; and the board, presented with a *fait accompli*, gave in. Consequently, Nine Elms had a school meals service for poor children seven years before the government first authorized local education authorities to offer these, and many years before school meals were introduced nationally during the Second World War (Linklater 1980, 98–9).

Enlightened discontent

As well as instituting alternative models, which later shaped the forms of state services, some of the more concerned missionaries moved towards socialism and feminism. R. H. Tawney's phrase, "enlightened discontent", describes this radical wing of welfare action, which in some cases not only sought to meet working-class needs, but also encouraged working-class organization and resistance, for example, the 1889 Dock Strike. Part of the rise of the new unionism of the unskilled received backing from Toynbee Hall. In 1902, women at the Robert Browning Settlement in Southwark co-operated with the London Trades Council, Poplar Trades and Labour Representation Committee (the Labour Party in embryo), in organizing a march of 3,000 working-class women, who carried banners reading "Bread for our Children" and "Work for our Men" (Vicinus 1985, 234).

This organizing among working-class women became a basis for links between feminists and the working class a few years later. When the socialist and feminist Sylvia Pankhurst took suffrage ideas to East London, she used the same combination of exemplary practical models: setting up a welfare clinic and a co-operative toy factory with a nursery, and campaigning through mobilizing demonstrations and lobbies (see Rowbotham 1973, 114–17). Her approach to welfare and the state, which emphasized participatory democracy while insisting that the state should serve workers, showed the influence of her background in the Independent Labour Party (ILP), an early socialist group formed in 1893.

The Independent Labour Party consisted of socialists with a wide range of views. It had developed in the context of local practical agitation for municipal reforms, but it had also attracted utopian-minded socialists influenced by William Morris. Its leadership, men like Philip Snowden and Ramsay MacDonald, were to develop the politics of the Labour Party. While one brand of ethical socialism was to move to the right, even after the Second World War the ILP retained elements of the earlier

utopian socialism, which had envisaged a transformation in social relationships, rather than simply putting the state, instead of private capital,
in the rôle of boss. So while the ILP was making demands on Parliament,
it was also committed to a qualitative change in society. This meant it
was not completely in accord with statist measures from above.

To members of the ILP and some other early socialists, local government seemed to be the best means of securing democratic control over
public resources. They were active in local councils, arguing for improvements in the Poor Law and education, and the provision of better
municipal amenities, from libraries to parks with bands and music, and
from gas lights to municipal transport. In the late 19th century, the
Women's Co-operative Guild, an organization of working-class house-
wives, was set up to improve the quality of food in co-op shops; it went on
to demand better conditions for maternity, birth control, equal pay, community laundries, and improved working-class education, presenting a
vision of a co-operative commonwealth based on caring and sharing.

By the 1900s there was sustained prodding for state intervention, both
locally and nationally, from a broad political spectrum which spanned
the Independent Labour Party, Labour Women's organizations, Karl
Marx's followers and the Social Democrats, through to social liberals,
some feminists, and social imperialists. The practical results became evident: in this period, the Liberal Party took up social reform and the new
Labour Party got its first members into Parliament. However, Labour
was denied access to trade union funds by a legal decision, and became
increasingly dependent on the Liberals, simply backing the state welfare
measures which they introduced; in this way, welfare was initiated from
above. This tendency hardened during the period of the coalition government during the First World War.

Democratizing society and the state

This was not the only strand in the labour movement, however. As the
social theorist Stuart Hall has observed, the pro-state tendency at the
time "had to contend with many other currents, including, of course, the
strong syndicalist currents before and after the First World War and the
ILP's ethical Marxism later with their deep antipathy to Labour's
top-downwards, statist orientation" (Hall 1984, 25). Within the anti-
statism of the syndicalists there were, of course, nuances: advocacy of the

amalgamation of unions; the belief that industrial unions, by organizing all the workers in an industry, could be the most effective means of defensive struggle; and the conviction that the industrial organization of workers was the key to revolutionary transformation and sometimes to the prefiguration of a socialist future, by developing the confidence and experience of freedom through action.

In the period before the First World War, there was considerable interaction between anarchism, syndicalism, left-wing members of the ILP, and socialist feminists, both through links generated by local organizing, and through wider networks such as the Herald Leagues, the social Clarion clubs, Guild Socialists, and the arts and crafts movement. In his history of the Labour Party, the socialist writer G. D. H. Cole said that in this period:

> Rising prices with wages lagging behind, were leading to a growth of industrial militancy and to a preaching of "direct action" doctrines which denied the effectiveness of parliamentary proceedings and denounced the Labour parliamentarians as "collaborationists" whose compromising tactics blurred the realities of the class war. Syndicalism and Industrial Unionism were in the air, and owed their vogue not only to the lag in real wages but also to the catchingness of the militancy of the women suffragists and of the Ulster diehards and their English Conservative allies. (Cole 1960, 2)

It was not simply that the phrase was "catching", though. Suffragettes, syndicalists and left-wing socialists in this period had reason to be impatient of representative democracy, because it did not address the issues they were concerned about – votes for women, workers' control, a radical solution to low pay, unemployment, the Irish question, health care, and housing.

The syndicalists' absolute dismissal of Parliament, however, meant that they failed to tackle the question of the state. They also enclosed the terrain of struggle with their emphasis upon the workplace, in ways that the utopian Morris tradition did not. Yet the syndicalists *did* engage with important problems: they asked whether this kind of social transition would require a transformation of consciousness, and how a desire for free and equal human relations could be developed within existing society. This concern about a new social order was also present in some

32

forms of ethical socialism and in feminism. Moreover, the organizational boundaries between these currents of thought were not tidy – there was always theoretical interchange. Indeed, some socialists were prepared to argue that the struggle in Parliament needed to combine with forms of direct action. As Leonard Hall wrote in *The syndicalist*, a synthesis was required: industrial democracy, consumer boycotts and the co-operative movement had to connect with electoral action through Parliament and local councils. Only this would prevent Socialism moving towards state socialism and bureaucratic "collectivism" (Hall 1912, 2). There was then an awareness of the need for interaction between direct democracy and central co-ordination in social and economic planning: this was a dilemma which the statist brands of socialism simply pushed under the carpet.

The outbreak of the First World War overturned many old alliances among both socialists and feminists. The crucial issue became each individual's attitude to the war, which necessarily involved an approach to the state. During the war, the state's powers were extended considerably in order to enforce conscription and to keep up production levels. Whereas previously the Special Branch had consisted of only about 50 men, the war saw a proliferation of small intelligence agencies, frequently in competition for spies, saboteurs, sloths, revolutionaries or pacifists, who might be undermining the production of munitions. In the climate of war censorship, *agents provocateurs* were acceptable to many people because of the exceptional circumstances of war production. In this way, the state intervened in industry for military reasons, as well as through the introduction of welfare measures. Some socialists came to support these changes, but others, like Bertrand Russell, an opponent of conscription, remained extremely critical. He wrote in *The ploughshare* in 1916:

> In economic home policy the old State socialism of the Fabian Society is somewhat discredited. There were socialists who rejoiced in the early days of the war, that now socialism had come. The Government controlled banks, railways, prices, everything. Now they have carried Socialism to the point of punishing all who will not take part in the war. If this is Socialism, the less we have of it the better. What is desirable is not increased power of the State, as an end in itself, but greater justice in distribution, and still more, better opportunities for initiative and self direction on the part of those who do not happen

to be capitalist. We need economic democracy as well as political democracy; we need the complete abolition of the system of working for wages. Something of the youthful revolutionary syndicalism is needed if labour is to have a free life. *The men who do the work ought to control the policy of their industry.* (Russell 1916, 137; emphasis added)

Women had views on this issue as well. In working-class women's organizations just before and after the war, the vision of a locally-based transformation of community life was emerging. At a meeting of the Women's Co-operative Guild in 1919, for example, Florence Farrow from Derby, the wife of a Labour Party railway clerk, said that every mother should receive a pension from the state for each child. She added that there should be municipal control of milk to keep prices down, that there should be municipal baths, better housing, heating and lighting, and greater democratic control over the supply of energy. She also advocated that teachers should be better paid, as a step towards improving the education of working-class children, and that there should be municipal cinemas, "where children could be shown pictures which would bring out the best in them and give them a love of things beautiful" (Farrow 1919, n.p.). The politics of the Women's Co-operative Guild sought ways of meeting the everyday needs of women through an eclectic mix of a kind of Fabianism from below and ethical and utopian strands of socialism. Like some ILP members, they regarded the presentation of municipal local demands as a means of democratizing state socialism.

Conclusion

The particular connection between the capitalist mixed economy and centralized state welfare, which emerged after the Second World War, is often seen as being in some way preordained – but it was not. Rather, it represented a political victory for a particular balance of social forces. As Stuart Hall observes: "One of the many tricks which the retrospective construction of tradition on the left has performed is to make the triumph of Labourism over these other socialist currents – the result of a massive political struggle in which the ruling classes played a key rôle – appear as an act of natural and inevitable succession" (Hall 1984, 25). The kind of welfare state that developed was not, and is not, the only conceivable approach to social wellbeing: it was an impressive achievement, but did not correspond to many of the earlier visions of socialism described in this chapter.

It is as necessary today as it was in those earlier decades to develop an effective and democratic strategy that will challenge the unequal distribution of resources and create new relations of freedom and equality, individual initiative and associative collectivity. Those new relations must take place *within the state itself*, as well as in the economy and the community, and must acknowledge and respond to the integral links between the reproduction of human beings and of daily life, along with economic production. It might then be possible to develop an alternative to both the authoritarian versions of welfarism, in which needs are decided from above, and the squandering of the creativity of human beings that results from giving exclusive power to the market and its beneficiaries.

References

Ashbee, C. R. April 1886. Manuscript journal, held at Kings College, Cambridge.

Black, Clementina (ed.) 1983. *Married women's work*. London: Virago.

Chew, Ada Nield (19 May 1894) in Doris Nield Chew (ed.) 1982. *The life and times of a working woman*. London: Virago.

Cole, G. D. H. 1960. *History of the labour party*. London: Routledge & Kegan Paul.

Farrow, Florence, October 1919. Derby Women's Co-operative Guild. In October 1919, *Derby Monthly Records, Women's Guild Congress Report*.

Hall, Leonard 1912. My version of syndicalism. *The syndicalist*, May. For the interconnections raised by Hall, see also Sheila Rowbotham 1986. *Friends of Alice Wheeldon*. London: Pluto.

Hall, Stuart 1984. The state, socialism's old caretaker. *Marxism Today* **28**, 11.

Hobsbawm, E. J. 1964. Dr Marx and the Victorian critics. In *Labouring men, studies in the history of labour*, E. J. Hobsbawm (ed.). London: Weidenfeld and Nicolson.

House of Lords Select Committee (1888) *First Report and Minutes of Evidence*. In J. Morris 1986. *Sweated trades, the origins of minimum wage legislation*. Aldershot, England: Gower.

International Labour Office, *Studies and reports*, Series 1, No 1, 15 October 1921, pp. 1–2, quoted in Sheila Lewenhak 1977, *Women and trade unions*, pp. 97–8.

Lewenhak, Sheila 1977. *Women and trade unions: an outline history of women in the British trade union movement*. London: Ernest Benn.

Linklater, Andro 1980. *An unhusbanded life. Charlotte Despard, suffragette, socialist and*

Sinn Feiner. London: Hutchinson.

National Anti-Sweating League n.d. *To secure a minimum wage.* Held at Fawcett Library, London Guildhall University, London.

Pigou, A. C. 1925. *Memorials of Alfred Marshall.* London: Macmillan.

Rankin, Mary Theresa 1914. Legislation and the living wage abroad. In *A series of lectures on the industrial unrest and the living wage*, The Inter-Denominational Summer School, June 1913. London: P. S. King.

Rowbotham, Sheila 1973. *Hidden from history.* London: Pluto.

Ruskin, John 1857 (rpt. 1912) Preface. In *The political economy of art.* London: Macmillan.

Ruskin, John 1862 (rpt. 1912) Unto this last. In *The political economy of art.* London: Macmillan.

Russell, Bertrand August 1916. Quoted in Challinor, Raymond 1977. *The origins of British Bolshevism.* London: Croom Helm.

Smith, Constance 1914. Wage movement in other countries. In *A series of lectures on the industrial unrest and the living wage*, The Inter-Denominational Summer School, June 1913. London: P. S. King.

Thönnessen, Werner 1969. *The emancipation of women, the rise and decline of the women's movement in German social democracy, 1863–1933.* London: Pluto.

Vicinus, Martha 1985. *Independent women.* London: Virago.

Walker, F. A. 1886. *A brief political economy.* London: Macmillan.

2

Lessons from the past: the rise and fall of the classic welfare state in Britain, 1945–76

Rodney Lowe

Introduction

The current debate on the future of the British welfare state is heavily informed by perceptions about its past. In particular, lessons are drawn from the so-called "classic" phase of the welfare state, which lasted from 1945 to 1976 – that is, from the election of the first majority Labour government to the abandonment by a later one of the commitment to full employment. Of course, there can be no "definitive" history of the welfare state: any interpretation of the past depends upon an individual's underlying theoretical assumptions. Furthermore, change – or lack of it – in any historical period is the consequence of circumstances unique to that time. None the less, a study of the past can stimulate new thought about the present and the future, by debunking certain myths and reviving forgotten perspectives.

This chapter has two aims: first, to define the term, "classic welfare state"; and secondly, to identify its major features, both positive and negative. There are opposing views on the overall record of state intervention during this period. On the one hand, there are those who – consciously or subconsciously – believe that the "classic" welfare state was a golden age of political consensus, economic growth, rising living standards and, consequently, social justice. Whatever the failings of particular policies, they argue, the essential framework and thrust of government policy was right. In stark contrast to the broken promises of 1919–21, the postwar Labour governments of 1945–51 courageously honoured the reconstruction pledges made during the Second World War; and in stark contrast to the record of the 1930s (and indeed of the 1980s), full employment was achieved, and both poverty and inequality were diminished (Morgan 1990, 424–8).

On the other hand, there are those who see this same period as being the root cause of Britain's accelerating economic decline and political ungovernability. They claim that scarce economic resources were badly misallocated, individual initiative was sapped and a further stride was taken along the "road to serfdom" by the creation of a dependency culture, or "nanny state". In the bitter words of one recent polemic (Barnett 1987, 304), the classic welfare state transformed sturdy, free-born Englishmen into a "segregated, sub-literate, unskilled, unhealthy and institutionalised proletariat hanging on the nipple of state maternalism".

What was the "classic welfare state"?

There is not, nor has there ever been, an agreed definition of the term "welfare state", let alone of the term "classic welfare state". All that can be said without contradiction is that over the past century, successive governments have committed themselves increasingly to the active promotion of individual welfare, and that, in the ebb and flow of such intervention, the years between 1945 and 1976 stand out as a coherent and distinct period. It was during this period that the term "welfare state" came into common use, first in Britain and later in the rest of the Western world (Lowe 1993, 10). The rapid acceptance of the term reflected a common realization that the nature of government intervention had changed fundamentally, so that conventional idioms were no longer adequate.

The key to this transformation, it has been widely acknowledged, was the government's acceptance of "comprehensiveness", the fifth principle behind the plan for social insurance that was proposed in the 1942 Beveridge Report (Cmd 6404 1942, para. 308). "Comprehensiveness" in this report had two distinct meanings. First, it required that in return for a weekly payment, contributors should be insured against all risks which might deprive them of their independent income. Everyone would thereby be guaranteed social security – freedom from the fear of absolute poverty – which had previously been the privilege of the rich alone. Secondly, it required that everyone should join the social insurance system. In this way, all citizens would be treated equally by the state and, in T. H. Marshall's phrase (1950, 40), be accorded an equal social status. This second element in the report's concept of "comprehensiveness" has become more commonly known as "universalism".

What was the *purpose* and *scope* of government intervention in this very active phase? Its chief *purpose* was the achievement of greater efficiency in the allocation of scarce resources. During the 1930s it had become apparent that, as society and the economy grew more complex, the unregulated market was becoming increasingly inefficient. Economists have since confirmed this conclusion: it is now recognized, in particular, that unregulated markets will underprovide services that are in the common, rather than the private, interest, because they cannot measure externalities (that is, the consequences for others, beneficial or harmful, of decisions taken by individuals or by firms in the market). Nor will they provide an optimum amount of public goods (goods which are in everybody's interest, such as public health, but for which prices cannot easily be charged). Moreover, unregulated markets misallocate resources: in the real world, it is simply not possible to justify theoretical assumptions about the perfect knowledge of consumers and perfect competition between producers. As Nicholas Barr has observed (1987, 421):

> The Welfare State does things which private markets for technical reasons either would not do at all, or would do inefficiently. We need a welfare state of some sort for efficiency reasons; and would continue to do so even if all distributional problems had been solved.

Government intervention to maximize efficiency led to an increase in the degree of equality within society. The acceptance of the principle of comprehensiveness, for example, as shown above, was seen to give everyone an *equal* right to social security and an *equal* social status. It has been argued, also, that by making labour relatively scarce, the commitment to full employment transformed the relationship between employers and the workforce and so effected the "transfer of power on a momentous scale" (Crosland 1956, 347). Such fundamental steps towards a more equal society tended to be overlooked later, when it became fashionable to concentrate on equality of outcome[1] in the distribution and income of wealth (which was thought to be more easily quantifiable). What should not be forgotten, however, is that the initial conception of the welfare state contained little commitment to a greater equality of outcome;

indeed, Beveridge specifically rejected such an intention (Cmd 6404 1942, para. 449). Equality of outcome was an objective that was grafted later on to the original package of welfare reforms – not least by revisionists within the Labour Party, such as Anthony Crosland, who identified it as a precondition for greater efficiency (1956, Ch. 9). This issue, and its implications for the rôle of the state, became the greatest source of ideological and political controversy in the Labour Party in the 1950s and 1960s. What was not controversial, however, was the belief that in relation to the unregulated market, state intervention was efficient.

In *scope*, the classic welfare state embraced the five core social services for which, in the 1990s, the term "welfare state" has become a synonym: social security, the National Health Service (NHS), education, housing and the personal social services (Lowe 1989, 155). It also embraced two other crucial areas of policy: employment and taxation. Integral to its conception was a commitment to "full" employment, which Howard Glennerster has recently described (1990, 12) as the "most important social policy in the postwar period". The Beveridge Report spelt out the two major reasons for this: by maximizing government revenue and minimizing outgoings, it was essential for the solvency of the social insurance system (as has been demonstrated by events in both the 1930s and the 1980s). Of even greater importance, however, was the realization that individual welfare depended not so much on government relief, as on the availability of a productive and rewarding job. Indeed, Beveridge argued that in relation to worthwhile employment, "income security which is all that can be given by social insurance is so inadequate a provision for human happiness that to put it forward as a sole or principal measure of reconstruction hardly seems worth doing" (Cmd 6404 1942, 440). There is little evidence here to support later charges concerning the wilful creation of a "nanny" state.

The second area of policy embraced by the classic welfare state was that of taxation. Beveridge largely ignored it, but in the 1950s, Titmuss (1958, Ch. 2) identified clearly the ways in which individual welfare could be affected by the financing, as much as by the targeting, of benefits. He drew particular attention to two types of welfare that were increasing surreptitiously: fiscal and occupational welfare. The former consisted of tax allowances for "approved" types of expenditure (such as the payment of interest on mortgages), by which individuals might reduce their liability to pay tax. The latter consisted of a similar reduction in companies' tax liability in relation to the provision of "approved" services for their employees (such as occupational pensions). Both types of welfare, argued Titmuss, doubly disadvantaged the poor. Not only were the poor unlikely to enjoy the income or the managerial positions which would entitle them to any (let alone the maximum) benefit, but also, as a result of the concessions, the tax base was eroded and the government was obliged to find alternative sources of income. As a result, rates of indirect taxation and insurance contributions rose, and income tax started to affect those on below-average incomes. Such changes in the incidence of taxation clearly raised questions of equity with which the welfare state was not directly concerned, and which, after the 1951–5 Royal Commission on the Taxation of Profits and Income, the Treasury and Inland Revenue, in particular, wished politicians not to discuss in public. Nevertheless they did defy contemporary conceptions of the welfare state which, as the government's Chief Economic Adviser in the mid-1950s noted (PRO 1957), was essentially concerned with "the provision of social services and progressive direct taxation".

The classic welfare state may therefore be defined as a distinct phase in British history between 1945 and 1976, in which the government sought in a particularly active and "comprehensive" way to promote individual welfare. The scope of government intervention covered not just a core of social services, but also a commitment to full employment and the maintenance of a progressive tax system; its purpose in the aftermath of the perceived wastage of the 1930s was to allocate scarce resources more effectively. This intervention increased the degree of equality within society, although there was no deliberate attempt to engineer a greater equality of outcome.

The strengths of the classic welfare state

The classic welfare state had three potential strengths: its functional efficiency; its acceptance of the constructive complementarity of economic and social policy; and its underlying assumption that state intervention was compatible with, and not inimical to, individual initiative and freedom. The degree to which the classic welfare state fulfilled these areas of potential is an issue on which social scientists and historians are likely to disagree. Looking back on past policy and judging it either by present-day standards or by ideal (or even polemical) criteria, social scientists instinctively tend to be critical. They might even be said, as Enoch

Powell put it of workers within the NHS in the 1960s, to have a "vested interest in denigration" (Powell 1966, 16).

In contrast, historians looking forward – in this case, from the inadequacies of the 1930s – and making judgements in the light of contemporary real-world constraints, tend to be more sympathetic (and possibly too sympathetic). They may, for example, highlight such achievements as the fall in unemployment: whereas the annual unemployment rate among the total workforce during the interwar period had averaged almost 11 per cent and peaked at 17 per cent, it rose marginally above 3 per cent only three times between 1945 and 1975. Poverty, as measured by Rowntree, dropped from 31 per cent of the working class in 1936 to a mere 2.8 per cent in 1951 and, even after its redefinition in the 1960s, is rarely considered to have exceeded 5 per cent of the population before 1975 (Lowe 1993, 139–41). Following the creation of the NHS, there was a rapid decline in the number of deaths caused by infectious disease and a reduction in infant mortality – the most sensitive of health indicators – from 56 to 16 deaths per thousand live births. The crude housing shortage also ended by 1956, and an opportunity was provided for the "biggest slum clearance and grant-aided improvement programme to be attempted anywhere in the world" (Donnison & Ungerson 1982, 187). Above all, women were given free access to health care, a right which had previously been limited to men in paid employment.

It has been argued, however, that these achievements would have taken place anyway, even without the development of the classic welfare state. Is it not possible, for instance, that full employment was the consequence of buoyant world markets rather than demand management (which many consider, in any case, to have been destabilizing)? Were not improved health standards the result of medical discoveries, such as the development of penicillin and antibiotics during the Second World War? Nevertheless, it is incontrovertibly the case that these achievements were attained under the classic welfare state and, as will be shown by reference to the education policy of the time, the state was far from being a passive bystander.

Before 1939, only 20 per cent of children received specialist secondary education, and of these, 52 per cent had to pay fees. All other children were locked into an "elementary" system, in which they attended an "all age" school from their fifth to their fourteenth birthdays. Any reform of this system was blocked by an administrative impasse in which church schools (responsible for the education of one-third of children)

42

competed with local education authorities as jealously as county councils (responsible for secondary education) competed with smaller local authorities (responsible for elementary education). The result of this in-fighting was a gross disparity in educational provision for children and in conditions of employment for teachers, which was exposed by the evacuation of children from the cities during the Second World War. These problems were addressed by the 1944 Butler Education Act, which marked a major advance in both policy and practice, despite its later reputation for conservatism (Simon 1986, 31–43). Institutional impediments to change were swept aside as the government assumed ultimate responsibility for the "control and direction" of policy, and county councils were entrusted with its overall implementation. Each child was assured of four years of specialist secondary education, and for the first time, teachers were guaranteed national rates of pay. Increased school rolls, caused by the baby boom and the raising of the school-leaving age, were matched by an efficient school-building programme. As a result, educational standards rose sharply: the average reading age of children aged 11, for example, increased by some 17 months between 1948 and 1964. Thus postwar educational policy provided clear proof of the superiority of state intervention over the previous combination of voluntary, market and local government provision.

A critical element in the efficiency of state intervention was its acceptance of the constructive complementarity of economic and social policy. That full employment was perceived as being essential both for the attainment of individual welfare and for the solvency of the social insurance system, has already been noted. Equally, social policy was seen not as the enemy of, but rather as a precondition for, economic growth. This view was argued most persuasively in a somewhat neglected epilogue to the Beveridge Report entitled, "Abolition of want as a practical postwar aim", which Beveridge produced in response to the Treasury's panic over the projected cost of his plan outlined in the initial draft of the report. Beveridge was persuaded to make several concessions (such as the withdrawal of the family allowance for the first child), so that the eventual cost of his proposals amounted to only one-fifth of the expenditure he had proposed (Harris 1990, 187). The epilogue to the report was intended to refute the pessimism of the Treasury, which had overshadowed interwar policy, and to argue the case for the economic benefits of increased social expenditure.

This case, which is as relevant in the 1990s as it was in the 1940s, had

three major elements. First, Beveridge attacked the enervating fatalism of
the Treasury. Poverty, he claimed, was a "needless scandal", which could
be abolished "easily within the economic resources of the community"

TRANSFORMATION SCENE

"Avaunt, foul sprite! and be no longer seen
I'll have you know I am the Fairy Queen!"

Beveridge according to Punch, *9 December 1942.*

44

(Cmd 6404 1942, para. 445). Secondly, he insisted that the cost of social policy looked prohibitive only if a static view was taken of society. "There are no easy carefree times in early prospect," he admitted, "but to suppose that the difficulties cannot be overcome . . . that technical advance has ended or that the British of the future must be permanently poor because they would have spent their fathers' savings, is defeatism without reason and against reason" (Cmd 6404 1942, para. 447). Thirdly, he rejected the other traditional Treasury objection: the threat of noncompliance. Employees would be willing to pay increased contributions, he argued, because comprehensive state insurance represented better value for money than the existing combination of compulsory and voluntary policies. Similarly, employers would be prepared to pay because they would be assured not only of a healthier, more mobile, better educated and hence more productive workforce, but also of the political stability that was essential for investment (Cmd 6404 1942, para. 449).

A prime example of productive expenditure, claimed Beveridge, was education. This was widely accepted: in contrast to their traditional concerns about the loss of family income and the fostering of unrealizable expectations, parents and policy-makers alike welcomed the expansion of education projected by the 1944 Act. Likewise, the 1963 Robbins Report – which recommended a doubling of the numbers of students in higher education – was also accepted within 24 hours of publication by a Conservative government, because of its perceived ability to halt Britain's relative economic decline. The contrast with education policy in the 1930s and 1990s could not be greater.

The final strength of the classic welfare state was its assumption that state intervention was compatible with, and not inimical to, individual freedom. This was the fundamental assumption behind the Beveridge Report which, while fully endorsing the need for state intervention to eradicate poverty, insisted that "the state in organising social security should not stifle incentive, opportunity, responsibility" (Cmd 6404 1942, para. 9). Hence, in defiance of the practice that was adopted in most other Western countries, state insurance was restricted to the provision of a flat-rate subsistence benefit. "To give by compulsory insurance more than is needed for subsistence," the Report asserted, "is an unnecessary interference with individual responsibility" (Cmd 6404 1942, para. 294 and appendix F). Earnings-related benefits, set up to maintain an accustomed rather than a minimum standard of living, were presented as a matter for private choice and thus voluntary insurance.

This fine balance between the principles of collectivism and individualism provides the key explanation for the immediate worldwide impact, and the continuing historical importance, of both the Beveridge Report and the creation of the classic welfare state – events which, in the view of at least one recent observer, are "equivalent in importance and stature to the French or Russian revolutions" (Baldwin 1994). The balance is best illustrated in the field of social insurance, where individualism was maintained by everyone's automatic right to social security depending upon the payment of a weekly insurance premium. The right to social security was not automatic, therefore, but *earned*, and it thereby reinforced the traditional middle-class virtue of self help. Nevertheless, *everyone* was covered by the insurance scheme – the rich were not excluded, as they had been during the interwar period, and select occupational groups could not contract out into their own exclusive schemes, as was the case in postwar Germany and France. There was thus a genuine equalization of risk and the maintenance of a certain degree of social solidarity. A middle way had been established between individualism (with its assurance of individual freedom but its tendency towards anarchy, in which the weak went to the wall) and collectivism (with its guarantee of security, but its tendency towards authoritarianism).

A similar balance was struck in other areas, including education. Here, central government claimed the ultimate power to "control and direct" policy and provided the funding that had been so markedly deficient before the war. In contrast to most other European countries, however, there was no core curriculum: both the formulation and the implementation of policy were delegated to a Central Advisory Council of professional experts and to independent bodies such as Local Education Authorities and the University Grants Committee. In this way, decentralization was effectively preserved within a theoretically centralist system.

The achievements of the classic welfare state were therefore considerable, particularly when compared with the regimes which immediately preceded and succeeded it. In each area of welfare policy, major advances were sustained; in addition, a genuine prospect was offered of a constructive, rather than a confrontational, relationship, both between the objectives of economic and social policy, and between the principles of individualism and collectivism.

By the mid-1970s, however, the welfare state was perceived to be not merely embarrassed by temporary difficulties, such as the fiscal crisis resulting from the increased price of oil and the subsequent slowing of economic growth, but to be fundamentally flawed. In 1976, the commitment to full employment was abandoned and all other policies came under attack from a wide range of sources. These attacks even included one on education policy by the then Labour Prime Minister, James Callaghan, in a notorious speech at Ruskin College, Oxford. Why was the classic welfare state, despite its apparent strengths, perceived to have failed?

The failures of the classic welfare state

There are two basic explanations for the disrepair into which the classic welfare state appeared to have fallen in the mid-1970s – managerial failure and political failure. Both sprang from the same source. In the 1940s, the rôle of government had been radically transformed, from the passive to the active promotion of individual welfare; but in order to discharge this new responsibility effectively, a parallel transformation was required both in the institutions of government and in popular attitudes towards state intervention. Neither was achieved – at least, not with sufficient speed. As a result, the full potential of active state intervention was never realized; and the spectre was raised that the reconciliation of both economic and social policy and of individualism and collectivism might lead not to the best, but to the worst, of all worlds.

The managerial failure was all the more damning because during the Second World War – as a result, in Peter Hennessy's words (1989, 88), of that "well known expert in public administration, Adolf Hitler" – Whitehall had been forced to reform itself. A dynamic blend of regular and irregular civil servants had created a ferment of ideas, of which the 1944 Employment Policy White Paper, drafted jointly by the Treasury and the economists temporarily employed within the Economic Section of the War Cabinet, was the most significant product (Lowe 1993, Ch. 5.1). Specialists were given access to top decision-makers, so that they might have an immediate and direct impact on policy. Skills in executive management, as well as in policy advice, were encouraged and rewarded. Above all, there was a pervasive enthusiasm, based on the belief that "everything was achievable". "Postwar Whitehall," Hennessy has observed, "was *the* place to be for the young and the clever with a high personal charge of public duty" (1989, 135).

This golden opportunity for permanent reform was lost, however. Absent from the steady flow of reconstruction White Papers between 1943 and 1945 was any attempt to address the issue of the machinery of government. As a result, there was no institutional blueprint (which many defeated nations enjoyed subsequently) for an active, interventionist state. The irregulars started to leave, specialists again became subordinate to generalists, and enthusiastic recruits were schooled not in management skills and risk-taking, but in the traditional virtues of policy-advice and crisis avoidance. The government was thus denied both the specialist skills and the vitality that were essential for the resolution of potential conflicts within policy, and for the effective taking of hard decisions about the allocation of scarce resources.

Education policy provides an apposite case study for managerial failure. There were some examples of good management, such as the Ministry of Education's school-building programme of the 1950s. However, the compromise between centralization and decentralization was a continuing source of weakness, rather than of strength. Decisions were evaded rather than faced. In the early 1950s, for example, central government failed to ensure that local government achieved parity of esteem between grammar, technical and secondary modern schools. It thereby helped to discredit a tripartite system of secondary education that has continued to work well for many of Britain's economic rivals, such as Germany.

Even more seriously, there was no consistent attempt to ensure the complementarity of education and economic policy. It had long been recognized that Britain's international competitiveness was being eroded by the technological inadequacies of both managers and workforce. The 1943 Education Reconstruction White Paper had observed that:

> Too many of the nation's abler children are attracted into a type of education which prepares primarily for the University and for the administrative and clerical professions; too few find their way into schools from which the design and craftsmanship side of industry are recruited. If education is to serve the interests both of the child and the nation, some means must be found of correcting this bias (Cmd 6458 1943, para. 28).

Although this problem was clearly identified, little action was taken by the government to solve it. County Colleges, which had been proposed by the 1944 Act as a focus for compulsory part-time education between the ages of 15 and 18, were never built, and a restricted experiment with technical secondary schools was abandoned in 1958. It was in just such areas of intermediate training that the educational strength of competitors, such as Germany, was located. These areas remained undeveloped in Britain largely because experts in Whitehall, with their own bias towards the liberal arts, appeared to lack both the will and the expertise to provide the necessary lead (Lowe 1993, 228–32).

Who, or what, was responsible for this managerial failure? Clearly the Treasury must take some of the blame. As the central economic ministry, it failed – at least until the mid-1960s – to develop the economic and statistical skills that were necessary for the effective management of an enlarged public sector, let alone the management of the economy. Even more culpably, it failed in its rôle as the department responsible for the management of the civil service until 1968, by not encouraging – and at times even actively *discouraging* – the development of such skills in high-spending departments (Lowe 1993, 85–8). Senior politicians were also to blame, because none of them took any serious or sustained interest in the machinery of government, from 1940 to the premiership of Edward Heath. This was a particularly curious oversight on the part of Labour ministers who, especially in the 1940s, had articulated such high expectations of centralized planning. There was also the constitutional impediment that ministers were conventionally responsible for all departmental decisions. This not only frustrated civil servants, who were denied legitimate scope for initiative, but also led to ministerial overload and, consequently, bad decision-making.

Even more important, however, were two fundamental issues that remained unresolved. The first was the issue of power within Whitehall. To control public expenditure, the Treasury without doubt needed an annual budget; but the cost-effectiveness of welfare policy depended upon long-term expenditure plans. How were these competing priorities to be reconciled? The Public Expenditure Survey Committee, with its five-year rolling programmes, was developed in the wake of the 1961 Plowden Report on the Control of Public Expenditure as an answer to this problem, but typically, it was inexpertly implemented (Cmnd 1432 1961). Secondly, there was the question of the power of Westminster. In economic policy in particular, success depended on long-term investment plans and corporate deals, which inevitably took effective decision-making away from Parliament. How was democracy to be safeguarded?

It was because fundamental issues such as these were neither directly confronted nor resolved that the potential effectiveness of active state intervention under the classic welfare state was progressively eroded.

The other major failure was political. It was not so much a failure of political leadership although, as has been shown, that did occur, but rather a broader political failure: the widespread absence of positive and informed support for active state intervention – in a country which, after all, had a tradition of public suspicion towards central authority. After 1940 there was a general welcome, and indeed demand, for a guarantee by government of such "rights" as social security and full employment. However, there was little parallel enthusiasm for, or acceptance of, any corresponding costs and "duties". Were active state promotion of individual welfare to proceed beyond the gratification of individual short-term interest to a mechanism for the rational, long-term allocation of scarce resources, a revolution in popular culture was urgently required.

The Labour governments of 1945–51 did, in fact, attempt to achieve such a revolution, but they were not successful. A major publicity campaign was launched on the appointed day of 5 July 1948, when the major postwar reforms, such as the NHS and social insurance, were formally implemented. It sought to win public acceptance for three major points: that the new welfare services were not free, but had to be earned through higher productivity; that social insurance, despite its higher premiums, was more efficient and cost-effective than the previous mixture of compulsory and private insurance; and that welfare expenditure would assist and not retard economic growth (PRO 1948). This campaign was not successful, however: it was curtailed by a press outcry, orchestrated by Lord Beaverbrook's *Daily Express*, over the misuse of taxpayers' money (a complaint which the paper failed noticeably to repeat when a very similar attempt was made to foster an entrepreneurial culture in the early 1980s).

In 1951, Hugh Gaitskell prepared a campaign to re-emphasize the warning given in the 1944 Employment Policy White Paper, that a "high and stable level of employment" was not wholly within the gift of government, but was dependent upon responsible behaviour from both sides of industry in the shape, for example, of wage restraint and the relaxation of restrictive practices (PRO 1950). This campaign was, however, brought to an abrupt halt by election defeat. It only resurfaced five years later, in a much attenuated form, in the Conservative White Paper, *The economic implications of full employment* (Cmd 9725 1956). Thereafter, policy-making became increasingly élitist, with an emphasis on the manipulation of public opinion, rather than the fostering of positive support for, and understanding of, the advantages of state action (Smith 1979, xi).

In consequence, public opinion remained largely faithful to the traditional British view that the rôle of government is to guarantee certain rights of the "free born Englishman". It was unsympathetic to the continental "organic" model, in which the government is seen to be an expression of the common interest and therefore not only dispenses rights, but also requires reciprocal responsibilities (Harris 1986, 233–63). Indeed, it is arguable that public attitudes became even less communally minded and more self-centred with the increase in affluence and consumerism, symbolized by the introduction in 1955 of advertising on commercial television.

This selfishness, Peter Baldwin has claimed, had already characterized the middle classes' acceptance of the welfare state in the 1940s. The increased cost of health care and pensions, as a result of advances in medical science and increased longevity, had convinced those who had formerly considered themselves to be self-reliant, that risk-equalization and social solidarity were desirable after all. Stigmatized benefits for the few were thus transformed overnight into worthwhile social rights for all (Baldwin 1990, 31). Similar attitudes characterized the affluent workers observed by Goldthorpe (Goldthorpe 1968–71). Positive support remained for those benefits from which the majority of taxpayers would benefit, such as the NHS and pensions; but increasing hostility was expressed against those services directed at the "undeserving" poor, such as single parents and the unemployed, who were seen to be largely responsible for their own misfortunes (Taylor-Gooby 1985, Ch. 2). This failure to create a culture more supportive of collective provision left the classic welfare state – or, at least, significant parts of it – extremely vulnerable to counter-attack in the mid-1970s. Just as managerial failure had failed to prove conclusively the positive advantages of collective action in many areas of policy, so political failure left the way open for cuts in welfare provision once public expenditure had been identified as a factor contributing to inflation.

Conclusion

The record of the welfare state in its classic phase, between 1945 and 1976, was considerable: during these years, many of the real advantages of active state intervention were clearly demonstrated. However, as a result of managerial and political failure, many other potential advantages were not fully realized. In order for them to be fulfilled in the future, there must be significant changes both in the management of state welfare and in popular attitudes towards it. In particular, administrative experiments such as the introduction of "quasi-markets" (which are discussed in Chapters 7 and 8 of this book), must be welcomed and monitored professionally in order to ensure the most cost-effective delivery of policy. In addition, resources must be recognized publicly as being scarce, and there should be an acknowledgement of the need for clear priorities. Above all, it must be understood by everyone that there can be no guarantee of social rights without an acceptance of the need for reciprocal duties.

Notes

1. Equality of outcome means that everyone in society has an equal amount of income, wealth, educational qualifications, and so forth.

References

Baldwin, P. 1990. *The politics of social solidarity*. Cambridge: Cambridge University Press.

Baldwin, P. 1994. Beveridge in the longue durée. In *Beveridge and social security 50 years on*, J. Hills et al. (eds). Oxford: Oxford University Press.

Barnett, C. 1987. *The audit of war*. London: Macmillan.

Barr, N. 1987. *The economics of the welfare state*. London: Weidenfeld & Nicolson.

Cmd 6404 1942. *Social insurance and allied services* (The Beveridge Report).

Cmd 6458. 1943. *Educational reconstruction*.

Cmnd 1432 1961. *The control of public expenditure*.

Crosland, A. 1956. *The future of socialism*. London: Jonathan Cape.

Donnison, D. & C. Ungerson 1982. *Housing policy*. London: Penguin.

Glennerster, H. 1990. Social policy since the Second World War. In *The state of welfare*, J. Hills (ed.), 11–27. Oxford: Clarendon Press.

Goldthorpe, J. 1968–71. *The affluent worker*, 3 vols. Cambridge: Cambridge

University Press.

Harris, J. 1986. Political ideas and the debate on state welfare. In *War and social change*, H. L. Smith (ed.), 233–63. Manchester: Manchester University Press.

Harris, J. 1990. Enterprise and welfare states: a comparative perspective. *Transactions of the Royal Historical Society* **40**, 175–95.

Hennessy, P. 1989. *Whitehall*. London: Secker & Warburg.

Lowe, R. 1989. The Second World War, consensus and the foundation of the welfare state. *Twentieth Century British History* **1**, 152–82.

Lowe, R. 1993. *The welfare state in Britain since 1945*. London: Macmillan.

Marshall, T. H. 1950. *Citizenship and social class*. Cambridge: Cambridge University Press.

Morgan, K. O. 1990. *The people's peace*. Oxford: Oxford University Press.

Powell, E. 1966. *A new look at medicine and politics*. London: Pitman.

PRO (Public Record Office) 1948. CAB 124/1016, *Economic Bulletin 21*, 26 November.

PRO (Public Record Office) 1950. T 230/294–6, Economic Section of War Cabinet papers on full employment policy.

PRO (Public Record Office) 1957. T 171/478, memo 25 by R. Hall, March.

Simon, B. 1986. The 1944 Education Act: a Conservative measure? *History of Education* **15**, 31–43.

Smith, T. 1979. *The politics of the corporate economy*. Oxford: Martin Robertson.

Taylor-Gooby, P. 1985. *Public opinion, ideology and state welfare*. London: Routledge & Kegan Paul.

Titmuss, R. 1958. *Essays on the "welfare state"*. London: Allen & Unwin.

3

Conservatives and consensus: the politics of the National Health Service, 1951–64

Charles Webster

The welfare state in Britain is thought to have been conceived and sustained by a broad political consensus which emerged during the Second World War and was maintained until it was fractured in 1979 by Margaret Thatcher's election victory. The position of the National Health Service (NHS) has been central to this argument.[1] It is generally believed that Conservative governments afforded a protected status to the NHS prior to the Thatcher era, and that its piecemeal dismantling since 1979 represents a break with this tradition. This chapter examines the evidence against such a view. It demonstrates the need to root historical interpretations in a detailed and systematic reading of contemporary sources. The chapter argues that for the Conservatives, the NHS was among the least regarded of the social services: it was the first candidate offered for sacrifice in the search for economies in public expenditure intrinsic to their plan to create an "opportunity state". Powerful forces within the Conservative government throughout the 1950s and early 1960s pressed continuously for significant departures from the principles adopted by the original architects of the NHS.

The Ministerial deliberations discussed in this chapter form part of a wider debate, from which emerged the philosophy destined to reach full fruition during the Thatcher period. For the progenitors of Thatcherite ideology, the NHS was one of the major targets of their criticism. As early as 1959, reacting to pressure from right-wing activists unsympathetic to the new health service, the British Medical Association (BMA) established a committee to draw up proposals for an entirely new form of insurance-based health service to supplant the NHS.[2] By 1964 the Conservatives were further along the road towards a radical reassessment of the NHS than is generally realized.

Until recently, interpretations of the rise of the welfare state have been dominated by the idea of consensus. As the acknowledged pillar of the welfare state, the NHS is thought to provide an ideal test case for the application of this "consensus hypothesis". Indeed, the first detailed applications of the idea of consensus were made with reference to the origins of the NHS. Superficially, the case for consensus appears to be compelling. For example, the vehement opposition of the Conservatives to Aneurin Bevan's policies led to the articulation of fears that Sir Winston Churchill's last administration (1951–5) would dismember the NHS.[3] Harry Crookshank, the Minister of Health appointed in 1951, seemed poised for this rôle. However, Crookshank was quickly superseded by Iain Macleod, one of the chief advocates of the "one nation" approach to Conservatism, which entailed adoption of a more positive approach towards social policy. Macleod was efficiently protective of the NHS. Building on Macleod's consolidation exercise, his stablemate Enoch Powell initiated a phase of expansion, particularly through the agency of the Hospital Plan (an ambitious programme for hospital building and modernization) launched in 1962. Conservative general election manifestos proclaimed their commitment to the health service: when the Conservatives left office in 1964, they handed over a service that appeared to be unchanged in its essential characteristics.

However, the whole notion of consensus is now being subjected to critical examination. With respect to the Second World War origins of the welfare state, the consensus approach has been subjected to a barrage of convincing criticism.[4] The weakness of the idea of consensus with respect to the *origins* of the NHS has already been demonstrated.[5] Although less attention has been paid to the postwar period, accounts of the 1945–51 Labour government give little support for the idea of consensus. The concept has thus retreated to the period between 1951 and 1979 but little detailed research into this period has yet been undertaken. One study by Anthony Seldon of the last Churchill administration is broadly supportive of consensus, but other commentators express reservations.[6] This chapter examines in detail the record with respect to the NHS of the Conservative administration from 1951 to 1964 – the period referred to by proponents of the consensus hypothesis as providing some of the strongest and most uncontentious evidence for the solidification of consensus in the welfare field.

A sterile regime

The new service was barely past its teething troubles when the Conservatives assumed office in the autumn of 1951. They inherited a neglected and war-damaged hospital system; an urgent requirement for medical facilities in new areas of urban development; a high birth-rate; a rising elderly population; an accelerated pace of medical innovation; higher expectations of health and treatment; and the target of a comprehensive, first-class service for all, largely free of direct charges. These objectives clearly could not be met without adopting a bold programme of development, and expanding the volume of resources devoted to the new health service.

However, the omnibus Ministry of Health established in 1919 had been split up by Labour in 1951, and the greatly reduced rump responsible for the NHS was consigned to an unattractive backwater of Whitehall. This demotion of the Ministry of Health was preserved by the Conservatives. The Minister of Health enjoyed Cabinet rank for little more than two years, from 1962 to 1964; the Ministry was therefore an unattractive assignment for ambitious politicians or the civil service élite. No fewer than seven Ministers were responsible for the NHS between 1951 and 1964, and most of them were of minor stature. It is commonly argued that Macleod and Powell were the exceptions. Both possessed obvious political ability, but Macleod lacked experience, and made little impact during his period of tenure as Minister of Health;[7] Powell adopted a Treasury-minded approach to his office, and was over-occupied with holding down expenditure. Officials of the Ministry of Health lacked confidence in dealing with their Treasury colleagues, while their Ministers were unable to compete with other spending Ministers, or to overcome the power exercised by Treasury Ministers. After its difficulties in controlling Aneurin Bevan, the Treasury became practised in the art of restraint, and it was rarely outmanoeuvred in its campaign to restrict spending on health. None of the relevant Ministers of Health rivalled the experienced and politically astute David Eccles, who was Minister of Education almost continuously from 1954 to 1962, and whose post carried Cabinet rank. This difference in status and greater continuity of ministerial responsibility help to explain why health languished and education became the government's primary social service priority.

Because of the dominance of Treasury authority over NHS policy, the

Conservative administrations were able to dispel convincingly the predictions of sceptics that the new health service would constitute a crippling burden on the Exchequer. In 1959, the Minister of Health pointed out to Cabinet colleagues the dismal record of the Conservative government. He indicated that, in real terms, the Exchequer contribution to the NHS had risen from £345m to only £395m between 1949/50 and 1958/59; this caused the share of the GNP absorbed by the health service to fall, from 3.84 per cent to 3.49 per cent, the lowest point of 3.24 per cent having been reached in 1954/55.[8] The meagre resources normally available for expansion were for the most part swallowed up in unavoidable expenditure beyond the control of NHS authorities, such as increases in pharmaceutical costs, in remuneration of doctors and dentists, and unanticipated emergencies.

These resource constraints rendered it difficult to realize the original remit for the service as defined by Bevan. Given the stringent regime of containment imposed on the NHS, the government obstructed expansion. Where concessions were unavoidable, their implementation was delayed to the maximum degree; when action eventually became unavoidable, improvements were limited to the minimum extent practicable in order to evade the accusation of bad faith. Treasury ministers tended to oppose all development initiatives indiscriminately, even where they represented enlightened and desirable objectives, and where they might lead to possible economies in expensive hospital services. The few imaginative initiatives emanating from the Ministers of Health elicited a blast of ritualized antagonism from the Treasury which effectively quenched any residual instinct for change. While it was appreciated that the new situation offered opportunities for trials of innovative approaches to care, particularly in the primary and community care fields, few efforts were made to realize these objectives.

One of the most notable shortcomings of the early NHS was the failure to implement the promise of a universal system of health centres, which were intended as the basis for the modernization of primary care and preventive services. Initially, health centres were not pursued on grounds of economy, but this argument rapidly lost its credibility. Although the health centre programme was never formally abandoned, only 10 health centres were established in the first 12 years of the NHS. By 1960, the health centre policy was effectively dead, and no Conservative minister in the period under consideration attempted its resuscitation. The first internal report on this issue boldly concluded that "the Ministry must

57

shoulder the main blame that the network of health centres over the whole country envisaged in the early days of the NHS failed to develop".[9] Failure to establish health centres restricted opportunities for the progress of primary care and for integration between doctors and local authorities in the creation of a framework of community care. The latter was left largely to the discretion of Medical Officers of Health and the Local Health Authorities – the most depressed arms of the new health service. Local authorities were not encouraged by the health department to develop their responsibilities in the fields of prevention, promotion and community care. The result was a generally low level of provision, and the persistence of notorious disparities in levels of local services.[10]

The bleak record of the Conservatives in the field of community care extended even to services involving negligible public expenditure commitment. For example, in principle under the NHS a chiropody service could be provided by Local Health Authorities. In practice, as an economy measure, the government limited this to the few areas that had provided the service before the inception of the NHS. In 1956 the Cabinet decided to relax this restriction in order to help the elderly, who as a class were not being exempted from a substantial increase in the prescription charge. But Treasury Ministers fought off until 1959 attempts to announce the chiropody concession, on the understanding that the extended service would not begin until 1961, and then with an estimated cost limited to £1m over five years.[11] A similar failure to stimulate local authority intervention occurred in the case of meals-on-wheels. This service expanded to a minor extent in the 1950s through the work of voluntary agencies; the rôle of local authorities was limited to providing subsidies for voluntary organizations. Members of Parliament exerted continuous pressure to allow the direct involvement of local authorities. In 1959, the Conservatives gave a general election pledge to make better provision for this service, but the necessary amending legislation was delayed until 1962. In 1964 local authorities and voluntary agencies were collectively providing less than five per cent of the estimated need for meals-on-wheels.[12]

The Hospital Plan is conventionally cited as an example of conspicuous initiative by the Conservatives, but here, too, we find less evidence for expansionism than appears on the surface. The hospital problem was the most serious issue confronting the new service. The ramshackle hospital system was approaching dereliction, and it urgently required a complete redesign in accordance with modern needs. However, from the outset capital expenditure was constrained to a minimum, and the Conservative administration evaded action in the interest of holding down health expenditure. In the first 10 years of the NHS, no new hospital was completed in England and Wales, and neglect of the hospitals caused an increasing professional and public outcry. Anxieties on this issue were supported by the Guillebaud Report (1956), which called for a long-term programme of capital expenditure at a level of £30m per annum; this under-represented the scale of need, but was three times the level of spending at the time. The government moved only slowly in the direction of the Guillebaud recommendations. Some concessions seemed necessary because of the obviously disadvantaged position of the health service compared to the education sector, where a large, long-term capital programme had been agreed for schools. Attempting to capture a fairer share of capital investment resources, the Minister of Health, Derek Walker-Smith, put forward in 1958 a demand for a development plan for hospitals, which evolved into his "Five Year Plan" for the health services; a main ingredient of this was an enhanced level of capital expenditure on hospitals.[13] This was the direct ancestor of the Hospital Plan published in 1962 by Enoch Powell, who deserves the credit for having secured for the first time the government's public commitment for a hospital building programme of extended duration. Nevertheless, Powell was far from being an uninhibited expansionist. In practice, despite grandiose publicity, the Hospital Plan was not a properly conceived planning exercise, and it involved in the short term only the most limited increase in capital expenditure. Treasury officials described Powell as being "more austere than anyone else" among the ministers, and as "a shining example of the policy of control".[14]

Powell's severity had already been demonstrated in 1958 when, as Financial Secretary, he joined the Chancellor of the Exchequer, Peter Thorneycroft, in resigning over failure to introduce public expenditure cuts. Powell intended to finance the Hospital Plan through charges levied on the sick. Also, to the surprise of the Treasury, he agreed to a "contract" limiting the increase of expenditure on hospitals to 2 per cent per annum, within an overall growth rate of 2.5 per cent for the NHS as a whole. This contract was still in place in 1964.[15] It imposed virtually impossible constraints on hospital development because of the higher costs of advanced hospital facilities. Any chance of meeting the imposed spending limits would have needed to rely on a rapid run-down of mental hospitals and the drastic expansion of community care; although both of these were objectives to which Powell subscribed, no effective steps were taken to achieve either.

Economy exercises

The Conservative government's campaign to contain expenditure on the NHS and minimize expansion was a main priority, and it absorbed much of their available energy. The second line of attack was the search for cuts, reduction of subsidies, or alternatives to funding from central taxation. These alternatives were pursued continuously and energetically, especially from 1951 to 1961. The context for this was mainly the annual round of negotiations over estimates, but special reviews of NHS or social services expenditure were also relevant. The NHS was a primary target for cuts because it was perceived to be the greatest potential source of demand for additional resources – a weak and easy target. It was also seen as an exemplar for a necessary shift in public attitudes away from a reliance on state-provided welfare services.

Special economy exercises were not a conspicuous success. After the abortion of the economy package evolved by Crookshank at the beginning of Churchill's administration, the Treasury became alarmed at the prospect of a rise of NHS expenditure above their adopted ceiling of £400m. As Chancellor of the Exchequer, Butler told Macleod that he was determined to avoid continually rising expenditure on the NHS, and that he intended to reduce its cost to the Exchequer.[16] Butler was particularly supported in Ministerial discussions by Lord Cherwell and by Thorneycroft. The result of these discussions was an independent committee, chaired by the economist, Claude Guillebaud; the long-drawn-out deliberations of the Guillebaud Committee effectively precluded government intervention until its report was published in 1956. The report itself became a barrier to retrenchment, because it was overwhelmingly complimentary about the NHS, detecting few avenues for economy, but many opportunities for additional expenditure.

While the Guillebaud Committee was still sitting, the NHS became caught up in the deliberations of the Swinton Committee, a small group of ministers convened in May 1954 to plan a £100 million reduction in civil expenditure. Ministers were asked to consider the effects of making a 5 and 10 per cent reduction in their programmes. The committee shortlisted six major savings for the NHS; these were eventually reduced to minor proposals for reductions amounting to £14m, a sum regarded as a reasonable share of the social service savings target of £20m.[17]

The lack of radicalism of the Guillebaud and Swinton Committees caused a renewed outbreak of alarm concerning the likely growth of social service expenditure, and the NHS was again singled out for particular attention.[18] R. A. Butler warned the Prime Minister that arresting the rise in social service expenditure would require "major changes of policy" and unpleasant decisions.[19] This issue was addressed by a further Committee of Ministers, the Social Services Committee, which deliberated between January and October 1956, and conducted a "Five Year Survey" of social services spending. This committee considered a wide range of economies with a target of £21m for the NHS, and £146m for the social services as a whole. The dominance of spending ministers on this committee resulted in conclusions that were disappointing to the Treasury ministers and the Prime Minister, with the result that the committee was wound up. The Social Services Committee was revived in 1959 to examine the financial structure of the NHS, with a view to proposing a permanent reduction in the Exchequer contribution.[20] The essential work of this committee was referred to a committee of officials chaired by Frank Figgures of the Treasury. This produced a draft report in May 1960, but preparation of a final report was deferred, pending guidance from ministers. The evident lack of enthusiasm of the committee for any of the changes favoured by ministers, the recess, and Cabinet changes in the summer of 1960 caused the report to be set aside, and the Social Services Committee was dissolved in October 1960. This was the final attempt of the Conservatives to utilize formally constituted committees as a strategy for identifying major economies in the NHS.

Cuts

The main test of Conservative attitudes to the NHS occurred in the course of the annual expenditure rounds conducted by the Treasury. Very little from these deliberations attracted public attention at the time, although it was obvious that the economies introduced represented only part of a much broader package under consideration. The voluminous official papers relating to control of NHS expenditure may be reduced to a relatively simple pattern. Treasury ministers drew up an extensive list of economies which were pressed in different combinations at each expenditure round between 1951 and 1961. In summary, the full package of health and welfare economies wanted by the Treasury comprised: elimination of allegedly less "essential" functions, such as the dental and ophthalmic services, falling back on substantial charges for these services; various forms of prescription charge; a consultation charge for general practitioners or outpatient departments; abolition of family allowance for the second child; a "hotel" charge for hospital beds; and elimination of the subsidies on school meals, school milk, welfare milk and other nutritional supplements given to pregnant women and young children. From 1957 onwards, the Treasury pressed for radical increases in the NHS element of the weekly National Insurance contribution (the "NHS contribution") paid by employed workers. These proposals were reinforced by regular demands for cuts in expenditure on existing services, and especially cuts in the allocation for capital development and maintenance.

The suggested economies were discussed frequently with the departments concerned, and periodically by groups of ministers as well. The Treasury line always received some support, but positive advocacy by

School milk was targeted in plans to save money (Topham).

certain ministers of the services concerned, or known public antipathy to the cuts, always resulted in drastic curtailment of the proposed economies. At the same time, considerable headway was made with direct charges for services. In 1952 a prescription charge of 1s. per form, without exemption for the elderly, and a flat rate charge of £1 for dental treatment, were both introduced. In 1953 the school meals charge was increased from 7d. to 9d. In 1956 the prescription charge was increased to 1s. per item on the prescription form, and school meals were increased to 10d. In 1957, the flat-rate NHS contribution, which had stood at 10d. since 1948, was doubled to 1s. 8d.;[21] school meals were increased to 1s. (this breached for the first time the principle that charges should be limited to the actual cost of ingredients); the cost of welfare milk was increased from 1½d. to 4d. per pint; and entitlement to orange juice was limited to pregnant women, nursing mothers and to children under two instead of five. In 1958, the NHS contribution was increased by a further 8d. to reach 2s. 4d.

Until 1960, the campaign for economies in the NHS was spearheaded by Treasury ministers, and ministers of Health were reluctant participants. This situation changed in July 1960, when Powell became Minister of Health. Powell's appointment meant that, for the first time, the Treasury and the Ministry of Health were agreed in their philosophy towards the welfare state in general, and the NHS in particular. Powell was ahead of his colleagues in advocating the elimination of subsidies for welfare foods, greatly increased charges for dental and ophthalmic services, and a doubling of the prescription charge. He was also supportive of the Treasury proposal for increasing the NHS contribution. He expressed his determination to place a brake on the increase in NHS expenditure, reducing the scope of the service and creating conditions for a reduction in taxation.[22] Powell believed that the Hospital Plan need not lead to an increase in the Exchequer's contribution to the NHS; it could be financed by charges on the sick. The Home Affairs Committee warned that the path advocated by Treasury ministers and Powell might face very considerable political objections, and the Prime Minister was concerned that the needs of the economy and the government's philosophy, involving a reduction of the burden on the taxpayer, entailed "increasing the burden on the least affluent and the present package gave apprehension on this score". Powell sensed the unpopularity of his proposals, but he warned that the "political effect of doing nothing to meet this [increased NHS expenditure] would be more damaging than going forward with the proposals".[23] With the exception of welfare milk, where sentiment towards mothers and babies prevailed, the Cabinet was guided by Powell. In 1961, the prescription charge was doubled to 2s. per item; minor increases were also made in dental and ophthalmic charges; the subsidy on orange juice and related supplements was removed; and a further 1s. rise in the NHS contribution was introduced, bringing this to a level of 3s. 4d.

A contributory health service

Among the various charges introduced by the Conservatives between 1956 and 1961, regular increases in the NHS contribution had by far the greatest quantitative significance. They reflected the germ of new thinking within the Conservative government about general principles governing the funding of the health service. This issue is worth considering in detail, because it illustrates the fluctuating state of opinion within the government, sharp divisions of outlook, and ultimately a move away from the principle of the Exchequer's funding of the NHS.

Bevan himself had championed Exchequer funding for the NHS on the grounds that general taxation involved the maximum redistributive effect. The more prosperous classes would make the highest payments to the cost of the service, whereas the poor would be its greatest beneficiaries. The idea that a subsidiary element in the funding of the NHS should derive from the weekly National Insurance contribution, derived from the Beveridge Report. The National Insurance Act (1946) provided that a contribution from the National Insurance Fund should be dedicated to the NHS. This was set at 10d. per week for each person covered by the scheme. Under the Labour government and during the early years of the Conservative administration, there were no proposals to raise this contribution, which declined in importance from about 9 per cent to little more than 6 per cent of the gross cost of the service. Treasury officials even considered eliminating the NHS contribution as an unwelcome complexity which served little purpose, except to result in the popular misconception that the NHS was financed entirely from the "stamp", as the NHS contribution was popularly known.

This continuity of policy ended abruptly at the very end of Harold Macmillan's tenure as Chancellor of the Exchequer, during the month before he assumed office as Prime Minister following the resignation of Anthony Eden. The Suez crisis forced Macmillan to approach the problem of NHS expenditure with renewed determination. Perhaps building on an obscure suggestion made by the Minister of Health in the Social Services Committee, in December 1956 he instructed officials to look into the possibility of financing "a greater part of the cost of the health service by raising the weekly insurance stamp".[24] Senior officials and the Financial Secretary were unanimous in urging Macmillan to reject this option. Macmillan replied tersely: "I do not agree. But we must argue it out. Remember that Britain is on the verge of bankruptcy".[25] As Prime Minister, Macmillan continued the impetus for major cuts in public expenditure, if necessary involving difficult policy decisions. In keeping with this spirit, Thorneycroft, the new Chancellor of the Exchequer, proposed an elaborate package of cuts in public expenditure based on a target of about £50m overall for civil expenditure economies in the year 1957/58. The Chancellor's proposals were dominated by items relating to the health and welfare services: abolition of the dental service; cuts in welfare food subsidies; increased charges for school meals; hotel charges for hospital beds; abolition of the family allowance for the second child; and an addition of 1s. to the NHS contribution. Thorneycroft's preferred options were scrapping the dental service, abolishing family allowances for the second child, and "hotel" charges. He argued that the NHS "must bear a large proportion" of the social services cuts.[26] Initially, and by contrast with Macmillan, Thorneycroft was lukewarm about increasing the NHS contribution. Even though the yield was considerable, it was "a regressive tax applied to wage earners, a poll tax which would be applied to a limited class of people in aid of a service available to all".[27]

Protracted Cabinet discussions took place in January and February 1957 before the package of economies was agreed. David Eccles and John Boyd-Carpenter (Minister of Pensions and National Insurance) conducted a spirited defence of the family allowance, while most of the proposals for NHS economies were rejected. Increases in the cost of welfare milk and school meals were agreed reluctantly.[28] This left raising the NHS contribution as a major option. The idea was discussed at a dinner party held by the Prime Minister on 29 January 1957, to which the Chancellor of the Exchequer was not invited, when Macleod (Minister of Labour) and Derick Heathcoat Amory (Minister of Agriculture) actively canvassed the view that:

what was wanted was a quite new policy for the Health Service
– not a policy to dismantle it but to put it on to a contributory

basis. The suggestion was that the present level of 10d. in the insurance stamp . . . could be eliminated. At the same time a new
Health Service stamp could be introduced starting . . . at a level
of 1s. 6d. . . . . In later years this might be increased to 2s. or 3s.[29]

Thorneycroft was persuaded by this argument. At the Cabinet Meeting on 31 January 1957, he suggested that an entirely new contribution
should be devised – one which would be more widely levied than the
existing NHS contribution, and which might become the vehicle for steering the NHS towards the contributory principle. Notwithstanding the
scepticism of Boyd-Carpenter, the Cabinet recorded "general agreement
that the NHS should now be established on a compulsory contributory
basis".[30] They agreed provisionally to aim for a new charge at 2s. (super-
seding the existing charge of 10d.), with provision for periodic increases
in line with whatever was determined to be the appropriate level of insurance contribution to the NHS. The idea of separate NHS insurance was
explored by officials, but found to be impracticable. Consequently, it was
decided to fall back on increasing the NHS contribution; a rise of 10d.
was agreed. As a concession to the idea of separate NHS insurance, it was
also decided that the more expensive National Insurance stamp should
be marked with a separate block indicating the level of the NHS contribution.[31] This represented a satisfactory conclusion for the Treasury,
because the £50m anticipated yield from the increase in the NHS contribution made up half of the £100m target adopted for the 1957 "cuts
exercise". Furthermore, the increase restored the NHS insurance contribution to the level of 9 per cent, where it had stood in 1948, and the
combined yield from direct charges and the NHS contribution covered 14
per cent of the gross cost of the NHS.[32]

Ministers were surprised by the ease with which the increased NHS
contribution was accepted in Parliament. It seemed that they had hit for-
tuitously on a painless way of raising substantial additional revenue for
the NHS, and had thus gained respite from the debilitating political
controversy which had surrounded proposals for even the smallest
increases in direct charges for health, or reductions in subsidy for the welfare services.

The government was tempted to try the same manoeuvre again in
1958, when a further increase of 8d. was introduced in the NHS contribution, taking it to 2s. 4d. This increase produced a yield of £32m in a full
year, and the combined yield from direct charges and the NHS contribu-

tion rose to almost 20 per cent of the gross cost of the NHS. This was about the level mentioned speculatively by Beveridge at the outset of planning for the new health service.[33] This particular increase in the NHS contribution was important politically because of its centrality to the package of £153m in cuts proposed by Thorneycroft in January 1958. It was the only substantial item to survive his departure from the government. His successor, Heathcoat Amory, was left to steer the proposal through the Cabinet, a process that involved protracted debate extending through four Cabinet meetings, and which provoked vitriolic criticism from Boyd-Carpenter. In defending his original proposal for a 10d. rise, the Chancellor conceded that the increase "would admittedly appear to penalise the NHS at a time when the Estimate for that service would show an increase considerably less than the new revenue which it was now proposed to obtain by means of the increase in contribution".[34] As on previous occasions, Boyd-Carpenter attacked this strategy as a "hypothecated regressive poll tax"; and he pointed out that it would represent the third increase in insurance contributions within a year, and would take the total amount of the National Insurance contribution above an acceptable level.[35] A reluctant compromise was eventually agreed, whereby the NHS charge was increased by 8d. rather than 10d., in order to keep the employee's total insurance contribution below 10s.

By the autumn of 1958, Heathcoat Amory was again under pressure from the Prime Minister to undertake a further cuts exercise. After ten years' experience of the NHS, Macmillan believed that they should consider "large and dramatic changes of a policy nature".[36] The Chancellor now proposed that they explore the insurance approach more thoroughly, with the idea of increasing the proportion of the NHS that was financed by direct charges and insurance, from one-fifth to one-third: "indeed, I would not mind seeing most of the services financed by something like a corporate insurance scheme, with the contribution varying either according to earnings or according to the number of the contributor's family".[37] This radical speculation set in train discussions which led eventually to the analysis conducted by the Figgures Committee; the consensus of the Committee was that the Chancellor's idea was feasible, but problematic, and politically contentious.

Unwilling to await advice from the experts, Heathcoat Amory pressed in January 1960 for a further increase in the NHS contribution. He suggested a 1s. increase to colleagues, but his proposal was greeted unsympathetically and rejected. On this occasion, Thorneycroft was strongly opposed by both the Minister of Health and the Minister of Pensions.[38] In a memorandum to the Social Services Committee, Boyd-Carpenter castigated the NHS contribution as being "a poll tax which, unlike income tax, disregards alike the means and family circumstances of the taxpayer",[39] while Derek Walker-Smith warned his colleagues that it would be "impossible to satisfy Government supporters that such an increase was financially necessary, politically appropriate, or equitable in its incidence".[40] Despite opposition within the Cabinet, and little encouragement from the Figgures Report, John Selwyn Lloyd, who replaced Heathcoat Amory in July 1960, quickly picked up the idea of increasing the NHS contribution. He was supported by Powell, the newly-appointed Minister of Health. Both Ministers found this measure attractive, as a sign of their determination to reduce general taxation and to "bring home to the public that the money must be found to meet the rising cost of the Service".[41] On this occasion the proposal for a 1s. increase in the NHS contribution, taking the total amount to 3s. 4d., was accepted by the Cabinet. The changed attitude among Ministers was prompted by the argument that substantial additional revenues were needed to offset the cost of the new Hospital Plan.[42]

This sequence of events reveals a new unity of purpose between the Treasury and Ministry of Health. A key feature in this was Powell's infusion into the Ministry of Health of the austere public expenditure philosophy he inherited from his brief period as Financial Secretary. A result of the new coalition was that Selwyn Lloyd and Powell successfully piloted through the Cabinet in January 1961 a package of health service economies similar to the one decisively rejected in 1958. On 1 February 1961 Selwyn Lloyd announced the 1s. increase in the NHS contribution; a further increase in the National Insurance contribution; a doubling of the prescription charge to 2s. per item; increased charges for dental and eye services; and the withdrawal of the subsidy on orange juice and other dietary supplements for children, pregnant women and nursing mothers.

These changes represented the most ambitious package of economies made in the NHS since the Conservatives took office in 1951. Although the entire programme was executed as planned, it met with fierce parliamentary opposition, and added greatly to the government's unpopularity. The Labour opposition immediately grasped the opportunity to move a Vote of Censure, which was debated on 8 February 1961. Indeed, the whole episode provided a much-needed stimulant to Labour morale, offering as it did evidence of the carelessness of a government which was visibly becoming accident-prone after a decade in office. After this embarrassment, the government abandoned its attempts to increase the insurance element in the funding of the NHS, and there were no further increases in charges or cuts in subsidies on nutritional programmes. Powell and Sir Edward Boyle, the Minister of Education, continued to press for economies in school meals, school milk and welfare milk as a trade-off for their programmes of capital expenditure. They argued their case in Cabinet, but their seniors were unwilling to comply. Selwyn Lloyd and Macmillan even went to the extent of making public declarations that there would be no further cuts in social services. These gestures were calculated to appease particularly the trade unions, but they were made without consultation with the departments concerned; the result was much ill-concealed anger, especially from Powell, who had relied upon the abandonment of the welfare milk subsidy to rescue his flagging initiative in community care.[43]

Conclusions

Close examination of the record of the Conservative government between 1951 and 1964 provides little support for the idea of a sustained consensus of support for the NHS as the principal pillar of the welfare state. On the contrary, the scale of the changes made between 1951 and 1964 constituted a substantial attack on the NHS, while resource starvation and lack of commitment to improving the service prevented the emergence of the range and quality of care intended by the original architects of the service.

Successive Chancellors of the Exchequer, Financial Secretaries, and Macmillan, as Prime Minister, called for major changes in policy with respect to the funding and organization of the NHS. They considered seriously the elimination of large parts of the family practitioner services, the introduction of charges for consulting general practitioners or outpatient attendances, and "hotel" charges for patients in hospital. The only one of these radical proposals to survive, in the attenuated form of the increased NHS contribution, was the idea of transferring the funding of the NHS on to an insurance basis. This represented a reversion from the principle of Exchequer funding, which had been crucial to the original conception of the NHS. Conservative intentions on this front were only incompletely worked out, but it was fully understood that the transition to an insurance basis was likely to undermine the redistributive aspect of the original system.

Conservative thinking developed on a piecemeal basis, depending on the vicissitudes of ministerial changes and the instincts of the dominant actors. There was no preconceived, systematic plan. Many key actions with respect to the NHS were the result of the direct initiative of particular ministers. Although wide discrepancies of outlook on general principles and particular issues were evident, there was a general underlying drift in favour of policies narrowing the remit of the NHS, cutting back Exchequer involvement, and encouraging the growth of the insurance principle and private health care. While economic constraints were influential, and some initiatives stemmed from civil servants, especially Treasury officials, most of the policies of the Conservative government were not necessitated by economic circumstances. The economic tribulations experienced during this period necessitated only temporary expedients of retrenchment. In other words, there was absolutely no reason why the health services should not have enjoyed the flow of resources and development initiative evident in such fields as housing, education, defence, or nuclear power.

The health service was demoted to a position of low priority by the Conservatives; in England and Wales it was supervised by a weak government department and a series of uninfluential ministers. The obvious exceptions were Macleod and Powell, but the former did little to arrest the slide, while the latter was more active as an agent of retrenchment rather than in optimizing the development of the health service. The most striking feature of Conservative management was the regime of severe resource constraint which precluded urgently needed improvement and modernization. The most spectacular casualties of this embargo on change were the promised programmes of hospital renewal and health centre provision. On these crucial fronts, virtually nothing had been accomplished by the time the Conservatives left office. Paralysis over urgently needed reform was endemic throughout the system, and the first 13 years of Conservative responsibility constituted an arrest in development, from which it was virtually impossible for the NHS to recover, and which placed Britain's health care system in a position of severe disadvantage compared with more adequately funded services existing in other Western countries.

The positive energies of the government were directed largely into a continuous programme of cheese-paring economies, many of which were minor in scale when looked at individually, but which amounted collectively to a considerable imposition on low-wage earners, larger families, and the elderly. These groups were adversely affected by increased charges on prescriptions, dental and eye services, school meals, welfare milk and nutritional supplements, while low-wage earners were hit heavily by the NHS contribution. The collective yield of the NHS contribution and charges specific to the NHS amounted to only 6 per cent of the gross cost of the service in 1950, while in 1961 increases had taken this to about 20 per cent. In 1961, the poor were paying approximately £170m more into the NHS than would have been the case had the original basis of funding been preserved. This represented a severe erosion of the principles of social justice embodied in the original decision to provide services without charge and dependent on general taxation. The way in which charges were introduced took no account of ability to pay and relied on flat-rate charges which were difficult for the poor to avoid. This was in contradiction to Butler's promise that "we shall make charges where they can best be borne".[44]

The Cabinet was aware that hospital modernization and tax reductions for the better-off were being carried by an expanding burden of charges on the poor. The repeated onslaughts of Boyd-Carpenter and Walker-Smith on the NHS contribution demonstrated some distaste among ministers for the imposition of a "regressive poll-tax" on the poorer members of the community. Not only were the charges a hardship in themselves, but they also acted as a deterrent to the use of services. Each rise in charges was followed by a fall in take-up. For instance, the small increase in the school meals charge in 1953 from 7d. to 9d. resulted in a decline in uptake from 51 per cent to 43 per cent of the school population in England and Wales, and from 39 per cent to 32 per cent in Scotland. This example is symptomatic of the general situation within the health and welfare services. The services were developed on a more limited basis in less affluent regions such as Scotland, and already depressed services were further eroded by the imposition of charges.

It was only the strength of public support for the NHS and the vulnerable electoral position of the Conservative government that precluded any wider assault on the fabric of the NHS. Official papers are rich in instances where proposals for more radical curtailment of the NHS were stifled, either because of disunity among ministers, or for prudential considerations. A Treasury official commented characteristically: "Ministers had repeatedly felt unable, presumably for political reasons, to accept the various recommendations" for increased NHS charges.[45] The pressure of public opinion, in particular, clearly limited the extent to which the Conservatives were able to put into practice some of their more radical ideas. The record of policy deliberations shows equally clearly that the government was favourable to further significant departures from the original conception of the NHS.

When the case is examined in detail, it is difficult to confirm the view of Rudolf Klein that the period from 1951 to 1964 brought the political parties into "prevailing consensus", "an overarching consensus about essentials" or agreement about the "underlying philosophy and basic structure" of the NHS.[46] Significantly, contemporary expert opinion was also sceptical about the Conservative record. No less an authority than Richard Titmuss described the 1961 package of economies as a "final charge of dynamite under the welfare state" and a "major blow at the principle of a health service as established after the war".[47] Despite the element of hyperbole, Titmuss was not describing a situation which could meaningfully be described as a prevailing consensus, fidelity to the original philosophy of the NHS, or confinement of disagreement to inessentials. The crisis of 1961 exposed the tension between Conservatives and Labour over health and social policy, and drew attention to the steady drift of the 1951–64 Conservative government away from the conception of the NHS upheld by its Labour architects. Titmuss's remarks provide a corrective to the tendency to minimize the significance of actions which seemed controversial at the time and which were potentially devastating in their impact on the lives of ordinary people.

Our preoccupation with consensus, and failure to pay attention to these distant roots of the Thatcher revolution, left informed opinion unprepared to react to the radical policy initiatives which surfaced during the next extensive phase of Conservative government beginning in 1979. In this sense, a more accurate reading of the Conservatives' record from 1951 to 1964 is essential to an understanding of current predicaments in the NHS and the welfare state more generally.

Notes

1. H. Eckstein, *The English health service. Its origins, structure and achievements* (Cambridge, Mass.: Harvard University Press, 1958); R. M. Titmuss, "Health", in *Law and opinion in England*, Ginsberg M. (ed.), 299–318 (London: Stevens,

1959); D. M. Fox, *Health policies and health politics: the British and American experience 1911–1965* (Princeton, New Jersey: Princeton University Press, 1986); R. Klein, *The politics of the National Health Service*, 2nd edn (London: Longman, 1989).

2. *Daily Telegraph*, 2 February 1959; D. S. Lees, *Health through choice* (London: IEA, 1961); J. Jewkes & S. Jewkes, *The genesis of the British National Health Service* (Oxford: Blackwell, 1962); Institute of Economic Affairs, *Monopoly or choice in health services?* (London: IEA, 1964).

3. Aneurin Bevan was Minister of Health from 1945 to 1951, then briefly Minister of Labour before resigning over the issue of health charges. For the period of Conservative government 1951–64, the following served as Chancellor of the Exchequer: R. A. Butler (1951–5), H. Macmillan (1955–7), P. Thorneycroft (1957–8), D. Heathcoat Amory (1958–60), S. Lloyd (1960–2), R. Maudling (1962–4); and as Minister of Health: H. Crookshank (1951–2), I. Macleod (1952–5), R. Turton (1955–7), D. Vosper (1957), D. Walker-Smith (1957–60), E. Powell (1960–3), A. Barber (1963–4).

4. Summarized in R. Lowe, "The Second World War, consensus and the foundation of the welfare state", *Twentieth Century British History* **1**, 152–82, 1990.

5. C. Webster, "Conflict and consensus: explaining the British health service", *Twentieth Century British History* **1**, 115–51, 1990

6. A. Seldon, *Churchill's Indian summer. The Conservative government, 1951–55*. 244–94 (London: Hodder & Stoughton, 1981); H. Jones, "New tricks for an old dog? The Conservatives and social policy, 1951–55", in *Contemporary British history 1931–1961. Politics and the limits of policy*, A. Gorst, L. Johnman,W. Scott Lucas (eds), 33–43 (London: Pinter, 1991); Lowe op. cit.

7. C. Webster, *Problems of health care. The British National Health Service before 1957*, 200–2 and *passim* (London: HMSO, 1988).

8. D. Walker-Smith, GEN 677/1, 5 February 1959, PRO, CAB 130/160.

9. Department of Health, Minute, 14 October 1960, 94203/2/14.

10. C. Webster, "The elderly and the early National Health Service", in *Life, death and the elderly. Historical perspectives,* Pelling, M. & R. M. Smith (eds), 165–93 (London: Routledge, 1991).

11. PRO, T227/666 and 744.

12. Home Affairs Committee, HA(59) 18th and 23rd mtgs, 30 October and 11 December 1959, CAB 134/1976.

13. Walker-Smith, C (58)158, 18 July 1958, CAB 129/94; Treasury, SS 267/491/01C.

14. Treasury minute, 1 July 1963, Treasury, 2 SS 21/786/01A.

15. Treasury, 2 SS 1/21/01D; 2 SS 21/786/01A.

16. Butler to Macleod, 13 January 1953, Department of Health, 94501/9/1.

17. CAB 134/783.

18. Butler, CP (55)188, 3 December 1955, CAB 129/78.

19. Butler to Eden, 11 November 1955, T 227/413.
20. CAB 134/2533; Treasury, 2 SS 21/36/01A–B, and 02.
21. The 10d. NHS contribution was split between the employee (8½d.) and employer (1½d.). This ratio was preserved approximately in the course of subsequent increases.
22. HA (60) 25th mtg, 16 December 1960, CAB 134/1980; Powell, C (60) 150, 14 December 1960, CAB 129/103.
23. HA (60) 25th mtg, 16 December 1960, CAB 134/1980.
24. Macmillan to Sir Herbert Brittain, 27 December 1956, T 227/425.
25. Macmillan to Henry Brooke, 31 December 1956, T 227/425.
26. Cabinet, CC (57) 2nd mtg, 21 January 1957, CAB 128/31.
27. Thorneycroft, C (57)16, 30 January 1957, CAB 129/85.
28. CC (57) 11th mtg, 15 February 1957, CAB 128/31.
29. Treasury minute, 29 January 1959, T 227/485.
30. CC (57) 5th mtg, 31 January 1957, CAB 128/31.
31. CC (57) 11th mtg, 15 February 1957, CAB 128/31.
32. Treasury, SS 1018/534/01A.
33. T227/426; SS 1018/534/01A.
34. CC (58) 5th mtg, 14 January 1958, CAB 128/32.
35. Boyd-Carpenter, C (58) 7, 13 January 1958, CAB 129/93.
36. T227/744.
37. Heathcoat Amory to Macmillan, 12 September 1958, CAB 21/3194.
38. CC (60) 5th mtg., 3 February 1960, CAB 128/34.
39. Social Services Committee, SS (60) 8, 15 January 1960, CAB 134/2533.
40. SS (60) 2nd mtg, 25 January 1960, CAB 134/2533.
41. Lloyd, C (160) 148, 12 October 1960, CAB 129/102.
42. Treasury, SS 1018/534/01A.
43. Treasury, 2 SS 1/1128/01C.
44. Butler, HC Debates, 29 January 1952, cols 54–5.
45. Treasury minute, 5 September 1957, T227/485.
46. Klein, op. cit., p. 62.
47. Titmuss, R. M. *Daily Herald,* 2 February 1961.

4

Local voices in the National Health Service: needs, effectiveness and sufficiency

Jennie Popay and Gareth Williams

Introduction

Over the past few years, the National Health Service (NHS) in Britain has been undergoing profound change. The most recent manifestation of this is the implementation of the reforms subsequent to the White Paper *Working for patients* (Department of Health 1989a). However, the context of health care provision has also altered dramatically since the inception of the NHS. Notwithstanding the challenges posed by HIV and AIDS, chronic illness and disability have replaced infectious diseases as the major health problems of the late 20th century. The demographic and social contours of Western society have been transformed, so that a larger proportion of the population live longer than ever before, and enjoy significantly higher average living standards (Jefferys & Thane 1989). At the same time, the experience of ill-health remains unequally distributed, as does access to material resources (Blane et al. 1990, Delamothe 1991, Pond & Popay 1993). The overall degree, nature and speed of change within both the NHS and its broader social context add up to a significant need for evaluating the organization and working of the NHS. This chapter examines the most recently introduced set of reforms, and asks what they are attempting to achieve and how likely they are to succeed.

In order to illuminate some of the issues involved in answering these questions, the chapter focuses on a single dimension of the recent changes – the drive to involve or "listen to" local people (as it is termed in NHS parlance). This particular aspect of the reforms is interesting for three reasons. First, it relates centrally to the changing politics of the welfare state, in that it is concerned with the relationship between the provision of public services and actual or potential recipients of them. It therefore raises the old issue of the nature of, and structures for, accountability within the welfare state (Webster 1993, Harrison & Wistow 1993). Secondly, it links the NHS reforms to social and political changes under way in the public sector more generally and, indeed, in society at large. In particular, it reflects a wider shift in the relationship between lay people and professional "experts" (Giddens 1990). Thirdly, it is a key aspect of many of the other changes happening within the NHS, and is therefore a useful analytical tool for considering these. Further, the moves within the NHS to involve local people and patients in many service issues raise important questions for social science theory and research, as well as for policy and practice.

The chapter begins by providing a brief guide to the policy background for readers unfamiliar with a rapidly shifting terrain. It then goes on to consider the three main arenas within which moves to involve local people in the NHS are most apparent: the process of health-needs assessment; the evaluation and monitoring of services; and the rationing of health resources. In a final section, the chapter comments on some of the key research and policy issues.

The policy context

Much of the publicity about the recent NHS reforms has highlighted changes in the status and economic position of hospitals. However, the reforms are about much more than this (Davey & Popay 1993). At their centre is the split between those providing health and social care – be they in the acute or community sector, or concerned with cure, rehabilitation, prevention or promotion – and those who are potential purchasers of these services. The effect of the reforms was to create an internal market in health care, with provider units (some of them, and eventually perhaps all, being trusts) holding contracts with purchasing authorities to provide services to geographically defined populations (Day & Klein 1991, Enthoven 1991).

As always, neat organizational models do not hold up to too much scrutiny. District Health Authorities (DHAs) and, to a lesser extent, Family Health Service Authorities (FHSAs; these used to be called Family Practitioner Committees) are mutating into health purchasing authorities with a strategic remit to commission services reflecting the measured needs of their resident populations. However, all FHSAs and some DHAs, to a greater or lesser extent, retain provider functions. In addition, an increasing number of general practitioner (GP) fundholders are both providers and purchasers of services, although given the limited size of their practice populations, they are less well equipped than DHAs and FHSAs to develop a strategic view of health needs. The NHS reforms have a number of more or less explicit objectives. The most prominent of these is to control health care expenditure, and to do this by removing power and control from the hands of individual clinicians who make decisions about individual patients, and to put it instead into the hands of general managers (Flynn 1992, Davey & Popay 1993). A range of other policy initiatives contributing to this objective have been introduced: these include resources management, quality assurance, audit, and contracting out of support services (Harrison et al. 1990, Maxwell 1988). Alongside the dominant aim of controlling expenditure, the reforms also aim to make services more responsive to the needs of actual and potential users, as patients and as local residents. In the White Paper, *Working for patients* (Department of Health 1989a), much was made of the shift in emphasis from professionals providing care to the concerns of those receiving services (Department of Health 1989b; Department of Health 1991). There was to be a move away from a service-led approach to providing health care, to a "needs"-led approach.

Consumerism is not entirely new to the NHS. Indeed, the last time it received explicit political attention, the result was the formation of Community Health Councils. But the recent reforms have involved a significantly renewed, and to some extent different, emphasis. This was advanced in policy terms with the publication of *The patient's charter* (Department of Health 1991), which described a range of "rights" people have within the NHS, and stressed the importance of obtaining users' views of services. But the new emphasis has not stopped with the patient. In January 1992, the NHS Management Executive (NHSME) published a document entitled *Local voices* which encapsulated the extended remit:

> This paper focuses on one aspect of [establishing a local corporate view of health needs] – taking account of local people's views – but not just in relation to needs assessment. Local people's views should also be used at other stages in the purchasing process, i.e. to help establish priorities, develop service specifications and monitor services: they represent a significant element of "purchasing intelligence" (NHSME 1992, 3).

We have here an ambitious agenda for NHS managers and other staff. They are to seek local people's views on health and health care needs; on the process and outcomes of the care people are receiving; on the priorities which should guide the future development of the NHS in different regions; and on the types of services which should be developed to meet these needs and priorities. Faced with this list, managers and other staff can be forgiven for feeling somewhat daunted. They were not to be allowed to treat the task lightly. As the NHSME paper made clear, in theory at least there was to be a significant break with tradition:

> To give people an effective voice in the shaping of health services locally will call for a radically different approach from that employed in the past. In particular, there needs to be a move away from one-off consultation towards ongoing involvement of local people in purchasing activities (NHSME 1992, 1).

The reasons for involving local people in the purchasing process were also spelt out:

> If health authorities are to establish a champion of the people rôle, their decisions should reflect, so far as is practical, what people want, their preferences, concerns and values. Being responsive to local views will enhance the credibility of health authorities but, more importantly, is likely to result in services which are better suited to local needs and therefore more appropriate . . . Moreover, as health authorities seek to bring about changes in services and make explicit decisions about priorities they are likely to be more persuasive and successful in their negotiations with providers if they secure public support (NHSME 1992,1).

The reference to "champions of the people" relates to the health authorities' rôle in *The health of the nation* strategy (Department of Health 1992). It is particularly associated with their activities beyond the confines of the NHS. According to the NHSME, if local people are involved in the purchasing process, then health authorities will be more effective in pursuing policies within, and outside, the NHS which reflect the needs of their resident populations. Additionally, health authorities will legitimate their rôle in resource allocation and rationing in the face of malcontent from service providers and the public.

The drafters of this influential NHSME document have avoided the discourse of consumerism. The notion of involvement does not bring with it the complex and critical baggage associated with the concept of consumers in health care more generally (McIver 1991; Steele 1991; Taylor 1990; Winkler 1987; Fitzpatrick & Hopkins 1983). But involving local people in the NHS on the "radical" basis described in the NHSME document leads unavoidably to complications; if there are no complications, then there is no effective involvement (Williams & Popay 1994). It is therefore important that those who would seek genuine involvement recognize and deal with this complexity and acknowledge the limits set on this by the present structures of the NHS.

What is the nature of the complexity that ensues when local people are involved in health care issues, and what are the structural limitations? They can be illustrated by looking in turn at the three key arenas in which health authorities are to involve local people: health needs assessment; monitoring the quality of services; and priority setting.

Assessing health needs: lay and professional epidemiology

The NHSME has recently defined health need as "the ability to benefit" from health care (NHSME 1991). They propose two strategies for assessing such needs. In the long term, they argue that it is important to develop a "strict approach" to methodology, which is derived from "a combined epidemiology and health economics standpoint". However, they suggest that a "pragmatic approach, blurring the distinction between need and demand and between science and opinion . . . is available to help decision-making in the short term". Such a pragmatic approach would involve bringing together the perspectives of various interests, including lay, medical, local authority and voluntary organizations.

The distinction between strict and pragmatic approaches to needs assessment echoes the conventional distinction between the scientific and the non-scientific, between "objective" need and clinical quality, on the one hand, and matters of opinion, preference and non-clinical issues, on the other. In the NHSME model, the opinions of local people are to be subordinate to the perspective of clinical epidemiology and health economics. This interpretation is supported by further reading of the *Local voices* document (NHSME 1991). After stressing the importance of local views, the authors note that:

There may, of course, be occasions when local views have to be over-ridden (e.g. on the weight of epidemiological, resource or other considerations) (NHSME 1991, 3).

But does epidemiology deserve this privileged position?

The limits of traditional epidemiology

The extent to which health and social care needs can be assessed using the theories and methods of epidemiology is constrained by the preponderance of chronic disease (Williams & Popay 1993). Three problems are particularly salient here: origin, prevalence and outcome. Taken together, these problems provide a powerful case for adopting the NHSME's "pragmatic approach" to needs assessment on a more permanent basis, and giving lay perspectives on health needs an emphasis that is at least equal to that of other perspectives.

First, as regards the origins of disease and ill-health, there are many examples of the difficulties posed in attempts to provide simple models of the causes of disease. These are most graphically illustrated in relation to coronary heart disease (CHD). Not only are the purported causes of CHD themselves multiple, posing complex questions about interactive effects at cellular, individual and social levels, but the relationship between these factors and the variable (CHD) they are alleged to explain, is highly uncertain. The major risk factors taken together, for example, explain only a small amount of the social variation in the disease, though they take up an enormous amount of NHS preventive effort (Marmot 1976). In addition, epidemiology has difficulty in conceptualizing behavioural and social factors such as class, diet and stress, because they are not easily reducible to simple, unitary variables (Popay et al. 1992, Popay & Bartley 1993). If stress is equated with a life-events score, class with occupation, and diet with the type of fat used on bread, it is scarcely surprising that a large amount of variance remains unexplained.

Secondly, with respect to the prevalence of health problems, ascertaining cases of disease and establishing prevalence are especially problematic in relation to groups of people who are, in one way or another, at the margins of society. In such situations, the population may be extremely variable, questions may be raised about the representativeness of those sampled, and response rates may be low. In the field of AIDS and HIV, for example, or in relation to homeless people, issues to do with recall of information about personal behaviour, how to generate a sample, and how to ensure an adequate response rate from people who have good reason to feel suspicious of official studies, raise major problems for the traditional epidemiological approach (McKeganey et al. 1990).

Thirdly, in relation to outcomes of disease, morbidity is more important than mortality in most of today's major health problems. Incidence is relatively low, and prevalence relatively high, but it is not always clear what we should be establishing the prevalence *of*. For most purposes, the concern is not with the prevalence of symptoms, but rather with the prevalence of the disabling consequences of ill-health. Once the focus shifts to the disabling consequences of disease, however, it is impossible to ignore the fact that the severity of a disability does not have a simple one-to-one relationship with the severity of a disease or impairment. Rather, disability is the product of an interaction between the impairment and a variety of psychological, social and economic factors (Landes & Popay 1993).

The concept which relates most closely to the assessment of health needs is that of handicap. This represents the interaction between individuals and social circumstances. It is defined as "a disadvantage for a given individual, resulting from an impairment or disability, that limits or prevents the fulfilment of a rôle that is normal (depending on age, sex and social and cultural factors) for that individual" (WHO 1980, 29). The concept of handicap relates to the experiences of chronically ill people in their daily lives. By definition, it requires us to move beyond biomedical parameters to encompass social and cultural factors. This must inevitably involve the perspectives of people experiencing the disability.

As the primary basis for assessing health needs, epidemiology has one final limitation which should be highlighted. As already noted, the focus of most epidemiological research is on disease rather than the experience of health and illness. In the recent White Paper, *The health of the nation* (Department of Health 1992), the NHS is being asked to move away from its preoccupation with the treatment of disease, towards a concern with the prevention of ill-health and the promotion of health. However, if it is to succeed in this endeavour, then the process of health needs assessment will require the input of other perspectives – not the least of which are those of lay people.

Lay perspectives on health needs

In late 20th century Britain, and in common with many other Western nations, increasingly lay people are challenging the power and status of professional knowledge (Beck 1992). Medicine has not escaped this movement (Gabe et al. 1994). The challenge to established professional interest within the health field is evident in a number of dimensions: the health problems that are given priority; views on the causes of health problems; and the chosen method for studying these. There are many instances where lay views reflect very different priorities on health problems from those of health professionals. One anecdotal example from day-to-day experience of the NHS illustrates this. In discussions about the findings of the growing number of Lifestyle Surveys conducted by, and for, the NHS, it is not uncommon to hear that local people stress problems associated with poor houses, unsafe roads, low income, pollution etc., as the most important factors affecting their health, rather than aspects of behaviour (Ong 1993). In a recent meeting attended by one of the authors of this chapter, to plan such a survey, the frustration of a senior public health doctor could be restrained no longer. Why, he asked, should we seek people's views on what affects their health, when we would only get told again that they wanted the rubbish and the rats removed?

The growing concern among lay people about the health hazards of the environment is a powerful indication of a widening gap between lay perspectives on health priorities and those of many health professionals (Williams & Popay 1994). A recent example of this is the response of the residents of Camelford when, in 1988, a lorry driver accidentally tipped 20 tonnes of aluminium sulphate solution into the local water supply. A local voluntary group was set up to monitor the effects of this spillage on health, and the group undertook its own research. The official expert committee (the Clayton Committee) concluded that many of the early symptoms reported by local residents could be attributed to the incident, but that any ill-health caused by aluminium was temporary; for lead, zinc, copper and sulphate, the amounts likely to have been absorbed, even on a "worst case assumption", would also have no long-lasting effects. The committee concluded that:

> in our view it is not possible to attribute the very real current health complaints to the toxic effects of the incident, except in

as much as they are the consequences of the sustained anxiety naturally felt by many people (Clayton 1989, 3).

The residents' group disputed the committee's report, and in February 1990 the Isles of Scilly Health Authority organized a conference at which three papers were presented which fuelled the debate: a clinical biochemist found high concentrations of aluminium in blood samples one year after the incident; a neuropsychologist reported evidence "consistent with the effects of minor brain injury"; and a clinical psychologist discovered significant memory defects (Cornwall & Isles of Scilly Health Authoritiy 1990).

The public outcry following this conference led to the Clayton Committee being reconvened to consider the evidence again. However, much to the dismay of local people, the committee was to have the same membership. In 1991, the committee reiterated its conclusion that there was no evidence that the ailments local people had attributed to the accident were caused by toxic water (Clayton 1991). The residents are continuing their campaign to have their views taken seriously.

Playing in the streets of London's East End, 1990 (Syd Shelton).

There are a growing number of similar examples of what has been termed "popular epidemiology", where local residents have taken action on an environmental hazard which they felt to be damaging their health (Brown 1987, Brown & Mikkelsen 1990, Brown 1992, Williams & Popay 1994). All these examples contain within them a more or less explicit challenge to the dominant position of medical and epidemiological definitions of the nature of health problems. For example, in September 1991, residents in the Limehouse area of East London launched a group action against the London Dockland Development Corporation for disruption by dust, noise, and television interference. Earlier, they had attempted to mount a research project into the health effects of the extensive construction work under way in the area, particularly the effects on mental health and respiration. However, at a public meeting, the Director of Public Health warned that it would be difficult and costly to prove the effects of pollution on health (*Guardian* 1991a). In the North-East, residents in Grangetown are taking ICI to court, claiming that the emissions from an ICI petrochemical plant have damaged the health of adults and children in the area (*Guardian* 1991b). An extensive study of the health effects of the plant is presently being undertaken, funded by the local authority (Phillimore & Moffatt, in press). A final example of lay action on environmental health hazards is the study of the effects of damp housing on health by Hunt et al. (1988). Residents on a Glasgow housing estate asked the researchers to get involved because they felt that respiratory problems among their children were caused by damp – a "lay belief" subsequently supported by research. The research showed that parental smoking is of considerably less significance in relation to children's respiratory illness than damp housing. This finding was at variance with the views of many health professionals.

Lay people are also questioning the conduct, as well as the findings, of research. This is very evident in relation to research on the experience of disability (Oliver 1992). Another example of this is the response of some of the women attending the Bristol Cancer Help Centre to the Cancer Research Fund's (CRF) clinical trial of alternative versus conventional treatment for breast cancer (Bagenal et al. 1990). These women have succeeded in discrediting the CRF study, despite the involvement of many senior medical researchers. Their ultimate aim of winning a charity commission complaint against the funders on ethical grounds has now succeeded (Bagenal et al. 1990).

Discordance between clinical and lay understandings of health needs is commonplace at the individual level. The possibility that somebody who is clinically ill can report excellent health, for example, has been noted many times in research (Blaxter 1990). In one recent study of the needs of older people with vision problems, some people with significantly impaired vision according to clinical measures reported no vision problems, and vice versa (Harries et al. 1992; Landes & Popay 1993). Obviously, such findings reflect immensely complex situations. In the vision study, the group of people who were clinically impaired but reporting no difficulties with sight appeared to be older, poorer and more likely than others to live alone. They were also more likely to be experiencing macular degeneration – a condition which would have affected vision slowly, so that the person involved may have simply learnt to live with the problem. Low expectations among older people may therefore be a powerful influence on the health and social care needs they report. These types of finding from research can be used to support a range of responses on the part of NHS purchasing authorities. On the one hand, NHS purchasers may accept the epidemiological evidence, but this would mean providing services for people who may not use them. On the other hand, the authorities could use the lay perspectives to justify not providing a service. Ideally, of course, they should be using both lay and clinical evidence to produce a picture of health and social care needs which does justice to the complex experience of health and illness.

Monitoring the quality of service

The second arena within which the move to listen to local people is being enacted is in relation to the quality of services. Three examples of the ways in which people are "being involved" in this arena will illustrate this: patient/consumer satisfaction surveys; user groups; and patients' assessments of the outcomes of the care they receive. Again, none of these is entirely new; as already noted, it is a question of a renewed emphasis rather than a totally fresh initiative.

Since the publication of *The patient's charter* (Department of Health 1991), studies of patients' satisfaction with services have become commonplace within the NHS. In a recent review of three types of surveys – lifestyle, patient satisfaction and public opinion, conducted over a five-year period in 70 district health authorities in England, information was received on more than 300 different studies (Popay & White 1993).

Patient satisfaction surveys were the most numerous. In the main, these NHS surveys were obtaining information on the process of care. Until very recently the focus was almost entirely on what have been termed the "hotel" aspects of care – the food, the sleep routine, visiting times, access to telephone, waiting times, etc. But more recently these surveys have started to include questions on other aspects of care, including, for example, whether people felt sufficiently informed about what was happening to them. However, they are a long way from representing a "radical" departure in patient involvement compared with what has gone before.

Approaches to involving consumers/service users in various aspects of their own care have also been around for a long time. However, it appears that the purchaser/provider split and the introduction of GP fundholding (the arrangement whereby GPs have a fund from which they are able to purchase directly certain types of patient care from anywhere they wish rather than through a health authority contract), may have created a climate within which the potential to promote active involvement of lay people might be more fully exploited. These groups can take many different forms. In Newcastle, for example, the purchasing authority has established a Mental Health User Group which has become something of a good practice example throughout the NHS. The group has a wide remit, covering a contribution to the assessment of needs through experiences of needing mental health services; suggesting quality measures from a user's point of view; monitoring the performance of quality standards via user visits to wards, day centres etc.; and participating in the planning of future service. The experience of the group has been reviewed in the book *Power in strange places* (Barker & Peck 1988). This account suggests that service users can have some influence and power within mental health services. However, it remains to be seen whether they can use this influence to achieve more than marginal change. A somewhat different example of user groups are the health forums/groups established by community health services units and general practices – that is, by the providers of community health services, rather than by the purchasing authority (Copperman 1992). As yet, however, there is little evidence that such groups are having any significant effect on the pattern and nature of the care provided. A recent innovative variant on the user group as a way of involving people in their care is the patient interactive video. This is the focus of considerable interest at the moment, perhaps in part because it raises the possibility of a technical fix to what is at heart a political problem. Using a video, people are informed about a particular intervention before they agree to undergo it. This information includes what is known about the effectiveness, the likelihood of negative outcomes and the possible side-effects of the intervention. A video on benign prostate disease is presently being piloted by staff at the King's Fund Centre in London.

Considerable work has been undertaken into the development of standardized ways of presenting patient-assessed outcomes. This includes measures of patients' perspectives on quality of life and functioning following the receipt of services of various kinds (Bowling 1991, Wilkin et al. 1992). In many studies, measures such as the Nottingham Health Profile, the General Wellbeing Index and, most recently, a measure developed in the USA and referred to as the SF36, are used alongside a condition-specific measure of outcome, normally with a more clinical orientation.

An important backdrop to the growing interest in patients' own assessments of the outcome of the care they receive is the interest shown by purchasing authorities in the development of outcome-oriented contracts. These are contracts which are purchasing the outcomes of a service, rather than the throughput. An example here would be a contract which required that an Ophthalmology Department demonstrated a positive improvement in the visual functioning of the people receiving the service, rather than simply doing a particular number of cataract operations. A vital aspect of these developments is the pressure from central government to evaluate the cost-effectiveness of the health services. Here the almost reified "QALY" – "Quality Adjusted Life Years" – should be mentioned. At the heart of this approach is a somewhat crude instrument for measuring quality of life, combined with information on the improved length of life attributable to a particular intervention. There are many complex and difficult issues to be resolved in relation to the use of quality of life measures. Endless person hours have been, and will continue to be, spent exploring the validity and other technical aspects of the measures in the hope that an instrument will be developed which is sufficiently robust to be used routinely in a health care setting to measure changes over time, for all age groups and in relation to all conditions (Ware 1993). Alan Williams, the father of the QALY (at the time of writing the most likely candidate for such an all-purpose measure), recognizes the crudity of his prodigy and many of the alternatives. However, he argues that "a sketch map is better than nothing when you are lost in the fog" (Williams forthcoming).

The use of standardized quality-of-life measures raises important research issues for social science. In an ongoing study of patient-assessed outcomes for services for older people, for example, a series of in-depth interviews are being conducted alongside structured interviews to explore the extent to which standardized measures capture the experience of the people involved. Structured interviews with people who have had cataracts removed suggest that, although the majority do have a significant improvement in their visual functioning, this does not lead necessarily to an improvement in the quality of life (Hill et al. 1993).

To some extent these issues are about refining the measures to be used, and they are also partly about using appropriate methods. But the move to obtain information on the outcome of care, from patients as well as from a clinical perspective, is also part of a changing process of rationing within the NHS. As such, it involves political and ethical issues as much as, if not more than, technical ones.

The final arena in which local people are being involved within the NHS is in priority setting.

Prioritizing health care

To question the need, or the desirability, of rationing within the NHS is generally considered at best to be naïve, and, at worst, stupid. The supply of health care will obviously always be limited, and demand, if not limited, will far outstrip the present supply, and perhaps also that of the foreseeable future. Hence, it is argued that some form of "rationing" is inevitable in any health care system (Gray 1993). But there is cause for concern over the process that is now developing whereby the rationing which has long been implicit within the NHS is made explicit, and in which local people are to be involved. The concern relates both to the methods being used to involve local people and to the apparent imperative to engage in rationing at all in the present context.

The method: involving local people
in prioritizing health care

In the past in the NHS, the rationing of limited resources has taken place at the level of individual clinical decisions about who should receive what service and what types of care should be prioritized. The recent NHS reforms have attempted to replace this with an explicit process of "prioritizing", in which local people are to be actively involved. In many ways, the previous informal system of prioritizing was remarkably effective; so much so, in fact, that formal attempts to prioritize between service areas has failed miserably. For example, policies aimed at moving more resources into the so called "Cinderella services" for the mentally ill or into community care, had little effect on resource distribution (Hunter 1993). But will this new system to formalize priority setting fare any better?

David Hunter of the Leeds-based Nuffield Institute has eloquently argued the case against the desirability, and the feasibility, of establishing a system of "explicit rationing" on the basis presently envisaged (Hunter 1991). He suggests that such a process, far from facilitating innovation and change, may make the re-allocation of resources more difficult, because of the overt conflict that will arise between professional groups. Additionally, he suggests that clinicians will circumvent any rationing guidelines that are produced when they feel it is necessary (as they always have), simply by redefining an individual's problems to fit the guidelines. Finally, he suggests that the limited success that professionals had in arguing the case for the most vulnerable groups may be lost in a system where the articulate middle class and the "worried well" shout loudest.

But what exactly does explicit rationing entail? The most famous recent example was the Oregon experiment in the USA (Dixon & Welch 1991), which is referred to in Chapter 5 of this book. Here, the commissioners responsible for administering the Medicaid public insurance scheme decided they would rank all the treatment and care options available according to their cost, improvement in quality of life, and effectiveness, and then start at the top of the resulting list and work down until the available money was used up. This, they argued, would ensure that the largest number of people got access to the most cost-effective service. The ranking was shaped by surveys of public opinion on health care rationing.

Some features of the resulting list are fairly predictable: top priority goes to life-threatening emergency conditions, such as acute appendicitis, choking or a ruptured intestine. At the bottom of the list are conditions such as very severe birth defects, extremely premature babies and very superficial injuries. However, even at the extreme, ranking problems arise; for example, people with terminal HIV illness would be offered no treatment or care, and in the middle there are many conditions that would be the subject of intense debate.

This or similar approaches to rationing or prioritizing (to use the more acceptable word) are quickly gaining in popularity. In Maryland, USA, for example, Medicaid was made available only to people who also accepted preventive services; in New Zealand and the Netherlands, core services are being identified which will be provided by the state health care system; those services that will not be so covered are also being identified, by exclusion. Both countries have canvassed public opinion to inform this process. In Britain, the NHS is slowly getting involved in this type of initiative. Some districts have already announced that they will not supply certain services (e.g. tattoo removal). Authorities are also canvassing public opinion on prioritizing decisions.

A wide range of methods, in addition to traditional surveys, are being used to obtain the views of local populations. In one district, for example, questionnaires were handed out to those who attended a series of public meetings held over 12 months. Another approach is a technique known as "priority search"; this has been used in a variety of situations. For example, public priorities for Accident and Emergency services were sought in a situation where consideration was being given to closing one of two sites (Wigan Health Authority 1992). In another district, this approach was used to try to identify the values that local people would wish the district to use when making decisions about priorities (Salford Health Authority 1992).

There are important methodological issues to be raised in relation to some of these exercises. For example, information that is not "representative" in any statistical sense of the views of local people may be used as if it were. Of equal importance, whatever method is used to involve local people in discussions about priority setting, the process will inevitably be ill-informed, due to lack of knowledge. As we have already noted, attempts to measure the outcomes of care may contribute to the valuation of one service against another in the future. At the present time, however, the information on outcomes, effectiveness and costs that would be required to resource a supposedly "rational" approach to decision-making about service priorities simply does not exist. Even if the techniques used could not be faulted on methodological grounds, considerable problems remain. In the final analysis, decisions about what health service priorities should be are political and moral, not technical, decisions. The process of explicit rationing as it is being developed within the NHS at the time of writing, therefore raises some fundamentally important issues about who will control the agenda for debate, what weight is to be given to the views of different "voices", and about the accountability of those making decisions.

There is unlikely to be a consensus among the population about priorities. It is perhaps obvious that if the ranked priorities of different groups within a local population were considered separately, there would probably be as many different lists as there were groups. Who will be the advocates for the more vulnerable groups in society – those who have traditionally had no voice in the NHS? Furthermore, people shift into different groups depending on the context – a woman may be a mother, a carer and a patient all at the same time or at different times over her lifetime. As already discussed, the views of local people may also conflict with those of health professionals. How are health authorities to resolve the conflict that will arise between different "local voices" or between lay and professional groups? As the authors of a recent study of the health service priorities of local residents and health professionals in a London district noted, "What will purchasing authorities do if their local population does not agree with what they want to do?" (Bowling et al. 1993). It is also important to ask whether local people will have any control over the agenda for debate, or whether they will simply be asked to respond to the agenda set by professional experts. The prescriptive and predictable targets contained in the White Paper on *The health of the nation* (Department of Health 1992) appear to negate the idea of local people, perhaps even local health authorities, setting priorities. Certainly, it is also apparent that the question of whether present funding for the NHS is sufficient is a taboo subject in many areas of the NHS. While there is considerable scope for internal savings within the NHS, by stopping interventions of unproven effectiveness, for instance, or through cost-improvement programmes, should local people not also be debating whether the present level of investment in the nation's health is sufficient?

Finally, if some of the responsibility for political decision-making about priorities is to be passed down to local level, should not the authorities carrying this responsibility be representative in some way of the local populations they serve? In many district health authorities, not a single member of the authority, and few, if any, of the executive directors, live in the district. At present, unrepresentative executive officers and authority members are seeking legitimacy from their local residents. While the involvement of local people in decision-making on priorities could be a very welcome development, mechanisms of accountability within the NHS at local level must be improved before this becomes a reality. Put simply, a more democratic service is needed.

Conclusion

The views of local people are being sought increasingly in the NHS, either as users of services or as residents of health authorities. To seek these views is not necessarily to hear them, and to hear is not readily equated with understanding, involvement or participation. If lay people are to be effectively "involved" in the NHS, either at the level of strategy or in individual services, then fundamental changes in policy and practice within the service, and in the research process, are required. Social science has an important contribution to make in improving understanding about the interface between lay and professional perspectives on health needs, and on the outcomes of care (Barnes & Wistow 1992). The policy shifts discussed in this chapter inevitably will bring these perspectives together to an unprecedented extent. Making sense of this borderland between what the NHSME chooses to call "science" and "opinion" is the stuff of social science. However, this borderland will only be illuminated and understood if there are developments in the theory and methods of the sociology of health and illness, and in particular in research on lay beliefs. The changing discourse within this field of work is both indicative of the problems and, it is to be hoped, illustrative of conceptual and theoretical developments. The concept of "lay beliefs" (Helman 1990) is giving way to the concept of "lay knowledge" (Blaxter 1983, Cornwell 1984). According to the dictionary, "beliefs" and "knowledge" are opposites. This is, perhaps, an indication that increasing status is being afforded to lay experiences. Most interestingly, the notions of beliefs and knowledge are being usurped in some arenas by the notion of "lay" or "popular" epidemiology with its connotations of science (Davison et al 1992, Brown 1987). This may signal the beginning of a much-needed rethink regarding the potential contribution lay people can make to understanding the experience of health and illness, the nature of health and social care needs, and the outcomes of health care. Such a rethink must, however, involve more openness to lay participation within research (Kelly 1990). This participation would need to go beyond lay discussion of the findings of research to include an active rôle in the conceptualization and specification of the nature of the problem, and the design and conduct of research. This process would involve widening the portfolio of methods considered legitimate within much health-related research, and acknowledging the important input lay knowledge can make to the design of conventional research measures (Williams & Popay 1994).

On the policy front, it is likely that many NHS managers and professionals will not have the skills necessary to listen to what local people have to say as residents or as patients. For those who would genuinely wish to listen, the multitude of voices they will hear may overwhelm them, and the poor attendance at public meetings or low response to surveys may disillusion them. Many will be selective about what they are hearing. Some professionals already talk in terms of having to "educate" people before they can even begin to listen to them. In a very real sense, effective lay participation within the NHS will only be achieved when there is a more democratic structure within the health care system. This may be a long way off, but what is clearly here is a widespread questioning of expert knowledge on the part of lay people both within, and beyond, the NHS.

References

Bagenal, F. S., D. F. Easton, E. Harris, C. E. D. Chilvers, T. J. McElwain 1990. Survival of patients with breast cancer attending Bristol Cancer Help Centre. *Lancet* **336**, 606–10.

Barker, I. & E. Peck (eds) 1988. *Power in strange places: user empowerment in mental health services*. London: Good Practice in Mental Health.

Barnes, M. & G. Wistow (eds) 1992. *Researching user involvement*. University of Leeds: Nuffield Seminar Series.

Beck, U. 1992. *Risk society: towards a new modernity*. London: Sage.

Blane, D., G. Davey Smith & M. Bartley 1990. Social class differences in years of potential life lost: size, trends and principal causes. *British Medical Journal* **301**, 429–32.

Blaxter, M. 1983. The causes of disease: women talking. *Social Science and Medicine* **17**, (2), 59–69.

Blaxter, M. 1990. *Health and lifestyle*. London: Routledge.

Bowling, A. 1991. *Measuring health*. Milton Keynes: Open University Press.

Bowling, A., B. Jacobson, L. Southgate 1993. Health service priorities. Exploration in consultation of the public and health professionals on priority setting in an inner London health district. *Social Science and Medicine* **37** (7), 851–8.

Brown, P. 1987. Popular epidemiology: community response to toxic-waste induced disease in Woburn, Massachusetts. *Science, Technology, and Human Values* **12**, 78–85.

Brown, P. 1992. Popular epidemiology and toxic waste contamination. *Journal of Health and Social Behaviour* **33**, 267–81.

Brown, P. & E. J. Mikkelsen 1990. *No safe place: toxic waste, leukaemia, and community action*. Berkeley, California: University of California Press.

Clayton, B. 1989. *Water pollution at Lowermoor, North Cornwall: report of the Lowermoor incident Health Advisory Group*. Truro, Cornwall and Isles of Scilly District Health Authority.

Clayton, B. 1991. *Water pollution at Lowermoor, North Cornwall: second report of the Lowermoor incident health advisory group*. London: HMSO.

Copperman, J. 1992. Barley Mow users group. Quoted in The Health Gain Standing Conference.

Cornwall and Isles of Scilly Health Authority, 1990. *Lowermoor water incident. Proceedings of the conference held on 3 February 1990 at the Postgraduate Centre, Royal Cornwall Hospital, Treliske, Truro*. Truro: Cornwall and Isles of Scilly Health Authority.

Cornwell, J. 1984. *Hard earned lives: accounts of health and illness from East London*. London: Tavistock.

Davey, B. & J. Popay (eds). 1993. *Dilemmas in health care*. Buckingham: Open University Press.

Davison, C., G. Davey-Smith, S. Frankel 1991. Lay epidemiology and the prevention paradox. *Sociology of Health and Illness* **13**, 1–19.

Day, P. & R. Klein 1991. Britain's health care experiment. *Health Affairs* (Fall), 39–59.

Delamothe, T. 1991. Social inequalities in health. *British Medical Journal* **303**, 1046–50.

Department of Health 1989a. *Working for patients*. London: HMSO.

Department of Health 1989b. *Caring for people: community care in the next decade and beyond*. Cmnd 555. London: HMSO.

Department of Health 1991. *The patient's charter*. London: HMSO.

Department of Health 1992. *The health of the nation: a strategy for health in England*. Cmnd 1986. London: HMSO.

Dixon, J. & H. G. Welch 1991. Priority setting: lessons from Oregon. *Lancet* **337**, 891–984.

Enthoven, A. 1991. Internal market reform of the British National Health Service. *Health Affairs* (Fall), 60–70.

Fitzpatrick, R. & A. Hopkins 1983. Problems in conceptual frameworks of patient satisfaction research: an empirical exploration. *Sociology of Health and Illness* **5**, 297–311.

Flynn, R. 1992. *Structures of control in health management.* London: Routledge.

Gabe, J., D. Kelleher, G. Williams (eds) 1994. *Challenging medicine.* London: Routledge.

Guardian 1991a. Dusting down to fight in Docklands. September 11.

Guardian 1991b. Battle over the breath of life. July 23.

Giddens, A. 1990. *The consequences of modernity.* Oxford: Polity.

Gray A. 1993. Rationing and choice. See Davey & Popay (1993).

Harries, U., R. Leventhall, J. Popay 1992. *Assessing the health and social care needs of visually disabled older people.* Interim Research Report. Salford: Public Health Research and Resource Centre.

Harrison, S., D. Hunter, C. Pollitt 1990. *The dynamics of British health policy.* London: Unwin Hyman.

Harrison, S. & G. Wistow 1993. Managing health care: balancing competing interests. See Davey & Popay (1993).

Health Gain Standing Conference 1993. *The public as partners – a toolbox for involving local people in commissioning health care.* Cambridge: East Anglia Health Authority.

Helman, C. 1990. *Culture, health and illness.* 2nd edn. Oxford: Butterworth–Heinemann.

Hill, S., U. Harries, J. Popay 1993. Unanswered questions remain. *British Medical Journal* **307**, (letter) 449.

Hunt, S. M., C. J. Martin, S. Platt, C. Lewis, G. Morris 1988. *Damp housing, mould growth and health status.* Edinburgh: Research Unit in Health and Behavioural Change.

Hunter, D. 1991. *Explicit rationing decisions – the pitfalls.* Paper presented at National Association of Health Authorities and Trusts Conference: The Oregon Experiment. 17 October. London: RIBA.

Hunter D. 1993. Care in the community. See Davey & Popay (1993), 121–142.

Jefferys, M. & P. Thane. 1989. Introduction: an ageing society and ageing people. In *Growing old in the twentieth century,* Jefferys, M. (ed.). London: Routledge.

Kelly, M. P. 1990. The role of research in the new public health. *Critical Public Health* **3**, 4–9.

Landes, R. & J. Popay 1993. 'My sight is poor, but I'm getting on now': the health and social care needs of older people with vision problems. *Health and Social Care in the Community* **1**, 325-335.

McIver, S. 1991. *An introduction to obtaining the views of users of health services.* London: King's Fund Centre.

McKeganey, N., M. Barnard, M. Bloor. 1990. A comparison of HIV-related risk behaviour and risk reduction between female street-working prostitutes and male rent boys in Glasgow. *Sociology of Health and Illness* **12**, 274–92.

Marmot, M. 1976. Facts, opinion, and affaires du coeur. *American Journal of Epidemiology* **103**, 519–26.

Maxwell, R. (ed.) 1988. *Reshaping the National Health Service. Policy Journals*. Berkshire: Transactions Books.

NHSME (National Health Service Management Executive) 1991. *Assessing health care needs: a NHS project discussion paper*. London: NHSME.

NHSME (National Health Service Management Executive) 1992. *Local voices: the views of local people in purchasing for health*. London: HMSO.

Oliver, M. 1992. Changing the social relationships of research production. *Disability, Handicap and Society* **7**, 101–14.

Ong, B. N. 1993. *The practice of health services research*. London: Chapman & Hall.

Phillimore, P. & S. Moffatt, in press. Discounted knowledge: local experience, environmental pollution and health. In *Researching the people's health*, J. Popay & G. Williams (eds). London: Routledge.

Pond, C. & J. Popay 1993. Poverty, economic inequality and health. In Davey & Popay (1993).

Popay, J. & M. Bartley 1993. Labour conditions and men and women's health. In *Locating health: sociological and historical dilemmas*, S. Platt, H. Thomas, S. Scott, G. Williams (eds). Aldershot: Avebury.

Popay, J., M. Bartley, C. Owen 1992. Gender inequalities in health: social position, affective disorders and minor physical morbidity. *Social Science and Medicine* **36**(1), 21–32.

Popay, J. & M. White 1993. *A review of survey research and related training and advice needs in the NHS in England*. Salford: Public Health Research and Resource Centre and University of Newcastle.

Salford Health Authority 1992. *Listening to local voices. The results of a priority search Survey of 1038 residents of Salford*. Salford DHA/FHSA.

Steele, K. 1991. *Patients as experts: consumer appraisal of health services*. Consumer Association, November.

Taylor, P. 1990. *Consumer involvement in health care: a review for the Swindon Health Authority*. Swindon: Swindon Health Authority.

Ware, J. 1993. Measuring patients' views: the optimum outcome measure. *British Medical Journal* **306**, 1429–30.

Webster, C. (ed.) 1993 *Caring for health: history and diversity*. Buckingham: Open University Press.

Wigan Health Authority 1992. *What should Wigan Health Authority bear in mind when planning the future accident and emergency services?* Wigan DHA.

Wilkin, D., L. Hallam, M. A. Doggat 1992. *Measures of need and outcomes in primary care*. Oxford: Oxford Medical Publications.

Williams, A. forthcoming. Priority setting in the NHS. In *Health and disease: a reader*, B. Davey, A. Gray, C. Seale (eds). 2nd edn. Buckingham: Open University Press.

Williams, G. & J. Popay 1993. Researching the people's health: dilemmas and opportunities for social scientists. In *Social research and public health*, J. Popay, G.

Williams (eds). University of Salford, Department of Sociology: Salford Papers in Sociology (no. 13).

Williams, G. & J. Popay 1994. Lay knowledge and the privilege of experience. In Gabe et al., 1994.

Winkler, F. 1987. Consumerism in health care: beyond the supermarket model. *Policy and Politics*, **15**(1), 1–8.

WHO (World Health Organization) 1980. *International classification of impairments, disabilities, and handicaps: a manual relating to the consequences of disease.* Geneva: WHO.

5

Priority setting for health gain[1]

Chris Ham, Frank Honigsbaum and David Thompson

Introduction

A key element in the recent reforms of the British National Health Service (NHS) is the establishment of District Health Authorities (DHAs) as the purchasers of health services for their residents. In their rôle as purchasers, DHAs are responsible for assessing the population's need for health care and for deciding which services to buy to meet this need. They operate within limited budgets determined by regional health authorities (RHAs) and have to agree priorities for the use of the resources they have at their disposal. In part, these priorities are intended to reflect the policies laid down by ministers and RHAs; and in part, they are meant to respond to an assessment of needs. Because it is impossible to do everything within the available resources, DHAs have to make choices about how to use their funds and which priorities to pursue.

This chapter reviews the ways in which six DHAs in England have approached priority setting in their new rôle as purchasers of health services. These DHAs are: City and Hackney, Mid-Essex, Oxfordshire, Solihull, Southampton and South West Hampshire, and Wandsworth. The six authorities are not typical of DHAs as a whole, but were selected because of the interest they have shown in this new challenge. The research for the study was carried out in the second half of 1992.

A brief history of purchasing

Working for patients (Department of Health 1989a), the White Paper that launched the health service reforms, contains little in the way of guidance for DHAs on their rôle as purchasers. As the reforms have been implemented, however, the nature of the purchasing function has become better understood. In this sense, DHAs have been "learning by doing". The NHS Management Executive (NHSME) has assisted this process by supporting development activities in various sections of the NHS, and by publishing reports summarizing the lessons learnt from experience (see NHSME papers on purchasing following the list of references on page 126).

As a result of this work, a clearer picture has emerged of the purchasing function (for further analysis, see Ham and Spurgeon 1992. It is evident that DHAs have a strategic rôle that extends well beyond placing contracts with providers; at the heart of this rôle is their assessment of the population's need for health care. Needs assessment provides the foundation on which DHAs draw up their purchasing plans and decide which services to purchase. In practice, it involves both the analysis of epidemiological data on patterns of mortality and morbidity in each area, and also the gathering of information on the views and opinions of local people, health care professionals and other interested groups. Through a review of both kinds of information, DHAs should be able to determine where to channel their efforts to achieve health gain for the population.

As part of this process, DHAs are increasingly forging alliances with local organizations and interests, such as Family Health Services Authorities (FHSAs), local authorities, voluntary organizations, employers and trade unions. It is vital that there is a dialogue between general practitioners (GPs) and the DHAs throughout the purchasing cycle: GPs refer patients to hospital for diagnosis and treatment, and DHAs determine where contracts should be placed. Also, GPs possess information of immense value to DHAs, in relation both to the population's need for health care and to the strengths and weaknesses of hospitals and other providers of care.

It is apparent that DHAs have to find ways of involving the public in their work, if they are to have any credibility as "champions of the people". This idea, which has been promulgated actively by ministers, draws attention to the rôle of DHAs in responding to the needs of the public, and not simply to the preferences of the providers. In pursuing this objective, DHAs have made use of a variety of approaches that include working with Community Health Councils (CHCs), involving voluntary organizations, undertaking surveys of public attitudes, and establishing locality purchasing arrangements (NHSME, 1992). Although these approaches are still at an early stage of development, they have helped to give legitimacy to the rôle of health authorities as purchasers.

Two different presentations of NHS reforms (top, Health Service Journal; *bottom, Camden and Islington Health Authority).*

Changes in management

DHAs have also been reshaping their management arrangements. This has often required the creation of organizations that bring together skills in finance, public health, planning, contracting, and general management. These organizations comprise a relatively small number of staff, many of whom hold senior positions. In many DHAs, the emphasis has been placed on flexibility and working in teams, rather than on the establishment of strong, functional departments. A high priority has also been placed on creating a style of working that is open to outside influences and which encourages alliances with other agencies.

The configuration of DHAs has been reviewed in many parts of the country. One consequence has been the establishment of fewer, larger DHAs, following the merger of existing districts. An alternative to mergers has been the creation of purchasing consortia or health commissions. These often involve FHSAs as well as DHAs. An important part of the rationale behind these developments is the perceived need to establish coterminous relationships between DHAs, FHSAs and local authorities. It is also argued that mergers enable DHAs to benefit from economies of scale and to make the best use of the scarce skills that are available.

DHA mergers have accentuated the differences between DHAs and GPs who buy services for their patients as fundholders. This has been brought into sharp focus by the lowering of the list size for practices entering the fundholding scheme. The sensitivity of fundholders to the demands of their patients and their direct knowledge of providers have resulted in a number of changes to service provision that are of benefit to patients. These changes have been facilitated by the careful selection of practices for entry into the scheme and the generous level of funding provided in the first year. So far, DHAs have struggled to keep pace with the innovative approach of fundholders.

A key issue in this respect is the future relationship between DHAs and GP fundholders. In view of recent ministerial statements, it can be anticipated that fundholders will be expected to work with DHAs in the development and implementation of local health strategies. It is unclear what this means exactly, or how it will be achieved. There seems little doubt, however, that fundholders will be required to use their resources to assist in the achievement of local policies and priorities that will themselves be shaped to reflect national objectives.

Purchasers and providers

One of the most problematic aspects of the reforms to date has been the relationship (or lack of it) between purchasers and providers. At one level, this reflects the primitive state of contracting arrangements. Most of the contracts placed by DHAs are block contracts, which represent little improvement over the global budgets under which providers operated in the past. As such, they do not offer the incentives for increased productivity that providers hoped would result from the reforms. At another level, purchasers and providers have not yet established effective contracting *relationships* that recognize the continuing nature of the arrangements that will exist in many parts of the NHS. An emphasis has therefore been placed on gaining short-term advantage in negotiations over particular contracts, rather than on building relationships from which both parties can benefit over a longer period of time.

To argue in this way is not to suggest that purchasers and providers should maintain existing patterns of service provision with minor disruption. Notwithstanding the emphasis placed on a smooth beginning and a steady rate of development in the first phase of the reforms, DHAs are beginning to reassess inherited commitments and to change the use of resources. As a consequence, there is bound to be greater uncertainty and unpredictability for providers. The most obvious examples are in London and other conurbations, where DHAs that have gained resources have started to shift contracts to alternative (often cheaper and more local) providers. Other examples include DHAs moving contracts for particular services when existing providers have failed to reach the standards laid down in contracts, and authorities seeking to shift the balance between secondary and primary care.

These changes are entirely to be expected as DHAs gain confidence in their purchasing rôle, achieve greater independence from providers as the establishment of NHS trusts gathers speed, and are allowed the same degree of freedom in using their resources that GP fundholders have enjoyed since the inception of the fundholding scheme. They throw up the challenge of how to manage the market, as some providers lose funds and others gain. Experience suggests that DHAs themselves, either singly or in combination, are playing an increasingly active part in market management, and that RHAs also have responsibilities in this respect (for example, in relation to arbitration). Even more than in the case of purchasing, however, the nature of market management remains ill-defined and open to different interpretations.

Setting priorities

In light of the developing understanding of the rôle of DHAs as purchasers, it is clear that one of their most important responsibilities is to set priorities for the use of resources. This responsibility is not new to DHAs, who have long been in the position of having to determine local priorities for service development. What is *different* is that as purchasers, DHAs may be able to make decisions which are less dependent than in the past on the demands of providers. They should be able to place greater weight on other factors, such as the views of local people and evidence regarding the cost effectiveness of different services.

In simplified form, the situation in which DHAs find themselves is displayed in Figure 5.1, which illustrates the main sources of pressure on DHAs as they seek to set priorities. In the past, national and regional "givens" and the demands of local professional interests (vertical axis) have been particularly influential. In the future, however, there will be an opportunity to attach greater emphasis to public views and evidence on cost effectiveness (horizontal axis).

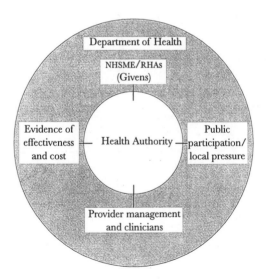

Figure 5.1 Pressures on Health Authorities (Heginbotham, Ham and others 1992).

Findings from six districts

Each of the districts included in this study has adopted its own approach to priority setting. One of the main reasons for this is that there has been no national initiative by the government to establish priorities for the NHS as a whole. While there are certain similarities between the districts, there are also important differences, so it is difficult to generalize about the work that has been undertaken.

In *City and Hackney*, the Director of Public Health has led a programme of work on priority setting. This has included an attempt to target development monies to meet health needs and to achieve health gain. Bids for development are ranked using a two-stage scoring system; the results are then discussed by the purchasing team and the DHA. In addition, a research exercise has been carried out within the district to explore the relative priority attached to 16 services or treatments by the public, GPs, consultants and public health doctors.

In *Mid-Essex*, the Director of Public Health has led a series of activities designed to help the authority approach priority setting. These activities stem in part from the North East Thames RHA's attempt to exclude certain services entirely from NHS provision. Drawing on work done in Oregon, USA (Honigsbaum 1991) and elsewhere, a number of tools and methodologies have been prepared to help in the ranking of bids for service development. These tools have also been used to identify values to guide priority setting. Within the district, a Public Health Forum has been created for the discussion of priorities. The involvement of GPs is secured through a GP advisory committee. In one part of the district, the rapid appraisal technique – involving an assessment of the views of local people on health issues – was used to understand the community's perception of needs and priorities. In *Oxfordshire*, there has been close collaboration between the DHA, FHSA and social services authority. Work on priority setting has been led by the Health Purchasing Committee. The DHA has produced a statement of the values which lie behind its purchasing work and has reviewed existing patterns of spending in relation to a number of services. Of particular importance has been the common needs project, which examined six priority areas (see below). In each area, the aim has been to assess the need for a defined condition, and to review spending patterns in the light of this need. As a result, it will be possible to identify potential changes in resource allocation and service provision. In *Solihull*, the Director of Public Health and colleagues have undertaken a survey of public attitudes in order to elicit views on the value of different health states and on priorities for service development. This work is supported by the RHA. A questionnaire has been designed for this purpose and has been distributed to 600 adults; a major effort has been made to secure a high response to the questionnaire. The Solihull approach is designed in part to test out this process of approaching priority setting, as well as to obtain information which will be helpful to the authority in making decisions. Work has also been undertaken to establish GPs' views. Authority members and the purchasing team have participated in a number of seminars on priority setting.

In *Southampton and South West Hampshire,* work on priority setting has been led by the Chief Executive and the purchasing team. In a simulation held in October 1991, the health authority worked with outside facilitators to explore priorities in three areas: coronary heart disease; the treatment of elderly people following stroke; and the balance of resources between care groups. In 1992, the authority issued three discussion papers to a wide range of local bodies. These enabled national priorities to be related to local opinion, in advance of the publication of a strategic purchasing plan. The formation of a Health Commission involving the FHSA has also led to greater attention to the balance between primary and secondary care.

In *Wandsworth,* which participated in the Department of Health's national network of purchasers, the development of purchasing was given early attention. In relation to priority setting, the district prioritized different categories of care and so identified values to guide purchasing. Bids for service development have been ranked using a number of criteria, including their likely contribution to health gain. The authority itself participated in a two-day seminar in May 1992, at which there was a discussion of the balance of spending between different services and care groups and a detailed analysis of services for the treatment of people with diabetes, and mental health services. More recently, the authority has been seeking to develop a strategy for coping with the loss of funding under the move to a new resource allocation formula.

Problems in priority setting

It is clear that work on priority setting is still at an early stage – even in districts that were chosen because they have been actively involved in this field. It is also apparent that priority setting is only one, albeit important, element in a range of activities being undertaken by DHAs in their purchasing rôle: priority setting has to compete for scarce management time and attention, along with a number of other demands.

To survive and flourish in such an environment, this work needs to be supported by top managers. In the six districts, there was a distinction between those authorities where priority setting was firmly rooted in the public health department and was led by the Director of Public Health, and those authorities where a corporate approach was adopted, involving the participation of the Chief Executive and other colleagues. This distinction should not be overdrawn, as in all districts the interest shown in priority setting extended beyond public health medicine. The extent to which top managers outside public health become involved, however, helps to account for differences in the attention given to priority setting and in the degree to which the work done enters the mainstream of health authority thinking and activity.

A related point is that three of the six districts have experienced significant organizational change in the past two years. This applies in: Mid-Essex, where three DHAs and the FHSA are now collaborating in the North Essex Health Consortium; Southampton and South West Hampshire, where the DHA has joined with part of the Hampshire FHSA in the Southampton and South West Hampshire Health Commission; and City and Hackney, where the DHA has been merged with two adjacent authorities, in order to create a new authority covering the whole of the City and east London. These developments have led to a preoccupation with structural changes and have diverted effort away from the establishment of the new purchasing function. This helps to explain why progress on priority setting issues has not been more rapid in some areas. On the other hand, the reconfiguration of DHAs and their closer alignment with FHSAs have opened up new possibilities for shifting resources in different directions.

Another important contextual issue is that DHAs have been pursuing their interest in priority setting against a changing financial background. Not only will the volume of resources available to the NHS grow more slowly in future years, but also the move to weighted capitation funding will have a significant impact in some districts. As a consequence, a number of authorities will be less concerned with the allocation of growth monies than with how to cope with substantial reductions in their budgets. This has had an important influence on attitudes to priority setting – some people question the value of trying to set priorities on a more systematic basis, in a situation where the real choices will be about how to *reduce* services, rather than to *develop* them.

Given the preliminary nature of much of the work reported here, it is worth emphasizing that the approaches pursued continue to be adapted in the light of experience. The initiatives taken are in this sense experimental and reflect a willingness on the part of those involved to test out various methods and to amend these methods as appropriate. To facilitate this process, a number of authorities have found it helpful to participate in networks through which they are able to compare and share experiences with other authorities.

Needs assessment

As noted above, priority setting is only one in a range of activities being undertaken by DHAs in their purchasing rôle. Almost everywhere, authorities are focusing their efforts on health needs assessment, with the aim of providing a framework for making purchasing decisions. This is led by Directors of Public Health, whose annual reports are the linchpins around which needs assessment is organized.

One of the most developed examples of needs assessment is operating in Oxfordshire. The common needs project seeks to improve the health of local people by using a needs assessment approach in priority areas of health care. The six priority areas chosen for examination are ischaemic heart disease, cancer, accidents, elective surgery, long-term disablement, and anxiety and depression. These areas were chosen on the basis of the following criteria: public health importance (frequency or severity of the problem); spectrum of services involved; availability of choice of services and real opportunities to change service pattern; high-cost services and/ or high volume of service usage; and services crossing organizational boundaries. It is recognized that some of the services required to meet identified needs will be provided by the DHA, some will be provided through the FHSA, and some by social services or the voluntary sector. Needs assessment is not seen as an end in itself: rather, the aim is to use the results of the work to make decisions about which services to purchase at the expense of others.

In 1992/3, it was agreed that the envelope of resources devoted to each area should remain fixed. This enabled attention to be focused on ways in which resources might be redistributed. In the case of heart disease, for example, it might be possible to spend less on in-patient admissions for myocardial infarction and more on coronary rehabilitation. Over time, as the process becomes more sophisticated, it will be possible to consider transferring resources between areas of need.

The framework for carrying out the common needs project identified eight areas in which potential changes could be made. These were:
- *care setting* – more day care and less in-patient care may, for instance, be beneficial;
- *cost of care* – the number of severe care cases requiring expensive treatment may need to be limited;
- *organizational responsibility* – in some areas, such as long-term disability, there may be an issue about whether the care is the responsibility of health or social services;
- *professional responsibility* – certain types of intervention may be more appropriately and effectively performed by nurses than by doctors, for example;
- *stage of intervention* – investment in prevention and health promotion may be more cost-effective than investment in treatment;
- *effectiveness / appropriateness of current interventions* – a particular intervention may have been shown to be ineffective, or intervention at a particular stage of a condition may be more effective than at another stage;
- *effective interventions not currently used* – there may be interventions which are not currently available but which have been found to be effective; and
- *equity of access* – it may be possible to distribute services more fairly across the county or improve their accessibility to particular client groups.

To investigate these issues, the project has made use of information gathering, discussion with interested organizations, and the formulation of recommendations for service changes and purchasing decisions. In practice, difficulties arose in acting on these recommendations, partly because of weaknesses in the development of the purchasing organization, and partly because providers were under significant pressure in coping with service changes.

Another example is Southampton and South West Hampshire, where much effort has been concentrated recently on the development of a purchasing plan for the Health Commission. The plan sets out a strategic approach to the development of health services in the district for the period 1993–8, based on national policies such as those in the area of community care, and those contained in *The health of the nation* (Department of Health 1992) and *The patient's charter* (Department of Health 1991). The needs assessment work carried out by the Director of Public Health and his colleagues made a significant contribution to the purchasing plan, as did consultation with GPs and other local interest groups (see below).

A major challenge in all districts in the development of purchasing plans and strategies, however, is how to reconcile pressures to increase expenditure on acute services with the perceived need to give priority to community services and primary care. At one level, this has been addressed through the "ring fencing" of resources for community services by identifying the budget for these services. This is intended to prevent these resources being raided by the acute sector (for example, in City and Hackney, and Wandsworth). At another level, authorities are seeking to use the results of consultation to support restraint in acute sector growth. Whatever the approach, it is widely acknowledged that the priorities set out in purchasing plans and strategies will have little meaning, unless they can be carried through into real changes in resource allocation.

Public participation

The authorities involved in the study appear to attach importance to public participation. So far, much greater attention has been given to this issue than to the use of evidence on the cost-effectiveness of services. The most structured approach to public participation has been pursued in Solihull. This has involved a postal questionnaire survey of 600 adults selected randomly from the FHSA register; a response rate of 80 per cent was obtained. The aim of the questionnaire was to elicit information about how the public values various health states and to establish the public's views on 11 possible priorities for service development. Preliminary results suggest a greater public preference for involvement in high-technology care such as liver transplants, rather than making improvements in access to basic services.

The City and Hackney Health Authority has also sought the public's views on priorities. This has been done through a research project based at the health needs assessment unit at St Bartholomew's Hospital Medical College. The project sought to explore how the public ranked 16 services. This was done via meetings with community groups at which 350 people were interviewed; a postal questionnaire survey and follow-up interviews; and a public meeting. The public's rankings of priorities were then compared with those of GPs, consultants and public health doctors. The results are displayed in Table 5.1, which shows that the public's views were in some cases significantly different from those of the medical respondents. This raises some questions: whose views should prevail when rankings differ in this way? And if the public's views are not reflected in resource allocation decisions, how does the health authority explain this and handle the expectations generated by consultation exercises?

Another important finding from the City and Hackney project was that the public's assessment of priorities depended critically on the wording of the questions put to them. For example, intensive care for premature babies was ranked highly when the survey questionnaire was piloted. Subsequently, when the question was qualified with the statement, "babies weighing less than one and half pounds are unlikely to survive", its ranking dropped markedly. This has important implications for the design of questionnaires and for the methods used to understand the public's views.

A different approach to public participation has been pursued in the Mid-Essex Health Authority, which has used various methods. These include collaboration with the CHC, working with voluntary organizations to discuss and rank priorities for service developments, and making use of the rapid appraisal technique in one part of the district to gather data about the community's views and values. Information from these different sources has been employed by the Health Authority to make best use of its growth funds.

Southampton and South West Hampshire Health Commission provides a further example. Following a simulation exercise held in October 1991 (Heginbotham et al. 1992), the Commission paid particular attention to local consultation with the public. When determining its strategic priorities for the period to 1998, the Commission prepared three discussion papers, which were used as a basis for debate with local groups that included the CHC. Each paper:

- gave an overview of national and RHA guidance, followed by the local perspective, and proposed a number of possible priorities for

Table 5.1 Main results of a public priorities survey in City and Hackney, 1992. Mean priority ranks (in order of priority 1–16, 1 = highest, 16 = lowest).

Services/treatments	Public	GPs	Consultants	Public health doctors
Treatments for children with life threatening illness (e.g. leukemia)	1	5	2	9
Special care and pain relief for people who are dying (e.g. hospice care)	2	4	4	8
Medical research for new treatments	3	11	8	11
High technology surgery and procedures which treat life threatening conditions (e.g. heart/liver transplants)	4	12	12	12
Preventive services (e.g. screening, immunisation)	5	6	7	4
Surgery to help people with disabilities to carry out everyday tasks (e.g. hip replacements)	6	8	5	5 equal
Therapy to help people with disabilities to carry out everyday tasks (e.g. speech therapy, physiotherapy, occupational therapy)	7	7	10	5 equal
Services for people with mental illness (e.g. psychiatric wards, community psychiatric nurses)	8	2	1	1 equal
Intensive care for premature babies who weigh less than one and a half pounds and are unlikely to survive	9	13	13	15 equal
Long stay care (e.g. hospital and nursing home for the elderly)	10	3	6	10
Community services/care at home (e.g. district nurses)	11	1	3	1 equal
Health education services (e.g. campaigns encouraging people to lead healthy lifestyles)	12	10	11	5 equal
Family planning services (e.g. contraception)	13	9	9	1 equal
Treatments for infertility (e.g. test tube babies)	14	14	14	15 equal
Complementary/alternative medicine (e.g. acupuncture, homeopathy, herbalism)	15	15	16	13 equal
Cosmetic surgery (e.g. tattoo removal, removal of disfiguring lumps and bumps)	16	16	15	13 equal
Number of respondents	322–35	63–66	112–16	4–6*

*Little can be construed from this sample as the numbers were very small. Bowling et al. 1993. Reprinted with permission from Pergamon Press.

local action, taken from the public health report, GP survey, strategy work, current experience of purchasing, GP fundholder plans and known social services priorities;

- presented these priorities in random order and without differentiating between those requiring investment, those for negotiation through contracts, and those for future work or analysis;
- covered topics and priorities as sequenced in national and RHA guidance;
- invited recipients to participate in a simple ranking exercise and to nominate any additional priorities.

The consultation process helped to inform the decisions taken on priorities by the Commission itself.

GP participation

As the Southampton and South West Hampshire example shows, DHAs have attached importance to the involvement of GPs, as well as of the public, in priority setting. Work undertaken in Southampton includes three questionnaire surveys of GPs, roadshows at which members of the purchasing team met GPs in different parts of the district, and visits to individual practices to discuss issues directly with GPs. There is also a district medical advisory committee, which acts as a forum for GPs and consultants to express views to the Health Authority. In Oxfordshire, emphasis has been placed on a countywide GP Advisory Committee and eight locality groups. Solihull and Wandsworth have developed their work along similar lines to Southampton and South West Hampshire and to Oxfordshire.

In Mid-Essex, GPs have worked closely with the Health Authority in setting priorities. Fundholders and non-fundholders alike have been involved in this process. This collaboration has helped the health authority handle an overspending of its budget for extra contractual referrals, with the support and co-operation of GPs. More significantly, the views of GPs have played an important rôle in identifying problems in service provision that need to be tackled by the DHA.

The importance of fundholding varies greatly between districts. Solihull is at one extreme, with 70 per cent of the population covered by fundholding practices from April 1993. At the other extreme, Wandsworth, and City and Hackney currently have few fundholders and do not expect coverage to increase significantly. Relationships with fundholders, as reported by GPs themselves and DHAs, vary from good to poor. There is widespread concern on the part of DHAs about their ability to pursue local health strategies, as the number of fundholders increases.

Fundholders, for their part, reported that they are already making changes in the use of the resources they control directly. Examples include the reduction of unnecessary out-patient appointments, making savings in expenditure on drugs, and altering referrals where local hospital services are unsatisfactory. One of the fundholders interviewed maintained that it was unnecessary to ration services through the exclusion of certain procedures from the NHS, because there was enough scope for freeing resources from existing budgets and redeploying these resources to respond to unmet needs. At the same time, he recognized that priorities had to be set, for example in relation to access to elective procedures; rationing through waiting for treatment would, therefore, still be necessary.

A potentially significant development in Oxfordshire is the establishment of a consortium of 10 fundholding practices. Through the consortium, the practices agreed a list of five hospital and nine practice priorities (see Table 5.2). These priorities were determined by the GPs involved, using their knowledge of the strengths and weaknesses of different services. Patients have not been invited to participate in this process, because the GPs held the view that there was plenty of scope for "getting the obvious basics right", before engaging in more elaborate methods of priority setting. One of the concerns expressed by DHAs was that services

Table 5.2   Priorities.

Hospital	1	Waiting lists reduced
	2	Waiting times for operations reduced – all within 9–12 months
	3	Outpatient waiting times reduced – all seen within 30 minutes
	4	Outpatient appointment times reduced – all within 8 weeks
	5	Monitoring of the above
General practice	1	Improvement in the physiotherapy service
	2	Improved chiropody service
	3	Monitoring of referrals
	4	Monitoring of re-attendance of outpatients
	5	Counselling
	6	Reduction in drug expenditure
	7	Improved dietetic service
	8	Improved district nursing service
	9	Greater scope for health visiting

for people with learning difficulties and mental health problems might lose out, because these were not perceived to be of high priority by most fundholders.

Tools and methods

A striking finding of the study was that a wide range of tools and methods have been developed to support work on priority setting. In Mid-Essex, examples include a list of priorities originally developed in the BBC "Public Eye" documentary programme, and a similar ranking exercise prepared in the district in which respondents are asked to rank 12 services. The purpose of these tools is to explore with a variety of interests (GPs, the CHC, voluntary organizations, etc.) the relative priority attached to different services. Those involved in Essex have also made use of material from the Oregon experiment in order to identify values that could be used to guide priority setting. Building on experience gained in Wandsworth, a list of criteria has been drawn up, against which the health authority will seek to prioritize health gain investment decisions.

In City and Hackney, the Director of Public Health has not only initiated research to investigate how the public views priorities, but has also developed a two-stage scoring method to help inform priority setting. In the first stage, bids are ranked on the basis of needs assessment, with the greatest weight being attached to services which respond to local needs. In the second stage, following the preparation of a short list, individual proposals are ranked using the following criteria:

Robustness/implementability of proposal	0–3
Promotion of equity	0–1
Evidence of effectiveness/cost effectiveness	0–2
Collaboration with/integration with primary care	0–3
Prioritized by CHC	0–1
Prioritized by GP/GP forum	0–1
Other possible/more appropriate sources of funding	0–5 (negative score)

As can be seen, the greatest weight is attached to whether other funding methods are available, using a negative score as low as five to cancel out the other weightings. The results of this process are then discussed by the purchasing team and the DHA.

A similar method is used in Wandsworth. In 1992/3, proposals were ranked using the following criteria and weightings:

Potential for health gain	40
Improves quality of service	20
In accordance with local views	20
Achievability in current year	15
In accordance with national and regional priorities	5
Total	100

In this approach, potential for health gain is an all-embracing factor, encompassing length as well as quality of life. The ranking exercise was undertaken among both the purchasing team and the non-executive members of the DHA. An agreed list of priorities was drawn up at the end of the exercise.

In Southampton and South West Hampshire, as noted above, there was extensive consultation on the purchasing plan, including an invitation to those consulted to participate in a simple ranking exercise and to nominate any additional priorities. The exercise was divided into priorities under each of the three national policies covered by the plan and published by the Department of Health: *Care in the community* (1989b); *The patient's charter* (1991); and *The health of the nation* (1992). The results of consultation (covering GPs as well as the public) are displayed in Table 5.3.

The Solihull health priorities project and the exercise in public consultation undertaken by the City and Hackney Health Authority illustrate the use of more formal tools to rank priorities. In the case of Solihull, a substantial investment of time and money has been made to produce a methodology which can be replicated elsewhere. In City and Hackney, the work was undertaken as a special research project, supported by external funding. In this case, the research concluded that a postal questionnaire survey was less valuable than interviews with a representative sample of members of the public. The City and Hackney project also demonstrated the difficulty of attracting the public to open meetings to discuss priorities in an inner city environment.

Oxfordshire has developed the use of ranking methodologies as part of a priorities network co-ordinated by the King's Fund. As in Mid-Essex, this has involved using material from Oregon to establish the underlying values behind purchasing decisions.

Table 5.3 Analysis of priority setting survey.

Priority in rank order (a)		Score (b)
Health of the nation	1. Smoking advice to schools	7
	2. Fluoridation	6
	3. Parent education	5
	4. Low back pain services	4
	5. Mentally disordered offenders	4
	6. Stroke care in the community	4
	7. Teenage family planning	4
	8. Diabetic advice	4
	9. Diabetic screening	3
	10. GP health promotion	3
	11. Family planning	3
	12. Risk factors	3
Care in the community	1. Elderly community services	8
	2. Respite/domiciliary care	7
	3. Rehabilitation services	6
	4. Discharge arrangements	5
	5. Care for mental illness	5
	6. Children Act support	4
	7. Day hospitals/transport	4
	8. Carers in care management	3
	9. Assessment training	3
	10. Replacing institutional services for learning disabilities	3
Patient's charter	1. GP based services	9
	2. Primary care training	5
	3. 13-week wait (outpatient)	5
	4. Direct access audiology	5
	5. Orthopaedic services	4
	6. Physical disability	4
	7. Hospital specialist services	3
	8. 12-month wait (inpatient)	3
	9. Less than 18-month wait (selected conditions)	3
	10. GP out of hours alternatives	3
	11. Hospital/GP prescribing	3
	12. Community/practice nursing	3
	13. Chronic pain relief	2

Outside expertise

In a number of authorities, use has been made of outside or specialist expertise. In Oxfordshire, health economists from the University were commissioned to assist the DHA in thinking through its strategy for allocating resources to coronary heart disease. However, an initial approach developed by the economists proved to be too complex, and the methodology had to be revised.

Rather more successful has been the use of economics expertise in Wandsworth. A health economist, who works on a part-time basis for the authority, produced valuable information as part of the work that has been done on the ranking of bids according to health gain criteria. In addition, his analysis of the use of resources in the district for the prevention and treatment of diabetes, and mental health care, was useful in illuminating the choices available in these two areas of service provision (see below).

In City and Hackney, the advice of an expert in medical ethics was sought in setting priorities for access to infertility treatment. Also, a team under the leadership of an experienced medical sociologist carried out research into the public's views on priorities. This work could not have been done without such specialist expertise and the additional resources provided by a charitable foundation. Similarly, Solihull received support from its RHA to bring in expertise in survey research, which enabled it to carry out a survey of the views of the public.

Beyond these examples, three authorities (Southampton and South West Hampshire, Wandsworth, and Oxfordshire) have called on outside help for assistance in organizing simulations of priority setting and in facilitating local discussion of values and priorities. Southampton's simulation was funded in part through company sponsorship. As these examples show, setting priorities on a systematic basis carries a cost, which has to be weighed against the anticipated benefits.

The shift to primary care

As DHAs work more closely with FHSAs, and as GPs are brought in to advise DHAs on purchasing priorities, interest is growing in a shift of services and resources towards primary care. There is evidence of this in the following areas: an increase in the amount of minor surgery and health promotion undertaken in general practice; the use of specialists to do some of their out-patient work alongside GPs; and the development of shared care protocols for common conditions such as asthma and diabetes. In a few cases, DHAs have moved considerably further and have allocated part of the hospital and community health services budget to support developments in primary care.

Notwithstanding these developments, some caution was expressed during the course of this study about the scope for a significant move away from secondary care services. This was partly because of the continuing pressure to expand acute services to accommodate new technologies and interventions, and partly because of the preparedness of GPs in some parts of the NHS to take on greater responsibility. The latter view was expressed with particular force in Wandsworth, and in City and Hackney, where it was argued that weaknesses in general practice precluded the kinds of change already taking place in districts where primary care standards are generally high. The implication is that in some areas, a major investment has to take place in primary care services before there can be a move away from secondary care.

The rôle of providers

While this study has focused on the rôle of purchasers in setting priorities, it is important not to ignore the contribution of providers to this process. Reference has already been made to the involvement of providers in Mid-Essex to the debate that has taken place in the Public Health Forum; these discussions have been supplemented by dialogue between the Director of Public Health and clinicians in individual specialties. Given the key rôle of providers in the implementation of priority decisions, it is vital that this kind of approach is pursued further – a point that was acknowledged by all six authorities involved in this study.

In some cases, providers themselves have taken decisions on priorities, in parallel with the decisions of purchasers. An example encountered in this study was the establishment of guidelines for the use of surfactant drugs in neo-natal care. A specialist unit had adopted a policy of withholding this drug for premature babies with a birth weight under 700 grammes. It is unclear whether this policy has the support of the DHA, and whether similar restrictions apply to other clinical services. Given that the main responsibility for priority setting in the past has rested with clinicians, it would be surprising if other guidelines of this kind did not exist; however, they may be implemented without the knowledge of purchasers.

A related point is the extent to which providers are able to vire resources within their contracts. In the two DHAs of City and Hackney, and Wandsworth, providers may switch resources between specialties up to a limit of 10 per cent and 5 per cent, respectively. This enables them to respond to fluctuations in activity levels. While the freedom to vire resources in this way is essential, given the complex and unpredictable nature of health care delivery, it may also distort priorities if there is a consistent change in a particular direction. For this reason, the GP adviser in one authority had recommended a reduction in the virement limit to 2 per cent.

The impact of priority setting

One of the questions that arises inevitably from the work done so far, is: what impact has it had on decision-making? In some districts, notably Solihull, where analysis is still in the preliminary stages, it is premature to expect any major changes to have occurred. In other districts, of which Mid-Essex is a good example, it is possible to point to decisions that have been shaped by the interest shown in priority setting. The decision to give higher priority to mental health services was a direct reflection of the discussions that took place locally with key interests. Similarly, in City and Hackney, the DHA decided to protect community services in the face of considerable pressure to allocate extra resources to acute services.

In the remaining districts, the impact of the work done has been real but less tangible. Managers in these districts refer to a change in the culture of their organizations and to a new approach to thinking about priorities, but are unable to cite specific examples of decisions that have been altered. No doubt this is due in part to the interest shown in exercises and simulations of priority setting, in districts such as Oxfordshire, Southampton and South West Hampshire, and Wandsworth. It is also because some of the analysis has been research-based and was not designed with the aim of influencing purchasing decisions directly at this stage.

Despite this, it is possible to show that the investment of time and effort has made a difference. In Oxfordshire, for example, agreement has been reached on the values which shape purchasing. In Southampton and South West Hampshire, the emphasis placed on widespread consultation on priorities illustrates how the *process* of purchasing has been influenced, and this in turn has helped to frame the strategic priorities set out in the purchasing plan. In Wandsworth, the development of criteria for ranking bids for development has made more explicit the basis on which decisions are made.

One of the issues to emerge from experience so far is the difficulty of comparing quite different services. In practice, DHAs have found it easier to take individual services or disease categories and to examine options for prevention, diagnosis and treatment within these areas, than to compare services across the board. This is not surprising, given the absence of a common currency for making these broad comparisons. The work being put in to the development of quality adjusted life years (QALYs) and cost-per-QALY league tables may, in time, provide such a common currency. These are techniques developed by health economists to compare the costs and benefits of different services. However, this study produced little evidence that QALYs were being used by DHAs, even where health economists had been hired as advisers. A more promising approach is to focus on choices within individual service areas or disease categories. In essence, this is what is happening in Oxfordshire in the common needs project (see above). The aim is to take as "given" the current envelope of resources allocated to any one area (elective surgery, for example), and then to examine the scope for redistributing resources within the envelope.

A similar approach to priority setting in terms of "bite-sized chunks" proved valuable in the purchasing dilemmas simulation undertaken in Southampton and South West Hampshire. In Wandsworth, too, work carried out into the use of resources for the prevention and treatment of diabetes, mental illness, and the provision of palliative care, demonstrated in a practical way the kinds of choice available when individual services are examined in detail. In the case of diabetes, available data suggest that a large volume of resources is spent on a small number of cases. These cases involve patients with multiple health and social problems, who are admitted to hospital for lengthy stays. Much less money is spent on a large number of cases looked after by GPs and diabetologists. This type of analysis shows the potential for using resources more effectively within individual disease categories.

Research for this study has indicated that on the whole, DHAs have avoided excluding services from NHS provision, a finding confirmed by other studies (Klein & Redmayne 1992). There are a number of reasons for this, including the advice issued by the Chief Executive of the NHS in response to the initiative taken by North East Thames RHA, that health authorities should not rule out whole categories of treatment. In place of exclusions, there is growing interest in the development of guidelines on *which* patients, with *which* indications, are most likely to benefit from the full range of services. This appears to be a promising path for development, given that almost all services are likely to benefit at least some patients in certain situations.

The rôle of guidelines

Guidelines may take a number of forms. At one level, they may be used in a hospital setting to help clinicians decide priorities for the use of limited or expensive facilities, or to ensure that the best professional practices are used. At another level, they may be drawn up by consultants and GPs, as part of the development of shared care arrangements. This includes identifying thresholds for referral or for particular kinds of treatment.

The value of clinical guidelines has been emphasized by the work of a government committee (the Dunning Committee), set up by the Dutch government to examine choices in healthcare. In a comprehensive review of different approaches to priority setting, the Dunning Committee made a number of recommendations of relevance to the UK. These include: the development of protocols and guidelines for appropriate care by professional and scientific bodies; the establishment of a rigorous system of assessment for new medical technologies; and the establishment of explicit criteria to determine access to elective surgery. There are clear echoes here of the report prepared by the Advisory Group on Health Technology Assessment (1992) for the Director of Research and Development.

As the Dunning Committee's recommendations make clear, guidelines have to be seen as only one element in a strategy for approaching priority setting. This is important because rationing has a number of dimensions. As this chapter has shown, there is a difference between allocating resources to different services, and allocating resources within individual service areas. Klein (1992) notes that there are at least two other dimensions: how to prioritize access to treatment between different patients; and how much to invest in particular patients, once access has been achieved. It is in these two areas that guidelines have the most significant contribution to make. To argue for the greater use of guidelines is to emphasize the importance of focusing on the *appropriateness* of inter-vention. As the Oxfordshire common needs project has demonstrated, appropriateness refers not only to the selection of patients, but also to the care setting (home, primary care, out-patient, day care or in-patient). By limiting interventions to those who clearly can benefit from the services concerned, and by delivering these services in the most appropriate set-ting, it should be possible to make better use of available resources. This is a central thrust of the argument of GP fundholders (see above), who maintain that they are already achieving improvements in services through the reallocation of resources in this fashion. The existence of wide variations in clinical practice (Ham, 1988) suggests that there is sig-nificant scope for change in this respect.

Information needs

The lack of information to guide purchasing decisions is a major prob-lem everywhere. In particular, information on the cost effectiveness of different services is often lacking or incomplete. The work of the Clinical Outcomes Group and of the clearing house on outcomes set up by the Department of Health may in time help to overcome this problem, but so far it has not made an impact on the six authorities that were visited during the investigation that forms the basis of this chapter.

The effectiveness bulletins commissioned by the Department of Health and produced by the Universities of Leeds and York have been of greater salience. They have started to fill some of the gaps in information on cost effectiveness, and more publications of this kind would be wel-comed by those involved in purchasing. Not least, the results of research need to be presented in a clear form which can be assimilated readily by busy managers and their colleagues.

One specific area in which information is needed is in relation to the shift between secondary and primary care. As shown above, DHAs are becoming interested increasingly in this issue as they work more and more closely with GPs. What is lacking at present is any summary of views on best practice, which would enable DHAs to decide what services can be provided most appropriately and effectively in and around a pri-mary care setting. Information is required on the following: issues such as the treatment of asthma and diabetes; the rôle of specialists in doing some of their out-patient work alongside GPs; the scope for extending minor surgery and investigations in primary care; and the use of staff such as physiotherapists, dieticians and counsellors in general practice. There was a strong feeling among those interviewed that much of this information is available, but it has yet to percolate through to those responsible for developing purchasing plans.

Given the high degree of emphasis that is attached to *The health of the nation*, DHAs also require information that would help them pursue the objectives outlined in the national health strategy. DHAs have no choice but to pursue these objectives, but they do have discretion in selecting the means for their achievement. At its simplest, this means identifying the comparative costs and benefits of the preventive and treatment strategies that might be adopted in working towards the government's targets for coronary heart disease, cancer and other priority areas. Although the Leeds/York bulletins are seen as useful, it is not clear why the topics they cover have been chosen – glue ear and screening for osteoporosis are hardly at the top of the NHS agenda. It would help DHAs if cost-effectiveness data were available in relation to services that are clearly at the centre of government policy.

One approach to this is illustrated by work done in Wales to produce protocols for investment in health gain. The stated purpose of these protocols is to address areas where further investment would bring worthwhile health gain. Areas covered include cancer, cardiovascular disease, maternal and early child health, and physical and sensory disabilities. Drawing on research findings and expert views, each protocol provides an assessment of need, and identifies options for meeting this need through changes in priorities or service delivery. As such, published reports provide a resource for use by health authorities. While elements of this approach exist in England (for example, the needs assessment work commissioned by the NHSME), there is no comparable work which brings together information on needs and service effectiveness in a form that is accessible to health authorities.

In this context, the research undertaken by James Raftery, which combines a disease-MAPping approach with evidence on cost effectiveness, appears to offer a promising way forward. Disease MAPs – (measurements on activity and price) – provide information on the number of patients suffering from individual diseases and thus contribute to needs assessment. Evidence on cost effectiveness is based on the Department of Health's cost-effectiveness register, drawing particularly on the literature on QALYs. In addition, Raftery has made use of comparative health service indicators data to illustrate patterns of use of health services facilities. A recent paper (Raftery 1992) illustrates how this approach can be applied to support work on priority setting for health gain.

The way forward

The six DHAs involved in this study have all sought to develop appropriate processes to support priority setting and to put these processes into practice. They have "leading edge" experience, which holds some pointers to the future development of the purchasing rôle. This chapter has attempted to draw from their efforts some lessons of relevance to the NHS as a whole.

It is still too early to identify what works, and what does not. At this stage, therefore, it is important not only to monitor current efforts and to learn from them, but also to investigate relevant issues. Research is needed, for example, into public participation and GP involvement in priority setting – on the wide range of approaches that have been used so far, and the extent to which the public and GPs can be empowered to play a part in shaping purchasing priorities. Another issue concerns the tools and methods developed to support work on priority setting; a bewildering variety of tools have been used, with only a limited exchange of ideas and experience between districts.

The rôle of providers in priority setting needs a full investigation. This issue was stumbled on almost by accident in the course of the research for this study, but was soon regarded as being highly significant. Little is known about the ways in which clinicians and others set priorities in provider units: the only example that emerged in this study was the use of guidelines for administering surfactants in a neo-natal unit. Research into this topic should proceed in tandem with research into the rôle of purchasers.

An issue of concern to both purchasers and providers is whether guidelines and clinical protocols can be used more extensively as part of the priority setting process. This was certainly the view of the committee set up by the Dutch government to examine choices in health care (Dunning Report 1992), and it was also the conclusion of the New Zealand core services committee (National Advisory Committee 1992). The underlying argument here is that by defining more precisely the patients who are most likely to benefit from clinical intervention and by concentrating scarce resources on those patients it may be possible to avoid the exclusion of whole categories of service from health care provision. If this argument is accepted, then a key challenge for the future is to encourage the health care professions to develop guidelines and protocols as a way of promoting the appropriate use of services. This will not be easy in circumstances in which the professions value their freedom to determine what is best for patients, but it may be unavoidable given the resource constraints under which health services will function.

Notes

1. This chapter is based on a report published by the Department of Health in 1994 (Ham et al. 1994). The research was supported by the Research and Development Directorate in the NHS Management Executive.

References

Advisory Group on Health Technology Assessment 1992. *Assessing the effects of health technologies*. London: Department of Health.

Bowling, A., B. Jacobson, L. Southgate 1993. Health service priorities: explorations in consultation of the public and health professionals on priority-setting in an Inner London health district. *Social Science and Medicine* **37**, 851–7.

Department of Health 1989. *Working for patients*. London: HMSO.

Department of Health 1989. *Care in the community*. London: HMSO.

Department of Health 1991. *The patient's charter*. London: HMSO.

Department of Health 1992. *The health of the nation*. Cmnd 1986. London: HMSO.

Dunning Report 1992. *Choices in health care*. Rijswijk, The Netherlands: Ministry of Welfare, Health, and Cultural Affairs.

Ham, C. (ed.) 1988. *Health care variations*. London: King's Fund Institute.

Ham, C., F. Honigsbaum, D. Thompson 1994. *Priority setting for health gain*. London: Department of Health.

Ham, C. & P. Spurgeon 1992. *Effective purchasing*. Health Services Management Centre, University of Birmingham.

Heginbotham, C., C. Ham & others 1992. *Purchasing dilemmas*. London: King's Fund Institute.

Honigsbaum, F. 1991. *Who shall live? Who shall die?* London: King's Fund Institute.

Klein, R. 1992. Warning signals from Oregon. *British Medical Journal* **304**, 1457–8.

Klein, R. & S. Redmayne 1992. *Patterns of priorities.* Birmingham: NAHAT.

National Advisory Committee 1992. *Core services 1993/4.* Wellington, NAC.

NHSME 1992. *Local voices.* Leeds: Department of Health.

Raftery, J. 1992. Disease mapping, comparative analysis and purchasing for health gain by disease. Unpublished paper.

Welsh Health Planning Forum 1990. *Protocol for investment in health gain – cancers.* Cardiff: Welsh Office.

NHSME papers on purchasing

1989   *Role of DHAs – analysis of issues.*
1990   *Developing districts.*
1990   *Starting specifications.*
1990   *Holding on while letting go.*
1991   *Professional advice for purchasers.*
1991   *Moving forward – needs, services and contacts.*
1991   *Assessing health care needs.*
1991   *Purchasing with authority.*
1991   *Purchasing together.*
1991   *Purchasing intelligence.*

6

Obstacles to medical audit: British doctors speak[1]

Nick Black and Elizabeth Thompson

Introduction

The reforms of the National Health Service (NHS), which commenced in April 1991, were designed to transform the provision of health care in Britain. These reforms included a commitment to medical audit, the formal evaluation of the practice of doctors, as part of a general move towards accountability and evaluation within professionalized health and welfare services. "The development and adoption of agreed standards of good practice," argues *The health of the nation*, which was published in 1992 by the Secretary of State for Health, "is particularly important. The recent developments in clinical audit are to be commended and should be built on" (HMSO 1992, 30).

The commitment to medical audit has been led by professional associations, such as the Royal Colleges, and encouraged by the UK Department of Health. It is supported by designated funding, which is distributed through the Regional Health Authorities (RHAs) in England, equivalent bodies in Scotland, Wales and Northern Ireland, and through the Royal Colleges. There is an accepted procedure for an audit cycle: first, the establishment of criteria and the setting of standards for high quality care; secondly, an assessment of the extent to which these standards are being achieved; thirdly, the implementation of changes; and finally, a reassessment to see if the quality of care has improved.

Unless the views of doctors are recognized and addressed, however, no amount of funding, persuasion and directives will achieve the successful implementation of effective medical audit. This chapter gives an account of a study that set out to discover and chronicle the views on audit of doctors working in general (internal), geriatric, and accident and emergency medicine. The discovery of their opinions and experiences should provide a more realistic basis from which to assess the measures most needed to implement audit fully.

Much of the current enthusiasm for medical audit is based on the belief that it is an effective means of improving the quality of medical care. Published accounts of audit tend to confirm this belief (Eisenberg 1986). But there may well be some publication bias: audits that fail to improve the quality of care are less likely to be reported. It has been suggested that concern about the effectiveness of audit acts to deter doctors from becoming involved (Baron 1983). Other potential obstacles to audit include: a reluctance to judge peers (Baron 1983); the danger of reducing public confidence in doctors (Baron 1983); a belief that doctors have been auditing their work for years (Paton 1987); inadequate data and information systems (Paton 1987, Gumpert & Lyons 1990); a lack of time (Paton 1987, Gumpert & Lyons 1990); the fact that the process can be threatening and boring (Gumpert & Lyons 1990) or require highly specialized medical knowledge (Jessop 1989); the difference between the educational needs of senior and junior doctors (Packwood 1991); and suspicions about managers' interest in audit (Tomlin 1991).

However, the identification of these obstacles has been based largely on the personal views of the authors who have written about them. There has been little effort to study systematically the knowledge, beliefs and attitudes of doctors towards audit: only two attempts have been made, so far as it is possible to tell, and neither of them has been published. One of these attempts is the only study that has considered the views of junior doctors (Sue Kerrison and Tim Packwood, personal communication). In the other study, consultant obstetricians and senior midwives were interviewed about their understanding of audit and the rôle of national and regional bodies; this also involved a non-participant observational study of obstetric audit meetings (Philip Banfield, personal communication). Overall, these studies have indicated that the views of the enthusiastic doctors who write about and promote audit may be a misleading representation of the beliefs and attitudes of many of their colleagues. It is salutary to note that in the USA, where audit was adopted some 10 years earlier than in the UK, the greatest obstacle remains the lack of support from physicians. A recent survey found that 8 per cent of physicians were hostile to audit and a further 60 per cent gave only grudging support (Casanova 1990).

The methods of the study

In the study which provides the basis for this chapter, interviews were carried out between August and October 1991 in four NHS district general hospitals in south-east England. These hospitals were taking part in a larger study of the cost effectiveness of an audit of the appropriate use of thrombolytics in people admitted with chest pain. Selection of hospitals for the audit study was based on the doctors having both an interest in the subject and a willingness to participate. Although the four hospitals are fairly typical of district general hospitals in England, their agreement to participate suggests that there may have been some selection bias in favour of audit.

All consultants and the junior medical staff (including registrars, senior house officers and house officers) working in general medicine were invited to take part. In addition, in each hospital, one consultant and two juniors in geriatric medicine, plus one consultant in accident and emergency medicine, were asked to participate. Sixty-two interviews were conducted by one of the authors of this chapter (Elizabeth Thompson) – about half with consultants and half with junior doctors (see Table 6.1). In all, 28 consultants and 34 junior doctors participated, including all the relevant consultants except one, who was "too busy", and about 50 per cent of the junior staff. Those junior doctors not participating were either on leave, not interested, or said they had insufficient time. It seems probable that the non-respondents were less supportive of audit than the respondents.

The interviews were relatively unstructured and lasted between 15 minutes and an hour. Respondents' views were sought on the following aspects of audit: its purpose; its impact on relationships between doctors; its help in day-to-day work; its impact on quality; the extra work it generates; its educational rôle; and its effectiveness and usefulness. Notes were

Table 6.1 Number of interviews by grade of staff in each of the four study hospitals.

	Hospital				Total
	A	B	C	D	
Consultant	10	5	7	6	28
Registrar	5	4	2	1	12
Senior House Officer	1	4	4	5	14
House Officer	3	2	1	2	8
Total	**19**	**15**	**14**	**14**	**62**

taken during the interview, and supplemented by additional notes made immediately afterwards. The data were analyzed by constant comparison, a method of generating themes from the data (Glaser 1964).

The results of the study

Before discussing the various difficulties identified by the respondents, it is important to recognize that it is only in the past few years that an effort has been made to persuade all doctors to participate in audit, although some doctors in the UK have been auditing their medical practice for many years. Also, many doctors consulted during the course of this study expressed enthusiasm for audit. Their concerns and criticisms should be considered in this context.

This chapter focuses deliberately on doctors' worries about audit, rather than on any satisfaction they might feel, on the grounds that the identification of problems is of most importance in the development of better methods of implementing audit. Generally speaking, adverse comments were made by doctors in a constructive spirit – in the hope that difficulties could be overcome and audit could be strengthened. The obstacles to audit that were identified by the respondents can be grouped into four categories: (i) perceptions of the need for, and the rôle of, audit; (ii) practical considerations; (iii) the effects of audit; and (iv) anxieties about the use of audit. Each category will be considered in turn.

Perceptions of the need for, and the rôle of, audit

Most doctors accepted the need for audit, associating it with good doctoring. However, they did not regard it as anything new, but as something they had been pursuing for years, long before the recent spate of interest from the government, professional associations and managers. The only change, they said, was the formalization of the activity. "[It's a] myth," said one registrar, "that we've never been doing it before." According to a house officer, "There is nothing new about audit. Now it's all written down and it's made more of an issue." A consultant remarked that:

> We have been doing audit for a long time. Clinical meetings have been going on for as long as I can remember. It is nothing new, we are not big stupid buffoons who do not question what

130

we do. By its very nature the medical profession is a very self-critical group. Audit is a more formal version, sometimes too formal.

Such widespread existence of audit should be encouraging to its proponents. However, most of the activities referred to were actually unsystematic, irregular, unstructured discussions of clinical subjects, with no clear agenda for action or attempts to reassess the problem after improvements in practice had been attempted.

A second perception that could impede the development of audit was suspicion about the motives behind the current encouragement from the government. Many respondents seemed to think that cost containment rather than improved quality of care was the real motive. The belief of doctors that improvements in quality could only be achieved by increased expenditure simply served to increase their incredulity regarding government motives. For example, they considered that consultations would need to be longer to ensure patient satisfaction, and that more time was needed in order to write legible notes and to ensure discharge summaries were dispatched promptly. Some doctors were afraid that the government and managers might use audit information to reduce resources, but would not be willing to increase resources if they were needed. "I'm suspicious," stated one consultant, "of the motives for audit. The package that it came in . . . it's like trying to squeeze more blood out of a stone." According to another consultant, "The latest reforms came in a packet. It's definitely a way managers can control their budget." Yet another consultant, who warned, "You may have caught me on a bad day!", asked:

> Do you want the truth? I think it's a government intervention, a political tool to discipline doctors and make them do more work. It's another initiative imposed by the Conservative government, well Mrs Thatcher really, to discipline doctors. It's an important political weapon with which to divide the NHS.

These doctors were sceptical about the real motives of those who were undertaking audit. One registrar said, "I don't know many real physicians who are interested in audit for the sake of medicine and patients. Those that do audit, most of them are struggling to satisfy the requirements of the hospital, to do audit." In the view of another registrar:

it attracts those who want to have less to do with patients and more to do with politics. It is for those doctors who are not so busy. It attracts them. Good doctors are always busy because they have many patients to see. This is rather rude but it's like the saying – those who can, do, and those who can't, teach.

A third problem was that many doctors wanted audit to be confined to *administrative*, rather than *clinical*, issues. This was partly on the grounds that clinical aspects were too difficult to audit, and partly because variations in clinical practice were seen as a reflection of differences in approach to medicine, which ought to be accepted, if not actively encouraged. In contrast, there was considerable support for the auditing of administrative matters. One consultant recalled an occasion when "the diabetic sister was studying the clinic list and suggested a reorganization to prevent patients spending too much time waiting. It was a very sensible suggestion. That sort of thing is useful". A registrar argued that, "Case review generally reveals things such as wrong GP's address, no letter to GP and so on. It's nearly always a clerical problem such as the wrong address and so on. The management of patients is good. It's usually other things such as a lost letter to the GP and then the patient ends up with the wrong drugs." A senior house officer said that in his opinion:

> audit should look at the management of things, the functioning of the hospital. There's a lot of red tape and bureaucracy in the hospitals and I think that when audit was set up it was set up to audit this. Also I think with medical conditions there are always reasons for and against, always arguments . . . it's difficult to reach a consensus. If audit looks at better and easier ways of management, then I think that the goal is clear and achievable. For instance, with streptokinase you could argue to give it less and there would be more heart attacks or you could argue to give it more and there would be a higher risk of complications.

The emphasis on administrative, rather than clinical, problems, led to a fourth – and intriguing – perception of the rôle of audit: namely, the question of *who exactly* was being audited. Since the junior staff perform the day-to-day duties of clerking and managing patients, they felt that it was only *their* work that was being monitored, and resented this state of affairs. "I know it has to be done," said one senior house officer, "but . . .

you get it in the neck a bit, really. It's enough strain as it is without added hassle . . . you're the one that's on the ground, the one who admitted him." Another senior house officer agreed: "At audit meetings," he said, "we look at topics such as GI [gastro-intestinal] bleed or case review . . . we look at the notes, whether they are dated, tidy, are they filed? It's probably important but it's very tedious. Often it comes down to almost the handwriting."

Some consultants approved of this focus on juniors, making no apologies for it. "The purpose of audit," argued one, "is to check standards, to look at the junior doctor's management and see whether it is acceptable. To look and see whether they have overtreated, undertreated . . . to review ongoing management." Another consultant observed that, "It is their [the juniors'] notes that are being audited. For instance, the other day we discovered that someone came in with epigastric pain and should have had an ultrasound scan because they had gallstones. These things come to light through audit." Other consultants, however, understood the resentment of the junior doctors, and were concerned about its implications for the process of audit. "It's seen as a junior bashing exercise," said one, who added, "I think that is one of the problems of audit. It is meant to find fault so that you can improve care. I think that it is difficult to be positive about negative things." Another consultant made the same point: "I think recently the junior staff have not got very much out of it. I think they felt that they were being got at, that it was inquisitorial."

Finally, there was a common, recurring, perception that the aim of audit was to convert medical practice – which was generally perceived to be an individualized, subtle art – into an unthinking, routine activity, largely based on guidelines and rules. Many doctors believed that a high degree of dependence on guidelines would have adverse effects for doctors. In particular, there was a fear that it would destroy the initiative of juniors, who would no longer think carefully through their plan for treatment, but simply pick up a form and tick the relevant box. Some doctors were also afraid that they would be obliged to comply with this sort of guideline in every case, even when they did not judge it to be appropriate. "I haven't been practising long," maintained one house officer, "but sometimes it's best to follow your own instincts. As you get more senior, you have to think of medicine as an art. I'd hate it to be constrained with form filling and following regular guidelines." A consultant presented the same view: "I feel you should do what you are happy with. You should not be foot-marching into something you do not agree with." Even those doctors who recognized the value of audit and, therefore, the need for compromise, worried about the introduction of strict guidelines. "If everything was rigid," warned one consultant, "then some of the fun would be taken out of medicine. We do need some framework, but would not want it to get too regimented."

Practical considerations

The previous section indicated the way in which doctors' views can obstruct the implementation of audit. This section will consider some of the practical issues that were identified as sources of anxiety by respondents. The first such issue related to the social environment within which the doctors worked. Because of the potentially sensitive nature of audit, it is desirable for it to take place within a co-operative, supportive situation. The need for this, and the corresponding dangers of carrying out audit in a hostile environment, were clearly recognized. "Doctors should not feel threatened," pointed out one consultant, "It's not a question of slagging each other off. It's criticism which should be constructive." According to another consultant, "At meetings you can get peer encouragement and bullying. It depends how supportive the group is. If you have a group who were already at each other before audit, well then audit will make it worse." Another consultant said that criticizing with "any degree of aggressiveness" would be "professional suicide".

Despite this awareness of the risks involved, apparently some unfortunate experiences had occurred. One registrar said that he did not think audit was "the best medium for providing peer support. In fact, in my last job, with the two chest physicians it caused discord". A senior house officer reported a similar situation: "[You] often find that if one team goes down quite heavily on the other team, then in the next session they'll do you quite heavily back." A consultant complained that, "When they audit me they pick on tiny little things like, maybe, I should have discontinued this treatment. I let it continue though, because I think it is progress. However, it is not a mutual admiration society."

Even if conflicts are avoided, the fear that they might develop can inhibit criticism and thus reduce the potential effectiveness of audit. Juniors reported that they had felt unable to challenge their seniors: according to a house officer, "the junior staff don't join in much. I think you feel a bit intimidated . . . you don't really like to criticize the consultants". The dependence of juniors upon their seniors for future jobs made them reluctant to criticize consultants. The consultants, in their turn, felt inhibited due to their lack of medical knowledge in particular areas: they felt it was inappropriate to audit their colleagues unless they were a specialist in the field under consideration. A consultant explained that, "It is hard for individual consultants to criticize another doctor unless they are an expert in that field." In his own speciality, said one, "I am the only person who practises and deals with HIV patients. I could pull the wool over someone else's eyes. How do others know or how can they judge what is good practice?" Not surprisingly, it was much easier for everyone to focus on organizational issues, where knowledge and experience were more equal.

Even if the working environment were conducive to audit, and doctors suffered no inhibition at the prospect of criticizing their colleagues, there was a third practical problem – the additional burden of work imposed by audit. "I get a bit annoyed with central government," complained one consultant, "when they say you must do audit, but they do not understand the different constraints upon doing audit." Another consultant complained:

> There are two problems with audit, and that is time and money. This change has been added to the health service with no resources to put it into shape. That part of it has not been thought through. It's piling more responsibilities on us. The secretaries are very busy and have not got time to pull more notes. The facilities are not there.

The lack of time was aggravated by other concurrent health service reforms, which had made further demands on consultants' time. Activities such as resource management and the collection of clinical information all took time. Even with the introduction of audit officers and assistants, which was generally appreciated, there was still insufficient time for an adequate analysis of results and preparation for meetings.

Some consultants claimed that seeing more patients, or devoting more time to teaching juniors, would be a much more effective use of their time. "It's not just the meetings," said one consultant, "it's the preparatory work that goes into it if it is going to be any good. There is pressure to do more work, do you leave the junior staff again? . . . you have to manage because managers cannot manage on their own or without us . . . and now there is directorship." Another consultant complained that,

"Every day this week I haven't been home before 10 pm because of management initiatives. This government induces meetings. I had to go to a resource management meeting and then a coding meeting before I came to you. I still have to see my patients."

Medical audit created extra work for juniors, too, who already felt over-committed. "The trouble," pointed out a house officer, "is that the juniors have to do it all. When you've had 20 admissions and then some psychiatrist asks why we hadn't filled in the forms . . . it's difficult." In principle, juniors agreed with the idea of audit, but maintained that it was impractical for them to get too involved. "Well, I'd get more involved," said a house officer, "if it was taken out of our time, not if it took up extra time in our day. If half a day was devoted to audit, then that's fine." In any case, complained a house officer, the extra work would be used for someone else's benefit: "We're at the front line. We're managing patient care. On top of that, audit creates extra things for us to do. We do all this so they can write up a paper or get their name added to something."

Many doctors thought that the additional work created by audit might be alleviated somewhat by information technology. Computers, they hoped, would make it easier to monitor the care of patients and

Many doctors hope that information technology will simplify audit (Julia Martin/Photofusion).

make audit an easier and more attractive task. However, several commented on the lack of sufficient information technology and support staff. A consultant complained that:

> If you have to make do with the present system of extracting information, it takes a long time. I would like to have a computer where I could have access to reports on patients and, say, out-patients . . . a system where I could get easy access to information.

A fourth area of practical difficulty arose from doctors' limited knowledge and understanding of audit. This was partly revealed through respondents' beliefs that they had been auditing their work for years, though without, evidently, any use of criteria, standards or reassessments. Some doctors were aware of their lack of training. "I'm not trained in audit," admitted one consultant, adding, "It might be easier for me if I was trained in audit. Others after me may find it easier." Another consultant wanted to see the employment of "an experienced person, who had experience of the health service as well, who could rotate round and set up sessions in a more structured way and dictate what we should be doing". A lack of understanding of audit was not universal, however. There were many doctors who knew about the audit cycle. But although these doctors knew what they should be doing, they admitted that they were failing to implement audit properly. "Really," said one senior house officer, "we talk about audit, rather than do it." A consultant remarked that, "The notes are not picked out of sheer randomness, they are biased. Slightly more interesting cases educationally. I think that this is probably not what should be happening." Another consultant complained that:

> At the moment it just confirms my gut feeling. It does not come up with anything unexpected really. It increases awareness and raises problems, but of the audits I've seen there are not enough cycles to change behaviour, and if that does not happen there is no point. I know it's fairly negative of a chairman of audit to say this.

Many doctors were highly critical of audit meetings, which was a fifth issue of practical difficulty. "The best thing about audit," observed one registrar, "is the sandwiches at lunch." There were two principal criticisms: first, that dull, administrative topics were selected rather than issues of clinical practice; and secondly, that often no decisions were made, or action taken, to improve the quality of care. According to a senior house officer, "At [previous hospital worked at] I didn't go to any meetings. At [another previous hospital] it was even worse. So boring. We used to have to hand in our bleeps so no one could escape. It was so boring. We looked at dull topics, like discharge letters, and we concluded that we weren't doing them quickly enough." A consultant concurred: "The medical meetings, with all due respect to Dr [X], tend to be terribly boring. It's case review week after week and if we suddenly come on to bed management they say, 'Oh this is not the forum for discussing this'."

Clearly, some dissatisfaction stemmed from a failure to follow the audit cycle properly. However, even when the cycle was completed, some juniors still found reason to complain. "I think it's important to re-audit," said a house officer, "but if you keep auditing it gets boring. If you want to find out if a problem has disappeared you need to re-audit." Some consultants were well aware of their juniors' lack of enthusiasm for audit meetings and were attempting to improve the situation. One consultant, who kept a checklist so that everyone felt obliged to attend, said, "I worry about the meetings . . . that the juniors feel that they are a waste of time. I think the difficulty is in getting audience participation . . . now I'm trying to get the juniors involved in thinking up a programme and actually to lead the meetings." Another consultant held the view that:

> I think it has to come from the top. There is no point telling the juniors to get involved if the consultant does not. I expect the registrar to be involved, in some areas I regard them as being more experienced than me. I think it is important for juniors not to look at it as some sort of ivory tower. That takes time.

Such strategies may increase junior participation. However, nothing can be done at present to change the sixth practical difficulty – the relatively short contracts of employment of junior doctors, which means that completing the audit cycle usually takes longer than their stay at the hospital. A registrar complained, "At grass roots level you resent having to write up all the forms and then you move on after six months and don't really see the changes or benefits that come out of it."

But the lack of participation was not confined to junior staff: as has long been recognized, audit fails to touch some of those it is meant to reach. Some respondents said that because audit was voluntary, it was too easy for consultants not to participate. There was a view that those who were most in need of auditing, whether senior or junior staff, would not participate. "In the past, anyway," said one consultant, "I think good doctors have practised audit and bad ones haven't." Another consultant made the same point: "It is, however, superimposed on an already heavy workload. Those that need disciplining don't go. Good doctors have an academic and intellectual audit of their own."

The effects of audit

When doctors were consulted on their views about the effectiveness of audit, two specific questions were asked: first, is audit effective in improving the quality of care; and secondly, if so, is it the most cost-effective approach?

Even the most ardent supporters of audit seemed to be uncertain about its effectiveness. "With things like audit," stated one consultant, "it is an act of faith. To practise it you have to be convinced . . . it's difficult." Another consultant said, "Take the quality of the notes. You find that they [juniors] make more entries, they are more legible. Whether or not this means that there is an improvement in patient care is difficult to say. The problem with audit is that the outcome of audits aren't necessarily reflected in the outcome for the patient. Maybe that will come later." A senior house officer expressed similar doubts, but added, "I have no evidence. It's a gut feeling. If we're completing the cycle, then it should improve care." Inevitably, those doctors who had little sympathy for audit were convinced it was ineffective. It was "Rubbish," judged one consultant, adding, "That's it. That is what I think. They think we are looking at how we manage ourselves. I think that nothing ever happens." Some believed that audit could even harm the quality of care: "Pharmacy did an audit on resuscitation," reported one consultant, "and as a result . . . a new policy was adopted. They told some people, but not us. On one of my wards a patient needed resuscitation and my staff went to the equipment and things were not there that are usually there. Audit did not cause that, but it was a consequence of audit."

As has already been seen, the ineffectiveness of audit was blamed frequently on the failure to complete the audit cycle. Audit seemed repeatedly to reveal similar problems with the quality of care, but there was no evidence that these problems were in fact being corrected. This failure was attributed to a lack of organization, poor management or the need for additional resources. According to one consultant, "We never correct the things that are wrong such as notes lost, changing notes and so on . . . because it is a management issue and nobody acts upon it." Another consultant observed that, "Sometimes you think there is no point if it does not lead to a change in practice. You can pat yourself on the back but there is no obvious mechanism for doing something about things. There is no accountability, no time, no motivation." Yet another consultant complained that:

> There is no mechanism for changing inadequacies identified by audit. Most things that are audited are already known. They are obvious and they don't need auditing to prove it. Take the thrombolysis study . . . Some people say, "Ah, if we audit it might show that we need a coronary care unit." Well, everyone knows that we need one and even after the audit the money won't be provided. It's very frustrating.

In any case, concluded one consultant, "If audit discovers things, reveals needs such as more nurses, more physio[therapist]s . . . the answer to that is more money which I suspect the government won't part with. Therefore, it is a waste of time." There was also the danger of doctors *appearing* to change their clinical practice to produce better audit results, while *actually* continuing to practise in the same way as before. In one of the hospitals, a house officer admitted that juniors had decided to modify their entries in the case notes, in order to influence the audit results and to maintain the appearance of reaching their targets.

Some doctors were worried about the cost effectiveness of audit, given the cumbersome nature of obtaining information in the NHS and the great commitment that was needed. Also, the possibility was put forward that practice could be improved through other, better means. "More and more time," complained one consultant, "is given up to go to meetings that weren't done before. It is assumed that this is all good news and no one is questioning whether they are beneficial and what they are replacing." Another consultant said that he could "learn that [the subject of the audit] from a paper in five minutes, instead of sitting through hours of audit meetings. Few people would argue with that." A house officer maintained that, "It's gone a bit mad. Everybody wants to audit everything. I think it's a good thing but if they paid us double, doubled our numbers, then there would be no need to audit." One consultant said he thought audit was useful, but wondered, "Is it the best thing to do, to spend money on?"

Anxieties about the use of audit

Doctors were concerned principally about the current practice of audit. In addition, though, many were anxious about the uses to which audit might be put in the future. They were afraid that audit could be used to intimidate doctors and that there would be further growth in expenditure on audit. Also, they were concerned about the possibility of legal implications for doctors and about an increase in involvement by managers and politicians.

Junior doctors' sense of being intimidated by consultants has already been referred to in this chapter, in the context of their reluctance to criticize their seniors. Even more strongly voiced was their anxiety about being humiliated at an audit meeting. A registrar reported that, "It has been stressful, certainly in other hospitals. In one review case an SHO [senior house officer] was reduced to tears by an auditing consultant." A house officer said that, "If a doctor was out of line, I think that if they were taken aside and it was explained to them, then I think that is better than exposing faults in front of everyone."

A second anxiety, which was shared by consultants and juniors alike, concerned the level of expenditure on audit. While most doctors expressed support for audit, they were acutely conscious of the competing demands of expenditure on direct patient care. "I think we have spent too much on audit," judged one consultant, adding, "The money could have better been spent on keeping beds open." A registrar thought that, "they are getting a bit carried away with it. We have got an audit facilitator, an audit analyst, audit department. I think they are getting a bit carried away". A senior house officer ventured the opinion that no more money should be spent on "audit or people for audit. If we did, it should be on educating doctors about audit, which would just mean a few extra sessions".

There were also worries about the legal consequences of audit in the long term. Some doctors were afraid that audit would increase, rather than decrease, their vulnerability to litigation: "The more structured and formalized it [clinical practice] becomes," warned one consultant, "the more it becomes an issue for medico-legal purposes . . . I can see more lawyers using failure to comply exactly with agreed guidelines as negligence." Another consultant said, "In the future, the legal medical implications [are my worst fear], because that is the way that some people earn a living. For example, you may follow 90 per cent of guidelines and if you do not follow 10 per cent because of clinical discretion, will you be sued?"

Finally, anxiety was expressed about the rôle of managers and politicians in the matter of audit. It has already been observed that some doctors were convinced that managers' and politicians' interest in audit was motivated by cost containment. There were even greater worries about the future behaviour of managers and governments:

> There is a lot of suspicion between clinicians and management. Doctors will fiercely defend their actions. They do not want to be dictated to by administration. I don't think that management should interfere, tell us how to run our clinics and so on. If a doctor is not seeing enough patients then fair enough, management should tell the silly man to pull his socks up.

Another consultant argued, "I don't think management should have access to all data. They should have access to information that they need to manage. If management had authority to move around, I mean to get information and make decisions, they wouldn't understand what clinical medicine is about. The reason I'm saying this is because I've been rather disappointed with management. They don't really understand what medicine is like." However, not all consultants took the likelihood of such developments so seriously. Two respondents took a more cynical view: "If you have been here as long as I have," said one, "then you usually find a way around things." Another believed that it was just "a phase in the NHS", adding that:

> It's a bit like TV franchises, the poll tax. It'll soon die down. It's a pain experiencing it. I think audit will change shape and form many times until it becomes disreputable. It's a shame because it distances doctors from enjoying their jobs. I don't want audit to occupy any more of my time. I think that there will be a new buzzword next year.

Discussion

Doctors have many criticisms of audit. On the one hand, this should not make proponents of audit despondent, as most critics accepted the general aims of audit and shared its objectives. Their criticisms were levelled more at the *way* audit was being implemented, than at the *principles* of the approach. On the other hand, it would be equally foolhardy to be complacent and to dismiss the criticisms as ill-informed comments generated from the respondents' self-interest.

In sum, 19 potential obstacles to audit, grouped into four categories, were identified in the course of this study. While some of these confirm previous anecdotal reports by writers on audit (Baron 1983, Paton 1987, Gumpert & Lyons 1990, Jessop 1989, Packwood 1991, Tomlin 1991), several have received little or no attention. Before considering the practical implications of the findings, however, two general observations need to be made. The first concerns the validity of the data. Should we believe what the doctors say? Much of the material can only be taken on trust. The recurrence of similar views from different doctors, often working in different hospitals, suggests that a particular opinion or experience was neither unique nor fabricated. For some issues, it was possible to confirm the respondents' comments. For example, when an examination of the minutes of audit meetings revealed that no attempt was being made to complete the audit cycle, this was confirmed by attending the meetings. For other issues it is not possible to be so confident. The dreadful, humiliating experiences of junior doctors at audit meetings generally seem to occur to "other people at other hospitals". It is possible that such accounts are the medical equivalent of urban myths, always happening to third parties elsewhere.

The second general observation is related to that of validity. Hundreds of accounts of audit by doctors have been published, ranging from general discussions of methods to descriptions of specific projects, yet all the authors speak about their subject in a way that is strikingly different from the doctors interviewed for this study. Why is this? It may partly be due to selection – authors of audit articles tend to be enthusiasts, and in any case, successful audits are more likely to be reported than failures. Another possible factor is the contrast between public rhetoric and personal experience, which was identified in the interviews. On initial questioning, respondents tended to provide well-accepted definitions of what audit was and why it was important. It was only after this "public rhetoric" had been produced that doctors started to give us their own views, based on personal experience. A similar contrast has been demonstrated in research into lay people's views of health and disease (Cornwell 1984).

What, then, are the chief lessons to be learnt from this study? The first is that factions or interest groups in organizations may subsume new initiatives for their own purposes. However well-intentioned and single-minded might be those who champion audit, they will have to contend with the different intentions of others. For example, if an individual doctor, or a group, is engaged in a long-running conflict with other doctors, audit may be hijacked and used as a weapon in their battles. Similarly, audit may be used in conflicts between doctors and managers or between consultants and juniors. In general, audit will be shaped by the prevailing, established environment, rather than the converse. Those who expect audit to resolve existing organizational difficulties are likely to be disappointed.

A second lesson that emerges is the extent of medical complacency that exists. This is best illustrated by the confidence with which doctors declared that the principal (or even the only) problems affecting health services are administrative and organizational, rather than clinical. This may reflect in part the difficulty of auditing clinical decisions and practice in the frequent absence of valid outcome measures. But it also reflects a general confidence in the field of medicine. It may also, of course, be the result of a failure to persuade respondents to reveal their deeper uncertainties about clinical practice. Given their readiness to offer frank views about audit, however, this is unlikely.

A third lesson, which has been noted previously (Baron 1983), is that many doctors are not convinced of the value of audit. They question repeatedly the cost of their time, of audit staff and of other resources, and resent being forced to undertake audit. They see little benefit to themselves or to their patients. These feelings are to some extent based on their own experience of audit which, as has been seen, is often a travesty of the way it should be done.

This is connected to a fourth lesson – that few doctors know how to undertake audit. This was also the case in the USA, where audit was introduced earlier. Only 46 per cent of doctors were judged to have a basic or a thorough understanding of audit (Casanova 1990). Some of our respondents recognized their lack of understanding and wanted advice and help. Training doctors in audit will be a major undertaking, however, given the general lack of scientific training they have received.

Finally, doctors seemed to confuse a knowledge of medicine with a knowledge of audit. Many juniors and consultants felt inhibited about commenting on the work of other doctors, because they thought their clinical knowledge of the area was inadequate. What they did not appreciate was that audit is largely about asking questions – about how and why medicine is being practised in the way it is. It is not necessary to know the correct answer; all that is required is the courage to ask simple, revealing questions.

Through interviews with practising doctors, this study has produced a taxonomy of their beliefs and attitudes. Some of the obstacles to audit could be overcome by simple practical measures; others could be solved by improving doctors' understanding of audits, and their skill at conducting them. However, many problems would remain, which will only respond to more profound changes in the beliefs, attitudes and knowledge of doctors. The difficulty of achieving such changes should not be underestimated. They are essential, however, if audit is to be used as a key tool in the reform of medical practice.

Acknowledgements

We would like to thank all the doctors who participated in the interviews; Mike Robinson and Phil Strong for their comments; and the Department of Health for funding. This study was carried out in collaboration with the Research Unit of the Royal College of Physicians in London.

Notes

1. Reprinted with permission from Nick Black and Elizabeth Thompson, *Social Science and Medicine* **36**(7) (Oxford, England: Pergamon Press,1993).

References

Baron, D. N. 1983. Can't audit? Won't audit! *British Medical Journal* **286**, 1229–30.

Casanova, J. E. 1990. Status of quality assurance programs in American hospitals. *Medical Care* **28**(11), 1104–9.

Cornwell, J. 1984. *Hard-earned lives*. London: Tavistock.

Eisenberg, J. M. 1986. *Doctors' decisions and the cost of medical care*. Ann Arbor, Michigan: Health Administration Press.

Glaser, B. 1964. The constant comparative method of qualitative analysis. *Social Problems* **12**, 436.

Gumpert, R. & C. Lyons 1990. Setting up a district audit programme. *British Medical Journal* **301**, 162–5.

Jessop, J. 1989. Audit: all talk and no action? *Health Service Journal* 31 August, 1072.

Packwood, T. 1991. The three faces of medical audit. *Health Service Journal* 26 September, 24–6.

Paton, A. 1987. Audit long overdue. *The Health Supplement* September, 3.

Secretary of State for Health, 1992. *The health of the nation*. London: HMSO.

Tomlin, Z. 1991. Grasping the nettle. *Health Service Journal* 27 June, 31–2.

7

Choice, needs and enabling: the new community care[1]

Jane Lewis

Introduction

Community care as a social policy is relatively new in Britain. The term itself came into use with the 1957 Royal Commission on the Law Relating to Mental Illness and Mental Deficiency, which recommended a policy shift from hospital to community care and emphasized the desirability of supported care in the family. The policy of shifting care from institutions into the community has been developed and promoted by successive governments since the 1960s. With the election of Margaret Thatcher's first administration in 1979, a new impetus was given to the idea of community care, although policy continued to provide incentives for institutional care until the passage of the National Health Service and Community Care Act in 1990. Implementation of the new policy is taking place in the context of the emergence of a mixed economy of welfare involving the private sector, the voluntary sector, the family and the state. This chapter explores the nature of these recent developments in community care and the shift in approach to the delivery of social services, in two sections. The first section traces the history and the formulation of government policy on community care and assesses the key objectives of the 1989 White Paper, while the second illustrates some of the more pressing issues of implementing the new policy on community care, by drawing on the work of two research projects designed to monitor the process of change.

The new policy of community care

The development of policy

The history of the policy of community care is a vexed one: it has been suggested (Walker 1982, 19) that the term's "durability probably owes much to its manipulation to encompass the widest possible range of institutions". Another commentator has concluded that the meaning of community care "has been changed to suit the new policies; its catchphrase character has obscured the complexities of care; it has invested a hotchpotch of policies and practices with a spurious sense of integration and consistency and because of its attractive connotations it has tended to escape close critical scrutiny" (Parker 1990, 22).

During the early 1960s, when prominent academic writers such as Peter Townsend (1962) were making moving and well-founded pleas for taking the elderly and the mentally ill out of institutions, another, Richard Titmuss, sounded a – by now, well-known – note of caution:

> What some hope will one day exist is suddenly thought by many to exist already. All kinds of wild and unlovely weeds are changed, by statutory magic and comforting appellation, into the most attractive flowers that bloom not just in the Spring, but all the year round . . . And what of the everlasting cottage-garden trailer, "community care"? Does it now conjure up a sense of warmth and human kindness, essentially personal and comforting, as loving as the wild flowers so enchantingly described by Lawrence in *Lady Chatterley's Lover*? (Titmuss 1968, 104)

The idea of community care, Titmuss recognized, carries an appeal based on a mixture of nostalgia and the promise of loving kindness. He warned, however, that good community care is not cheap.

Despite the endorsement given to the idea of community care from the late 1950s, however, little progress was made in making it a reality. In 1961, Titmuss questioned the government's commitment to the policy. Local authorities (LAs) were slow to acquire new powers in the field of community care: it was 1959, for example, before they were permitted to provide chiropody services, and 1968 before they were obliged to provide home helps (Means and Smith 1985), although most authorities had taken steps to establish such services before they were made a statutory

responsibility. The 1963 Health and Welfare Report (Cmnd 1973) continued to define the concept of community care to include residential
care for the mentally disordered; it followed the other major planning
document of the 1960s, the 1962 Hospital Plan (Cmnd 1604), which was
generated in part from a desire to reduce the in-patient population in
mental hospitals, and which therefore required the planned extension of
community care. It has been pointed out (Walker 1982, 1989; Humble
and Walker 1990) that local authority institutional care became the
health authority's community care. Local authority plans produced in
response to the Health and Welfare Report showed a forecast rise in
home helps of 45 per cent between 1962 and 1972, compared with a rise
of 87 per cent for residential staff (Walker 1982, 16).

Not only was the *definition* of community care confused, but the *whole
attempt to shift resources* from the National Health Service (NHS) to local
authorities for community care, using formal planning machinery that
was refined during the 1970s, has been roundly condemned as a failure
(Glennerster et al. 1983; Webb and Wistow 1987; Wistow 1990). For
example, the percentage of domiciliary and day care expenditure, as a
proportion of total expenditure by social services departments, on the
elderly stood at 33 per cent in 1973 and the same figure in 1985: significant amounts of money did not shift across into local authority community care budgets. Nor did those budgets expand sufficiently to take
account of demographic change after the economic crisis of the early
1970s. The annual rate of growth in the personal social services was restricted in 1976 to 2 per cent, which was barely sufficient to maintain the
then current levels of provision.

None the less, the promotion of community care received a new
impetus at the end of the 1970s, with the election of the first Thatcher
administration. One reason was the publicity accorded to demographics,
which showed that between 1971 and 1981 alone, the number of people
aged over 75 years – the age group commonly agreed to be in need of
the most care – had increased by 20 per cent, and was projected to rise
by 30 per cent by the year 2001, with the percentage of the over-85s set
to double (Ermisch 1983). Also, it may be argued that the promotion of
community care was integral to what has been described (Wicks 1985) as
the Thatcher government's attachment to "an inter-connected trinity of
family, private market, and voluntary sector". In fact, community care
had always been by far the most "mixed economy" of all the welfare
services, relying as it did on provision by family and neighbours – the

voluntary and private sectors – as well as the state.

A 1981 White Paper, *Growing older*, stressed the importance of informal care:

> Whatever level of public expenditure proves practicable, and however it is distributed, the primary sources of support and care for elderly people are informal and voluntary. These spring from the personal ties of kinship, friendship, and neighbourhood. They are irreplaceable. It is the rôle of public authorities to sustain and, where necessary, develop, but never to displace, such support and care. Care in the community must increasingly mean care by the community (Cmnd 8173, para. 1.9).

At the same time, changes in the social security system in 1981 and 1983 effectively gave an open-ended grant to those entering private or voluntary homes, resulting in an enormous (138 per cent) rise in the number of private residential beds. Ironically, this vast increase in private provision was achieved only at an increase in cost to the government in terms of the board and lodging allowance, which rose from £10m to £1000m between 1980 and 1989. Encouragement had been given to certain kinds of "community care", but as the influential 1986 report of the Audit Commission remarked, some of this encouragement was "perverse".

The report of the Audit Commission argued strongly for the removal of the social security "perverse incentives" to institutional care, pointing out that, at best, all that had been achieved was a shift from hospital-based to community-based residential care, funded by supplementary benefit (Audit Commission 1986). The Commission also stressed that provision of community care was uneven between different local authorities and that it had not kept up with the run-down of long-stay institutions. The Commission evidently regarded community care as being cheaper than residential care. It calculated that the care of a frail elderly person cost the state only £135 per week in a domiciliary setting, but £295 per week in a NHS geriatric ward.

The formulation of policy

As a result of the Commission's report, Sir Roy Griffiths, of Sainsbury's, who had already reported on management in the NHS, was invited to report on the financing of, and arrangements for, community care, which he did in 1988 (DHSS 1988). The Griffiths Report recommended making local authorities responsible for community care. Immediate reaction to the report expressed the belief that it would not find favour with government ministers, because of the powers it proposed to give to local government. However, the report *could* be read as advocating greater central control (Lewis 1989; Walker 1989): at the centre, firm patterns of responsibility and accountability for community care would be established via a minister with responsibility for community care, who would specify objectives and provide resources to match them; at the local level, local authorities would identify need, and plan and co-ordinate provision; and at the level of the individual, a care manager would be responsible for assessing need and arranging care "packages".

While Griffiths was anxious to avoid central government "prescription", he nevertheless envisaged central government as providing the "framework" within which local authorities would operate, in terms of both policy aims and finance. A specific grant set at 40 or 50 per cent of agreed local spending was to be made available to LAs, on the submission of community care plans which were judged to provide satisfactory evidence of local needs, collaborative planning, and the promotion of a mixed economy of care. Local authorities were to be made the managing agents and given the responsibility of implementing central government policy which, as Griffiths made clear, would also involve their becoming the organizers, rather than the providers, of care.

The legislative framework that followed the Griffiths report underlined the government's determination to terminate the open-ended social security commitment to funding residential care and to promote a mixed economy of community care, in which local authorities became *enablers* rather than providers – which meant that they would co-ordinate and purchase care, rather than provide it directly. But the 1989 White Paper, which set out government proposals for improving community care, abandoned both Griffiths' idea of making political accountability at the centre explicit and, more significantly still, the link between planning and resource allocation. The perverse incentive to institutional care was to be removed by transferring to local authorities the care element of social security support to residential and nursing homes, in the form of a special transitional grant. However, this did not amount to new funding, because of the slippery definition of community care which has included residential care. Indeed, many social services departments (SSDs) have found themselves implementing the 1990 NHS and Community Care Act (as well as the 1989 Children Act and the 1991 Criminal Justice Act) in the face of local authority budget cuts.

The government experienced considerable difficulties with the Griffiths Report, of which reluctance to make local authorities responsible for implementing the policy was the most obvious. The reasons for these difficulties are important in that arguably they served to weaken Griffiths' design in two crucial respects. The 1989 White Paper stated a firm commitment to community care and to many of the mechanisms favoured by Griffiths, in particular the promotion of care management and the idea of the "enabling authority" which co-ordinated and purchased care, rather than providing it directly. But the implicit, unstated objectives of the government involved the capping of growth in social security expenditure: hence the ending of social security support for institutional care and a means of financing the reforms which broke Griffiths' link between planning and financing. The government was also reluctant for ideological reasons (Baldcock and Evers 1991) to expand the rôle of central government in relation to community care, and to make a minister responsible for it.

It has been suggested (Wistow and Henwood 1991, 89) that "in many crucial respects the plans [in the White Paper] are naive". Certainly, both the White Paper and the subsequent guidance showed that policy had not been thought through in many significant respects (for example, *how* exactly an "enabling authority" was to transfer its budget internally from providers to purchasers), which was only to be expected given the relatively untried and untested nature of many of its key elements.

Griffiths (1992) insisted that the community care changes are primarily about management change. His claim for the political neutrality of his proposals is in line with similar claims for the "new public management" more generally (Hood 1991), with its stress on accountability, results, competition and efficiency. However, academic commentators have suggested that the new managerialism has served to transform local/central government relations, extending to the public sector the decentralization of production and centralization of command made possible by the revolution in information technology that has characterized the private sector (Hoggett 1990). Moreover, the ideas of the new managerialism will inevitably be subject to political manipulation in the context of local authorities (Gray and Jenkins 1993).

The government's community care policy may well be strong enough to secure profound change at the local level. The 1989 White Paper has firmly stated values, goals and a strategy for implementation. It is unlikely that the main elements of the policy can be remade by "street level bureaucrats" (Lipsky 1980). Yet some sort of interactive model would still seem to be appropriate for understanding what is happening in the field of community care. The government's unstated policy concerns weakened the managerial logic of Griffiths, which resulted from the pursuit of the single goal of setting up a "business plan" for community care. As a result, the White Paper and the guidance read as a strong statement of intent, with considerable attention to the changes needed within local authorities (albeit, in line with the Griffiths Report, remaining non-prescriptive), while the overarching mechanisms for ensuring implementation – assured finance linked to planning and full lines of accountability to central government level – are absent. Local authorities must change the way they deliver community care, but the ways in which they do so will be various. In addition, there must be a question mark over what kind of community care can be achieved, since all the responsibilities Griffiths gave local authorities – revolving around the identification of need – remain, while central government responsibility for making sure that resources are consistent with objectives, does not.

The objectives of the 1989 White Paper

The 1989 White Paper listed six objectives: the promotion of domiciliary, day and respite care to permit independent living at home; making support for informal carers a high priority; making the assessment of need and good "case management"[2] the cornerstone of high-quality care; promoting the development of a flourishing independent provider sector; clarifying the responsibility of agencies to increase accountability; and securing better value for money by introducing a new funding structure (Cm 849, para.1.11). In brief, the White Paper asked local authorities to establish the needs of the clients (or the "users", as they became in this document and the subsequent official guidance) and to devise ways of meeting them that would secure for the users the greatest possible choice and independence; this would also, it was believed, improve quality and cost effectiveness. The first of these objectives assumed that there were people in institutional care who should not be. Since there was no new money and also a clearly stated objective of promoting domiciliary care, it followed that money had to be shifted from residential to domiciliary provision. Whether there are indeed people in institutions who could be cared for in their own homes is a vexed issue, and given that there is conflicting evidence, it is possible to cite selectively. In 1988 the Committee of Public Accounts (1988) suggested that if appropriate domiciliary services had been available, only 77 per cent of those entering institutions would have needed to be admitted. Price Waterhouse's study of one-third of residents in Hampshire's residential homes came up with a figure of 86 per cent (DH, SSI, NHSME & PW 1992, vol. II). But a review of the evidence has also indicated (Schorr 1992; Henwood 1992a, 32–4) that comparatively few people are inappropriately placed in residential care, and two-thirds of the 103 elderly people on the brink of entering institutions who were interviewed by Allen et al. (1992), said that they did not feel they could stay at home, even with more help.

The White Paper's "independence" objective also assumed implicitly that it is possible to keep people (and here the focus is understood to be on *elderly* people, not least because of the open-ended social security commitment to this group that was so important in prompting the review of community care) out of institutional care. However, the research literature has been quite clear about the necessary preconditions for this. It has been shown (Davies et al. 1990) that the effects of increasing community care resource inputs (for example, home helps and respite care) alone are relatively few and weak. Improving outcomes requires substantial investment in the management of change and specifically in the development of rigorous care management, which may in turn be expensive.

Finally, this first objective assumed that people (again, primarily elderly people) *want* to stay at home. This may be so, but there has been very little research investigating what elderly people want in reality. The character of the vastly increased demand for residential care during the 1980s is hard to determine. After all, people *had* to "choose" residential care, because this was what social security monies would pay for. Health professionals, too, played a part in manipulating a demand which served to free hospital beds. However, there is also the possibility that some proportion of elderly people genuinely want residential care. As has been stressed (Stevenson and Parsloe 1993, 15), there is a problem of treading the fine line between autonomy and protection: while all the emphasis in the official documents has been on autonomy, risk makes protection equally important.

The White Paper's second objective – to prioritize support for those

Helping to care (Nursing Standard).

caring for dependants – represented at least partial acknowledgement of the strong campaign mounted by carers' associations (especially by the National Council for Carers and the Association of Carers, which merged in 1988 to form the Carers' National Association), feminist researchers (Finch and Groves 1983; Ungerson 1987; Lewis and Meredith 1988) and the Equal Opportunities Commission, to put carers' needs, both for money and services, on the political agenda. Research showed clearly that the presence of an informal carer significantly lessened the chance of someone receiving statutory personal social services (Evandrou et al. 1986).

The third objective, to make services needs-led, was of central importance in promoting a radical change in the way SSDs work. It has been a common criticism of social services departments that they have been pre-occupied with delivering a limited range of services, rather than respond-ing to what clients in fact need (e.g. Smith 1980, Webb & Wistow 1987). Nevertheless, it was surprising to find the concept of need so centrally placed in the new approach to community care. "Need" has always been subject to criticism from a variety of points of view. Economists have tended to see it as impossible to measure and have put their faith in "wants" which can be met through the market (Nevitt 1977). New-right theorists (e.g. Barry 1990) have tended to dismiss the idea of "need" as being inherently paternalistic. Certainly, it is a "contested" concept (Fraser 1989) and inevitably so, given scarce resources. In the context of community care, the needs of users and carers may be pitted against one another, as well as being contested by the authorities. The White Paper made assessment of need and care management – the process by which the user would be shepherded through the personal social services system – the "cornerstone" of the needs-led service. Certainly, assessment was one of the few specific duties laid on local authorities by the 1990 NHS and Community Care Act (Part III, 47 (i)).

Assessment was also promoted in the official guidance following the Act, as a means of advancing user choice (DH 1990a, para. 3.18). But the Act specified that it is the local authority that will decide whether, and how, to meet need. The process of assessing need thus encapsulates the tension between choice and rationing. In particular, despite the priority given to the needs of carers, resource constraints mean that services must be targeted to those in greatest need, who hitherto have been defined as those *without* carers. The 1990 guidance advised: "local authorities also have a responsibility to meet needs within the resources available and this will sometimes involve difficult decisions where it will be necessary to strike a balance between meeting the needs identified within available resources and meeting the care preferences of the individual" (DH 1990a, para. 3.25). The government's guidance made it clear that the way to ensure that the user's need will be represented fairly lies in the other main strategy contained in the new approach: that is, the separation of purchasing and providing, such that the local authority becomes an ena-bling authority. The 1991 summary guidance on assessment and care management advised that the separation of the process of assessing need from service provision "does not solve the conflicts between needs and resources, but it does ensure that the respective interests of user and pro-vider are separately represented' (DH, SSI & SOSWSG 1991a, 15.30).

The separation between assessing need and purchasing or commissioning services on the one hand, and providing services on the other, is thus conceptualized as an internal split made by SSDs. It is also linked, however, to the White Paper's fourth objective, the stimulation of independent provision. Making SSDs into "enablers" who purchase more than they provide, and so promoting a mixed economy of care, was seen as being central to the creation of user choice, and services that are both high in quality and cost effective (DH & SSI 1991a, para. 1.8–9).

The evidence regarding whether contracting out services cuts costs, is equivocal (Walsh 1989, 42–3), and quality will depend in large part on the effectiveness of regulation and inspection. With regard to the promotion of choice, the House of Commons Social Services Committee (Social Services Committee 444, paras. 21–2), drawing on evidence presented to it, observed that it was not the user who would do the choosing, since it was going to be the local authority that would decide whether and how to meet need. It also pointed out that an increase in the number of people providing care did not necessarily mean an increase in the different types of care available. A report prepared for the Joseph Rowntree Foundation in 1992 wryly pointed to "cognitive dissonance" around the issue of choice: "true choice depends . . . on whether the care that is preferred will be paid for" (Schorr 1992, 22). However, as the guidance made clear, it was intended that choice should consist in increasing the range of providers and in the menu of services the social services staff (not the user) can choose from (DH 1990a, para. 4.22). The idea of making services needs-led is not the same, therefore, as making them user-led.

What has happened in the field of the personal social services, as in housing, education and health since 1988, is the introduction of what academic research has labelled a "quasi-market". Quasi-markets are different from markets on both the supply and demand sides. The supplier is not necessarily out to maximize profits, nor is the ownership structure necessarily clear. On the demand side, consumer purchasing power is not expressed in cash (purchasing is not financed by the consumer, but by taxes), nor is it the consumer who exercises the choice in purchasing (Hoyes and Le Grand 1991; Hoyes et al. 1992; Le Grand 1993).

Le Grand (1991, 1963) has described the introduction of quasi-markets in social services as a response to critics on both the political right and the political left. Critics on the right had charged that welfare bureaucracies were wasting resources on excessive administration and protecting their own interests at the expense of those of users, and that they offered the client little choice in services and hence were not meeting needs. Critics on the left were concerned with equity as well as efficiency, and maintained that the welfare system was particularly unresponsive to the needs and wants of the very people it was set up primarily to help – the poor and disadvantaged.

The academic research on the phenomenon of quasi-markets is important for understanding the dimensions of choice that are, and are not, offered. If it was intended, as the government guidance insisted, that enabling will provide the user with greater choice or, further still, as the guidance on assessment and care management suggested, will *empower* users and carers (DH, SSI & SOSWSG, 1991a, 9.6), it is important to be clear what the user can, in fact, do. He or she cannot be sure that preferences will be met. It will not usually be possible for the user to "exit" from the system and take his or her custom elsewhere, as would be the case in a market. What the reforms give the user, as opposed to the care manager or other social services officials, is a limited amount of "voice" via the assessment and care planning process, and the complaints procedure, which it is obligatory for SSDs to provide.

The fifth objective of the White Paper was to clarify responsibilities between the authorities involved in the provision of community care. This recognized the historical difficulties in securing joint planning and joint working between health and local authorities; for community care to become needs-led, it has also to become a "seamless service" (DH 1990a, para. 1.8–9). Consensus has perhaps been strongest in criticism of the joint planning efforts of the 1970s and 1980s, which resulted in objectives expressed in terms of levels of service production derived from professional judgement, rather than from assessment of user need (Webb & Wistow 1987; Wistow 1990). Both the White Paper and subsequent guidance articulated the government's intention to move away from the idea of joint planning as it had emerged in the 1970s, and to build instead on the new enabling framework: "The Government proposes to base future national policy on planning agreements rather than joint plans" (Cm 849, para. 6.10).

The other main duty laid on local authorities in the Act (in addition to assessment) was to consult other authorities (DHAs, Family Health Services Authorities (FHSAs) and housing authorities), voluntary organizations, users, and carers, in the production of community care plans. The draft guidance on planning indicated that the emphasis must be on partnership and on the production of planning agreements between authorities that were grounded in their purchasing functions (DH 1990b, 12). In other words, there had to be agreement on who should do what for whom, when, at what cost, and who should pay. Given the breaking of the link between planning and finance, the House of Commons Social Services Committee expressed doubts: "We remain to be convinced that without greater incentives to work together the risks associated with the introduction of competition in community care will outweigh the benefits claimed for it by Government" (Social Services Committee 580-I 1990, para. 93). The Committee felt that the boundary between health and social care would continue to be a vexed issue and that there would remain incentives for health and local authorities to "cost shunt" across their borders, rather than to co-operate.

The new funding structure referred to in the White Paper's final objective came into being on 1 April 1993, together with the duty imposed on local authorities to assess. The social security monies that would have been spent on new residents in nursing and residential homes, together with a sum in respect of additional costs, were transferred to local authorities in the form of a special transitional grant. Half of these transferred monies were allocated according to the current residential/nursing home care spend from income support in the independent sector, and half according to the standard spending assessment formula. Thus those local authorities with the fewest residential and nursing home beds found themselves worst off.

Implementing the changes in community care

The official guidance accompanying and following the 1990 Act has been copious. Social services departments have faced, and continue to face, huge changes. In 1992, the Audit Commission acknowledged the complexity of the agenda they faced and their "right to feel intimidated. It is difficult to know where to start" (Audit Commission, 1992a, 39). In order to illustrate some of these difficulties of implementation, this chapter will now draw on two research projects designed to monitor the changes in community care. The research from these projects has been used in the following ways: first, to identify the issues that are treated; and secondly, to provide specific illustrative examples. Eventually the research will provide a systematic analysis of the process of implementation, set against the policy guidance. Given the stage of the research and uncertainties of the implementation process, what follows should be taken as being tentative and indicative.

The first study, a pilot project, began in 1990 and traced the experience of four voluntary organizations belonging to the same national organization, in dealing with their local authorities as the latter moved to contracting for services. The second project began late in 1992 and consists of a two-year project monitoring all aspects of the changes in five local authorities, one shire county, one inner London borough, and three outer London boroughs. Both projects used the methodology established by Glennerster et al. (1983) and called by them "administrative anthropology". It consists of intensive observation of meetings in the authorities and records of informal contact, as well as formal interviewing.

The process of implementation

The government's policy guidance set out the process of implementing the 1990 Act as a series of rational steps. The logic dictates that a local authority will assess need, both at the level of the individual client and for its population, decide what services should be provided, separate its provider and purchaser functions, and then set about securing the best services for clients in terms of both commissioning services and preparing individual care plans. In fact, social services departments are being asked to think about an enormous range of issues at the same time: assessment, care management, purchaser/provider splits, contracting for services, construction of community care plans, quality assurance, complaints procedures and inspection, and new forms of joint planning. It was not easy to decide where to start, and in fact local authorities started in very different places at very different times. The shire county and one of the outer London boroughs (both Conservative controlled) went for a model of total reorganization and began by restructuring their departments into purchaser and provider streams. The remaining three London boroughs decided to implement the changes more gradually, focusing initially on assessment and care management.

Department of Health circulars in 1992 (widely known as the Foster/Laming letters) laid out eight key tasks for local authorities to accomplish before April 1993. These highlighted the need for local authorities to make sure that the following were in place: assessment systems for individuals; agreements with health authorities regarding new arrangements for hospital discharge and for clients in residential and nursing homes; purchasing arrangements for nursing and residential home beds; and information for the public about the arrangements for assessment and care provision in the form of the community care plan (Community Care Support Force 1992). The fact that progress on these was monitored by the Social Services Inspectorate and the Regional Health Authorities made them centre-stage activities from the middle of 1992. But, depending on what the SSDs had already decided to do, and depending on existing priorities and work cultures, the process of implementation looked very different. This was acknowledged in the 1992 Audit Commission Report, which talked about the difficulties of managing the *"cascade of change"*: "the process of implementation inevitably generates new difficulties and requires other adjustments which in turn trigger further requirements in an ever increasing cascade of change" (Audit Commission 1992a, 19).

Social services departments set up pilot projects – mainly on assessment and care management – but found it difficult to generalize from what were usually well-resourced and certainly small-scale endeavours, to services as a whole. Departments faced a problem of timing, in that they had to begin implementing a system before the results of the pilots were fully known. If departments had had time for another phase of pilot projects, they might have been able to build better models. They also found that the guidance, while copious, was not prescriptive. There were some 12 models of care management to choose from, for instance, and details were given of six levels of assessment. Four of the SSDs involved in the research underwent restructuring in face of the changes (and another one is about to do so), although none so completely as the shire county.

In some cases restructuring was intended also to cut the total number of posts, because implementation of the changes was going on at a time of severe budgetary restraint. In any case, it has been observed that in none of the local authorities is there any management "fat". While all created a division whose functions could broadly be described as strategy/quality assurance, the number of people available to think through the changes required has been very limited. The Audit Commission reported that 44 per cent of the local authorities they surveyed had no one spending even as much as 50 per cent of their time managing the implementation of community care (Audit Commission 1992b, 22). In the research authorities, the people required to think through the changes are often swamped with operational issues and there have also been problems of communication between "thinkers" and "doers". Perhaps as a result, there has been a tendency on the part of some authorities *first* to create the system required – for example, care management – and *then* to think about what it means. Thus authorities who appear advanced on paper may in the end be no better off than others who appear to be laggards (this may also be true for other pragmatic reasons: for example, software for information systems, on which so much depends, is bound to improve, and late starters will benefit from this). Thus, there was a logic in the guidance offered for the process of implementation; but in practice it has proved far less straightforward.

Assessment and care management have been lumped together in the guidance, which may account for the considerable confusion surrounding the two issues, especially care management. The summary guidance defined care management as a *process* consisting of seven elements, which *includes* assessment. The elements were listed as: the publishing of information (in the community care plan); determining the level of assessment; assessing need; determining the care plan for the user; implementing the care plan; monitoring; and review (DH, SSI & SOSWSG, 1991a, 9.7). However, it is questionable whether it is feasible for the care manager to undertake all aspects of the care management process and, in addition, to act as a purchaser of service, as was intended in the newly devolved purchasing arrangements (see below).

The White Paper and the guidance made it clear that the government wanted assessment kept simple: "The Government does not wish to see an elaborate and bureaucratic pattern of costly and time-consuming case conferences established, nor does it want to see a duplication of effort" (Cm 849, para. 3.2.11; see also DH 1990a, para. 3.35). The guidance also specified that the process of assessment had to be needs-led and therefore separated from the provision of service. In a review of the assessment systems of four local authorities published in 1991, the Department of Health (DH) and Social Services Inspectorate (SSI) made the usual comment that, in the past, assessment had been service-led, adding that it had been "undertaken by a person with a *vested interest* in supplying that service" (DH & SSI 1991b, 17 [emphasis added]). The intimation was that the service provider has a self-interest in giving the user access to his or her service. However, in the shire county there is some indication, in the case of home care, that where assessment has passed to a care manager/purchaser to carry out, s/he is less willing to restrict or ration care than were the service providers. All but one (an outer London borough) of the research authorities have separated the work of assessment from providing. In that outer London borough, no firm decision has been reached regarding whether care managers are purchasers or providers, and assessments can still be carried out by providers. Such a mixed system allows a flexible approach, based on proximity to the user, and may also prevent duplication and/or overload on any one group of workers.

From the SSDs' point of view, the issues around assessment are: what it consists of in terms of levels, the criteria and content of each level of assessment, and who does it. It should be pointed out in passing that the issues from the users' point of view are rather different. First, it may seem that the duty to assess those appearing to be in need constitutes an entitlement to service, which may in turn result in conflict, given resource constraints (Utting 1993). Secondly, there is no statutory right to appeal against assessment: the only recourse is through the department's complaints procedures. Thirdly, while users and carers are required to be involved in the assessment process, the motive seems to reach beyond the idea of empowerment emphasized by the guidance on assessment and care management. In the same 1991 DH/SSI review of assessment systems in four LAs, social services staff were encouraged to trust the user's perception of his or her need. The review argued that the historical tendency of social workers to look for underlying needs could no longer be justified in the context of both user empowerment and budgetary restraint (DH & SSI 1991b, 45).

The levels of assessment have proved hard to establish. Service-led assessments often operated according to informal rules; needs-led assessments, however, must be formalized and their accompanying criteria published. While the guidance referred to six possible levels, the four London authorities participating in the research seem to be settling for two. The shire county has as yet no explicit formalized levels of assessment. Given the duty to assess where there appears to be need, SSDs face the difficulty of determining whether the client is eligible for assessment. The answer seems to lie in screening, which the 1990 guidance said might be included as part of the assessment process (DH 1990a, para. 3.20). But in its model for purchasing care for elderly people, the Department of Health emphasized the importance of screening as a means of avoiding unnecessary expensive assessments (DH, SSI, NHSME & PW 1992, vol. I, 9). All the authorities involved in the research are using clerical staff for screening.

Beyond screening lie varieties of limited, specialist and comprehensive assessment, which seem to be defined chiefly in terms of whether the input of more than one professional is required, and whether the clients' level of dependency is such that there is a question about their ability to continue living in the community. It has also been difficult for authorities to decide on a common assessment form to be used by different professionals and agencies. Misapprehensions and confusions regarding the purpose of such a form and difficulties in integrating it into existing practices led to the creation of an impossibly complex form in the shire county. In one of the outer London boroughs, a simulation exercise on limited and comprehensive assessment showed that similar results were produced from both forms of assessment. In another outer London borough, early commitment to multidisciplinary working for the purposes of assessment resulted in objections from some of the agencies that it was time-consuming and costly when the system was generalized borough-wide. In all the authorities except one outer London borough, some or all of the decisions reached by assessors are being vetted by a panel. The function of these is hard to generalize and they may well prove to be a transitional form, but in two of the authorities their rôle includes keeping the authority within budget and checking that the process of assessment is needs-led. Panels existed in the past to determine entry to local authority residential care. They are not discussed by the guidance, but it seems that they have found a rôle within the new system.

The requirement to separate the process of assessment from provision has also raised numerous issues about the nature of assessment and its relationship to social work. Broadly, it is accepted that care managers will do assessments. But the guidance on their rôle has been exceptionally vague. The inner London borough decided that care managers primarily require social work skills; while the shire county has appointed social workers and occupational therapists to the posts. One of the outer London boroughs had been considering the concept of a care co-ordinator rôle before the changes were introduced. It has persisted in the use of this term to describe a function which can be taken on by a range of agencies and staff (and even the user/carer him/herself), according to the user's circumstances. In another outer borough, the appointment of care managers was preceded by a reduction in the total number of social workers. Those social workers who were unsuccessful when re-applying for their old jobs were invited to become care managers, rôles thus seen from the start as being inferior to those of social workers. The struggle over the relationship between the tasks of care manager and social worker has crystallized into a battle over titles: whether to opt for social worker (care management) or care manager (social work).

But more than professional status is at stake. Attention has been drawn (Stevenson & Parsloe 1993, Smale et al. 1993) to the danger that assessment could become mechanical. Similar concerns have prevented the shire county from formalizing levels of assessment. An example has been given (Stevenson and Parslow 1993) of an assessment for a young physically and mentally disabled person about to leave school, which amounts to drawing up a life plan and may take some 60 hours to complete (it should also be noted that assessments for people with learning difficulties are likely to be very different exercises from those for elderly people, but the guidance did not distinguish between client groups). It has been argued (Stevenson and Parsloe 1993, 33) that "assessment is not just an orderly cerebral process, it is conducted within the context of a relationship". A similar argument has been made (Smale et al. 1993) that a "procedural model" for assessment, which gathers information to see if the client fits certain criteria that make them eligible for "x" or "y", will not empower clients. At a training day held in an outer London borough, staff protested that it was not possible to move from the assessment to drawing up the care plan, "without a period of social work". By this they meant that the forming of a relationship between user and staff member was crucial to working out how to meet need.

This set of issues also enters review, which is the final stage of care management as a process. In the past, reviews (when they took place at all) were performed informally by service providers, who usually decided whether the client required more of a particular service. Pushing the idea of needs-led assessments into the reviewing process, the importance of which was emphasized by the guidance (DH 1990a, para. 3.51), requires considerable change. Again, a non-provider should carry out the review. But in the county, some providers have observed that they are closer to the user and this can create tension when someone has to come in "from the outside" to carry out reviews. In addition, the process of formal review is new and therefore expensive; no authority has decided whether it can afford to have all reviews performed by care managers. But if the idea of review by a named worker gets lost, so does one of the most important aspects of the care management process.

Finally, given the inherent tension between needs and resources, it is not surprising that unmet need became a major issue during 1992. If services are to become responsive to need, logic dictates that unmet need should be recorded. The summary guidance on assessment and care management spoke of the importance of identifying the disparity between assessed need and availability of service (DH & SSI 1991a, 9.5). However, a letter on assessment from Herbert Laming, Chief Inspector in the SSI, to local authorities (SSI & DH 1992), cast doubt on whether unmet need should be recorded: "Practitioners will, therefore, have to be sensitive to the need not to raise unrealistic expectations on the part of users and carers." LAs have reacted variously: the inner London borough split its assessment form so that the assessment was recorded on one side and the service decision on the other; one outer borough decided to record service deficit (but not service unavailability) but not to reveal this to clients; and another outer borough will record unmet need on an individual basis, shared with the client, as well as on an aggregate basis, the point being to identify the problem, not the service response. The service response will be recorded when: (i) the customer wants a service but it falls outside the eligibility criteria; (ii) there is a dispute about the quantity of service provided; (iii) the assessor agrees that the service provided is not ideal; or (iv) all agree on the service but there is a waiting list. The remaining outer borough has yet to make a decision, while the county has decided to record service deficit, broken down into budget insufficiency, and/or market failure (i.e. no service available), and/or non-priority on a separate form. It is therefore far from clear to what extent unmet need will inform the future development of services.

Local authorities have been forced to seek tools that will help them to reconcile the tension between needs and resources. The Audit Commission's 1992 report on managing the changes located resource implications in the middle of its "cascade of change", but it would be more realistic to put these firmly at the top. The question of how assessment and service criteria interlock with budgets is of crucial importance. As the Audit Commission put it in its report on the "community revolution": "Priorities and targets between and within user groups must be set together with eligibility criteria for the receipt of care. Budgets must then be allocated which attempt to square the circle between needs, targets and resources" (Audit Commission 1992b, 2). As the report went on to acknowledge, lack of financial and management information could be the rock on which the new community care system founders.

The inner London borough has made an effort to follow the District Audit's 1992 advice on needs-led budgeting in respect of its special transitional grant. This method requires SSDs to define levels of need as low, medium and high; to estimate the numbers of users at each level; to define the care components for each level of need; and to agree and to cost standard service levels. For most authorities, such a method is too sophisticated for both the existing information technology and the degree of organizational change that has taken place. However, the method does highlight the importance of pitching the eligibility criteria for service at the correct level: for if a user is deemed to be eligible, the authority must supply service. If an authority finds itself running out of money for a particular service, therefore, it is possible that eligibility criteria will have to be revised. There is also the political problem that the money available may stretch further for one client group than for another. In the inner borough, the eligibility criteria for care management have been pitched so that the service goes only to those with high levels of need.

The shire county has rejected explicitly the idea of an indicative level of expenditure related to a particular level of need, on the grounds that this introduces unwelcome rigidity in prescribing the level of expenditure for a client. Two users with similar needs may be very differently placed with regard to carers and informal support systems, for example, which may be relevant to pricing the services they require. The county has concentrated on addressing the issue of eligibility for service by developing what it has called a "risk/needs matrix". The vertical axis records the area of primary need, physical taking priority over social, and the horizontal axis records the risk run by the client within the area of his or her primary need. This, as with the greater part of the changes, seems to be easier to apply to some client groups (the elderly and those with physical disabilities) than others (children and those with learning difficulties).

It appears that the process of developing the various stages of care management is serving to *redefine need*. The guidance defined "need" variously as "the requirement of individuals to enable them to achieve, maintain or restore an acceptable level of social independence or quality of life, as defined by the particular care agency or authority" (DH & SSI 1991a, 12.11) and as "the ability of an individual or collection of individuals to benefit from care" (DH & PW 1993, 6). While these are rather different, they are centred on the needs of the individual. However, after the definition of priorities and application of eligibility criteria, need gets redefined as a high level of dependency.

Enabling

The White Paper set out various ways in which SSDs could promote the mixed economy of care: by determining clear specifications for service, stimulating the independent sector, and floating off self-managing units (Cm 849, para. 3.4.6). A report on a survey of the meaning of enabling in 24 local authorities and SSDs (Wistow et al. 1992) found only three "enthusiasts" for the policy. Similarly, four of the five research SSDs showed little enthusiasm for enabling in 1992. However, attitudes seem to have changed considerably during 1993, with all departments developing policies on commissioning, chiefly as a result of central government's decision that 85 per cent of the social security element of the special transitional grant should be spent in the independent sector.

Guidance on the purchase of service advised that relationships between purchasers and providers were best conceived of as "being a contract culture involving close on-going relationships with providers rather than being based upon anonymized short term price competition" (DH & PW 1991, 11). The creation of a market solely in terms of price, and a firm division between purchaser and provider, were not intended. However, SSDs still had to separate their purchaser and provider functions and to work out how to become "enablers". The guidance provided three possible models for achieving the former (DH & PW 1991; DH & PW 1992). The shire county adopted a "high and firm" purchaser/provider split (operating from the second management tier right down through the department) in 1991 in a reorganization that involved 1,200 people changing job descriptions. One outer London borough also adopted this model early in 1992, but by regrouping divisions, and the inner borough has been moving towards it in an incremental fashion, again since 1991. Another outer borough adopted a different model, separating purchasing from providing only within the community care division. This followed from the fact that the SSD reorganized in 1992 to reflect the Children Act and Community Care Act, creating two main client group divisions: Children and Families, and Community Care. However, this authority is now also moving towards creating a "high and firm" split. The remaining outer borough commissioned a consultants' report on reorganization in 1993, which recommended a "high and firm" split, but the prospect of achieving it in one step, as the shire county did in 1991, has proved somewhat daunting.

Such reorganizations have not been easy to accomplish, especially since SSDs were juggling so many other changes. In the county, the SSD also localized its services at the time of the reorganization, which may have resulted in some blurring between geographical and purchaser/provider lines of accountability that have yet to be made clear. Reorganization in this local authority and elsewhere was accompanied by cuts in middle and senior management, and the flattened hierarchies that resulted might not always have been best at coping with the implementation of the changes. In addition, departments went through a phase of firm purchaser/provider separation, during which communication between the two "sides" tended to be limited. The two early starters have now (mid-1993) come through this and have seen the value of purchaser/provider alliances, but the inner borough, pursuing its more incremental pattern of change, seems to be just entering such a phase. SSDs have historically been dominated by provider cultures, but in the new order power has shifted to purchasers, leaving some providers within departments anxious and uncertain.

The pressure to adopt a "high and firm" purchaser/provider split has come in large part from the injunction to SSDs to become enablers. Community care has always been a mixed economy, in that the voluntary and private sectors have played an important part in provision. But the guidance set out major changes in how SSDs would undertake their new commissioning rôle. Purchasing is envisaged at both the macro and micro levels. In other words, the SSD can develop a central purchasing function but is also encouraged to devolve budgets down to care manager level (DH & SSI 1991b, 15. 31–33), something Le Grand (1993) has identified as being crucial to the success of a quasi-market in community care.

While the guidance assumed that budgets will in the first instance be transferred to purchasers, there has been virtually no advice given to SSDs on how to accomplish this. The managers' guidance on assessment and care management merely states that the transition must be managed "to minimize the underutilization of in-house services while expanding the choices available to users" (DH & SSI 1991b, para. 1.17). Given that so great a proportion of the budget is tied up in existing in-house provision, SSDs have found it difficult to move the money across. Forms of "shadow trading" are being developed, whereby expenditure is tracked and purchases are invoiced without budgets being transferred. But it has proved easier to develop internal trading for new services, such as those for HIV/AIDS, than for long-standing services. By developing internal

169

service level agreements, purchasers of HIV/AIDS services in the inner borough have been able to buy on the basis of hours rather than posts, which has caused considerable rethinking on the part of providers.

The issue of how far to devolve budgets and of what balance to strike between macro and micro purchasing (at central department level and at the level of the individual care manager), is pressing and difficult. The five research authorities vary in the extent to which they have mapped the market, by visiting independent providers and collecting information on the types of provision and prices. Authorities need a purchasing strategy, in which mapping the market is a necessary first step. Yet the authority that has gone furthest in contracting-out services, largely as a result of member commitment to such a policy, has done so without performing such a mapping exercise and without considering the balance between macro and micro purchasing.

Commentators are agreed that micro purchasing by care managers is likely to offer more choice to users than centrally negotiated block contracts (Knapp & Wistow 1992). The Department of Health's circular of December 1992, giving the direction to social services that clients have the right to choose where they go for residential care (DH 1992), added to the pressure towards spot-contracting. On the other hand, there are equally strong pressures pushing purchasing decisions towards the centre: the macro pattern of health authority purchasing; the reluctance of local authority finance departments to permit radical devolution; the concern of senior managers within the SSD to retain budgetary control; the belief that centrally placed negotiators may get a better price; and the practical problem of deciding how to divide the budget between a large number of care managers. Some of the London boroughs are considering proposals to devolve budgets as far as senior service managers, joint commissioning groups, or local team managers, who will provide care managers with a menu of services. Given the lack of adequate information and financial systems, however, the timescale for achieving this is uncertain. The shire county is committed to devolving budgets to its 16 local offices.

SSDs have already had to reach purchasing decisions on residential and nursing home beds, often in the absence of adequate information. It is likely that those who can maintain maximum flexibility in what is an uncertain period of transition, will do best. Thus those who are saddled with large block contracts, or who have little by way of in-house residential care left, could face problems. Again, laggards may in the end derive benefits from their delay.

The movement to service level agreements or contracts, both internally and with independent providers, may be conceptualized as a process of formalization, just as the process of assessment makes criteria explicit for the first time. Such a process has consequences for independent providers as well as for the SSD. In particular, voluntary organizations are concerned that it may be harder to get financial support from local authorities for campaigning, advocacy, advice and core administration – in other words, anything that is not service provision, despite the protection assured to these activities in the guidance (Cm 849, para. 3.4.14 and DH 1990a, para. 4.4). They are also concerned that service-level agreements will impose more "professional" standards on volunteers and require new administrative and management skills (Lewis 1993). In the case of a voluntary organization in one of the outer London boroughs, which signed a three-year contract to provide day care in 1990, the management of the contract was greatly affected by the "cascade of change" experienced in the SSD. The organization began by continuing the regular contact with an SSD social worker that had been maintained when the service was provided under grant; once the SSD introduced a firm purchaser/provider split and appointed a contracts manager, however, the relationship became much more formal. The organization also lost its volunteer day care centre managers, who did not like having to complete the new quarterly returns and other more "managerial" aspects of their jobs under contract.

As SSDs develop the mixed economy of care, it is possible that local authority provision will become residual and the independent sector will provide the bulk of social care. It is likely therefore that voluntary organizations, which are highly dependent on local government funding, face a major shift in their rôle from complementary and/or supplementary, to alternative providers. And, given that residual providers have in the past been the innovators, this rôle may pass from the voluntary to the statutory sector in the future.

Joint planning/working/commissioning

The origins of the joint planning of the 1970s and 1980s were to be found as much in the search for rational comprehensive planning as in the pursuit of collaboration (Webb & Wistow 1986, 56). Moreover, the process was more about the allocation of joint finance at the margins, which by the 1980s was favouring NHS over local authority services, than planning (Audit Commission 1986, para. 68; Wistow et al. 1990). There have been impediments to joint planning at the level of mechanisms: the incompatibility of local authority and health authority information systems, planning and budget cycles, and geographical areas, are most commonly cited (one of the two research authorities that have moved to joint commissioning happens to have coterminous LA and Health Authority (HA) boundaries). But both academics (Webb & Wistow 1986, 158) and the Audit Commission (1986, paras 117–30) have agreed that the most important impediment to collaboration in the form of joint planning has been the powerful urge to protect organizational interests, philosophies and priorities. Different cultures, styles and patterns of accountability between LAs and HAs have made the always expensive and usually cumbersome joint planning machinery a kind of adversarial talking shop.

Joint collaboration in the production of a community care plan was set out as the first step in the process of implementing the community care changes. The government guidance denied any possible tension between promoting a mixed economy of care and quasi-market principles on the one hand, and a "planned economy" on the other (DH & SSI 1991a, para. 2.1.12). However, doubts have been raised about whether non-statutory provision *can* be incorporated into a national planning framework (Wistow & Henwood 1990). The guidance eschewed prescription on how to plan, saying that this should depend on the local situation and local needs (DH 1990a, para. 2.6). However, the implementation document on planning showed that the priority was to reach agreement on who was to provide what, because planning was intimately linked to the creation of enabling authorities (DH 1990b). Authorities remained free to decide whether to produce joint or separate plans, with the proviso that they agree principles and a framework for financing and provision. A review of 25 local authorities carried out for the SSI found that half of the second round of community care plans were "jointly owned" (Wistow et al. 1993). Most authorities revamped their joint planning machinery to give greater place to the FHSA, voluntary sector, users and carers (and more recently in response to a Department of Health circular (DH 1993), the private sector), although whether as equal partners or on a consultative basis, has been a point of contention. But the logic of the process of implementation demanded a course of action so far adopted by very few authorities: the establishment of mechanisms to ensure both joint planning and joint commissioning.

Yet the problem of insular cultures remains, and is particularly strong at senior management level; joint working at the level of service delivery, it has been observed, was always more successful than joint planning (Hunter et al. 1988). One of the outer London boroughs had conspicuous success in joint working around assessment, although it has proved to be time-consuming and costly. The boundaries between health and social care remain remarkably difficult to define; an attempt to do so by the West Midlands Regional Community Care Steering Group in 1990 allocated a large number of tasks to both authorities. It is especially difficult to establish clear lines of accountability for services during a period of budgetary cutbacks, when it is uncertain as to what extent continuing care will be purchased by health authorities (Henwood 1992b) or community nursing by General Practitioner (GP) fundholders.

The movement to "joint commissioning" in such a climate is made more difficult, given the different purchasing structures of HAs and LAs. The outer London borough with coterminous boundaries agreed to set up joint commissioning teams as early as 1991, but the meaning of the term was ill-defined, with the result that the degree to which the teams commission and/or plan is far from clear. It has been suggested (Knapp & Wistow 1992) that, at a minimum, joint commissioning should mean compatibility of specifications, compatible assessments of population needs and mappings of available provision, and common values. However, the other outer borough with a joint commissioning structure is aiming to achieve joint agreement on priorities and hence on how each agency spends its budget, which may be as significant an achievement as joint specifications. A move towards the pooling of money and the joint buying of services, which participants tend to assume is the chief goal, will require a quite different order of effort.

Conclusion

The government's legislation on community care requires local authorities to assess individual need and to consult with other authorities in order to identify need at the community level. Other aspects of government community care policy have been promoted not only by the publication of guidance, but also by specific directives, perhaps the most significant being the requirement that LAs spend 85 per cent of the social security element of the special transitional grant in the independent sector. LAs are being forced to change the way they deliver community care, although the pace at which they do so varies considerably. Furthermore, the process of achieving change is far from uniform, depending on local circumstances such as member and officer commitment, work cultures and existing organization, and relationships with health authorities, as well as specific decisions about how to approach implementation and the subsequent problems of managing the "cascade of change". While authorities have appointed care managers and have for the most part separated purchasing from providing, care management and purchasing mean different things in different places. Perhaps most significantly, the central meaning of a needs-led service is being redefined in a context of severe resource constraint. The government's decision to retain control over resource allocation at the centre while giving LAs the responsibility for planning services has resulted in a fundamental tension between needs and resources, which LAs are struggling to resolve. To this extent, the community care policy is being shaped from the bottom up.

At the time of writing this chapter – mid-1993 – the outcomes of the changes, which are incomplete, are necessarily uncertain. From the clients' point of view, it may be that fewer people eventually receive a service, but the service will be better. As early as 1990, SSDs participating in the King's Fund mutual aid implementation network felt that "more precise targeting of services is almost certain to mean that some people receive fewer services – or nothing at all – at the same time as others receive help more precisely geared to their requirements" (Beardshaw 1991, 7). It seems inevitable that only need that is defined as high dependency will receive service. This must raise questions about the treasured, albeit notoriously hard to define and measure, "concept of prevention". As one home care organizer put it: "if you don't do the preventive work, the person becomes a crisis" (Meredith 1993, 61).

However, research has shown (Davies et al. 1990) that more social services in and of themselves have little effect without the application of a thorough system of care management, which local authorities are finding expensive to implement for all stages of the care management process. We thus return to Titmuss's observation of over 30 years ago, that good community care does not come cheap. If the government's aim was cost containment, it is doubtful that the community care changes were the way to achieve it. Keeping costs under control within the new community care system must mean delivering care (although possibly of a higher quality) to fewer people.

Social services departments have been, and are, working under enormous pressure. The injunction to change their rôle from that of provider to enabler has involved considerable reorganization and uncertainty, and the formalization and change in meaning of processes such as assessment have caused professional confusion. In many respects the community care reforms showed an admirable determination to get away from the traditional postwar British practice of changing the structure in the hope of producing the desired change. LAs were asked to focus on the user and the promotion of need and choice. However, the fact that the separation of purchasing and provision was seen as a necessary prerequisite for achieving a needs-led service and greater choice, meant that in practice, SSDs underwent substantial reorganization. In addition, the process of making procedures explicit and formal has threatened to make certain forms of professional practice, especially in the social work field, merely routine procedures.

The summary guidance on assessment and care management stressed the importance of managers and practitioners not feeling "deskilled or daunted by the scale of pace of change" (DH & SSI 1991a, 27.105). However, it is clear that care management has threatened social workers' sense of professional identity in some departments. Frontline workers have been observed to be suffering isolation and difficulties, and there is a danger of squeezing out professional discretion (Schorr 1992, 52); research has also shown (Wilson 1993) that social workers are dissatisfied with the co-ordination work necessary for good care management and wish to remain in close contact with clients. In addition, providers are feeling uncertain about their futures. This is in line with the more general observation by academics that the new public management appeals to the dedication of staff, while tending to undermine the structures that promote that dedication (Pollitt 1990, 113; Hood 1991, 16). The unhappiness of staff may well have an impact on the quality of service.

Social services departments have historically been "doers". The shift to enabling and purchasing is therefore a major change. As purchasers, SSDs are also in the shadow of the health authorities. In 1986 the Audit Commission recommended a single health and local authority budget for elderly people. This advice was ignored, but the extent to which there will be convergence between health and social services as the latter chiefly become purchasers, must be on the agenda.

Social services departments are being asked to perform a tricky balancing act. During 1993–4, the DH expects them to continue to develop assessment and care management systems, increase the involvement of users and carers, begin to shift the balance of resources towards non-residential care, further develop joint planning and commissioning (to include GP fundholders), develop a positive relationship between purchasers and providers, and improve collaboration with housing authorities (DH 1993). On the other hand, the DH also wants a degree of steady state. In particular, it is anxious to avoid market failure on the part of private residential home providers and "bed-blocking" in the NHS. It was, after all, the failure of arrangements for hospital discharge that caused the NHS contracting simulation exercise (the "Rubber Windmill") to fail in 1990 (Audit Commission 1992b, 57). To achieve change is a major challenge, but to achieve change without noise may be impossible.

Notes

1. This chapter draws on two research projects funded by the ESRC and gratefully acknowledges the work of the research officers on one of the projects: Penny Bernstock and Virginia Bovell.
2. The term "case management", imported from the USA, was changed to "care management" in the policy guidance.

References

Allen, I., D. Hogg, S. Peace 1992. *Elderly people: choice, participation and satisfaction*. London: London Policy Studies Institute.

Audit Commission 1986. *Making a reality of community care*. London: HMSO.

Audit Commission 1992a. *Community care. Managing the cascade of change*. London: HMSO.

Audit Commission 1992b. *The community revolution: the personal social services and community care*. London: HMSO.

Baldcock, J. and A. Evers 1991. Citizenship and frail old people: changing patterns of provision in Europe. In *Social Policy Review*, N. Manning (ed.), 1990–1, 101–127. Harlow: Longman.

Barry, N. 1990. *Welfare*. Milton Keynes: Open University Press.

Beardshaw, V. 1991. *Implementing assessment and care management: learning from local experience 1990–1991*. London: King's Fund College Papers 3.

Cm. 849 1989. *Caring for people. Community care in the next decade and beyond*. London: HMSO.

Cmnd. 1604 1962. *Hospital plan for England and Wales*. London: HMSO.

Cmnd 1973 1963. *Health and welfare: the development of community care.* London: HMSO.

Cmnd 8173 1981. *Growing older.* London: HMSO.

Committee of Public Accounts 1988. *Twenty-sixth report.* London: HMSO.

Community Care Support Force 1992. *Implementing community care: delivering the key tasks.* London: Price Waterhouse.

Davies, B., A. Bebbington, H. Charnley and colleagues 1990. *Resources, needs and outcomes in community based care.* Aldershot: Gower.

DH (Department of Health) 1990a. *Community care in the next decade and beyond. Policy guidance.* London: HMSO.

DH (Department of Health) 1990b. *Community care implementation documents. Planning.* London: Dept of Health CCI 6.

DH (Department of Health) 1992. *National Assistance Act 1948 (choice of accommodation) directions.* Circular, LA (92) 27, 23 December.

DH (Department of Health) 1993a. *Community care plans (consultation) directions.* Circular, LAC (93) 4, 25 January.

DH (Department of Health) 1993b. Implementing caring for people. Letter, El (93) 18/C1 (93) 12, 15 March.

DH & PW (Department of Health & Price Waterhouse) 1991. *Implementing community care. Purchaser, commissioner and provider roles.* London: HMSO.

DH & PW (Department of Health & Price Waterhouse) 1992. *Feedback on the purchase of service and purchaser/provider workshops.* London: Dept of Health.

DH & PW (Department of Health & Price Waterhouse) 1993. *Population needs assessment good practice guidance.* London: Dept of Health.

DHSS (Department of Health and Social Security) 1988. *Community care: an agenda for action.* London: HMSO.

DH & SSI (Department of Health & Social Services Inspectorate) 1991a. *Purchase of service guidance.* London: HMSO.

DH & SSI (Department of Health and Social Services Inspectorate) 1991b. *Assessment systems and community care.* London: HMSO.

DH, SSI & SOSWSG (Department of Health, Social Services Inspectorate & Scottish Office Social Work Services Group) 1991a. *Care management and assessment. Practitioners' guide.* London: HMSO.

DH, SSI & SOSWSG (Department of Health, Social Services Inspectorate & Scottish Office Social Work Services Group) 1991b. *Care management and assessment. Managers' guide.* London: HMSO.

DH, SSI, NHSME & PW (Department of Health, Social Services Inspectorate, National Health Service Management Executive & Price Waterhouse) 1992. *Implementing community care: model for purchasing care for elderly people.* London: Department of Health.

DH, SSI & SOSWSG & PW (Department of Health, Social Services Inspectorate, National Health Service Management Executive & Price Waterhouse) 1992.

Implementing community care: Model for purchasing. London: Department of Health.

District Audit Service 1992. *Constructing budgets for purchasing community care.* London: Audit Commission.

Ermisch, J. 1983. *The political economy of demographic change.* London: Heinemann.

Evandrou, M., S. Arber, A. Dale, N. Gilbert 1986. Who cares for the elderly? Family care provision and receipt of statutory services. In *Dependency and interdependency in old age: theoretical perspectives and policy alternatives*, C. Phillipson, M. Bernard, P. Strang (eds). London: Croom Helm.

Finch, J. & D. Groves (eds) 1983. *A labour of love.* London: Routledge.

Fraser, N. 1989. Women, welfare and politics of need interpretation. In *Politics and social theory*, P. Lassman (ed.), 104–22. London: Routledge.

Glennerster, H., with N. Korman & F. Marsden-Wilson 1983. *Planning for priority groups.* Oxford: Martin Robertson.

Gray, A. & B. Jenkins 1993. Markets, managers and the public service. The changing of a culture. In *Markets and managers*, P. Taylor Gooby & R. Lawson (eds), 9–23. Buckingham: Open University Press.

Griffiths, Sir Roy 1992. With the past behind us. *Community care.* (16 January), 18–21.

Henwood, M. 1992a. *Through a glass darkly. Community care and elderly people.* London: King's Fund Institute Research Report no. 14.

Henwood, M. 1992b. Twilight zone. *Health Services Journal*, 5 November, 28–30.

HMSO 1990. *National Health Service and Community Care Act 1990.* London: HMSO.

Hoggett, P. 1990. *Modernisation, political strategies and the welfare state. An organisational perspective.* Bristol: School for Advanced Urban Studies.

Hood, C. 1991. A public management for all seasons? *Public Administration* **69**, 3–19.

Hoyes, L. & J. Le Grand 1991. *Markets in social care services.* Bristol: School for Advanced Urban Studies.

Hoyes, L., R. Means, J. Le Grand 1992. *Made to measure? Performance measurement and community care.* Bristol: School for Advanced Urban Studies Occasional Paper 39.

Humble S. & A. Walker 1990. Constructing a new welfare mix in the United Kingdom: the role of the voluntary sector. In *Shifts in the welfare mix: their impact on work, social services and welfare policies*, A. Evers & H. Wintersberger (eds), 237–71. Frankfurt: Campus Verlag.

Hunter, D. J., N. P. McKeganey, I. Allen 1988. *Care of the elderly: policy and practice.* Aberdeen: Aberdeen University Press.

Knapp, M. & G. Wistow 1992. Joint commissioning for community care. Paper presented at Commissioning for Community Care Conference, 10 July.

Le Grand, J. 1991. Quasi-markets and social policy. *The Economic Journal* **101**, 1256–67.

Le Grand, J. 1993. *Quasi-markets and community care.* Bristol: School for Advanced Urban Studies.

Lewis, J. 1989. "It all really starts in the family . . .". Community care in the 1980s. *Journal of Law and Society* **16**, 83–96.

Lewis, J. 1993. Developing the mixed economy of care: emerging issues for voluntary organisations. *Journal of Social Policy* **22**, 173–92.

Lewis, J. and B. Meredith 1988. *Daughters who care*. London: Routledge.

Lipsky, M. 1980. *Street level bureaucracy*. New York: Russell Sage Foundation.

Means, R. & R. Smith 1985. *The development of welfare services for elderly people*. London: Croom Helm.

Meredith, B. 1993. *The community care handbook. The new system explained*. London: Age Concern England Books.

Nevitt, D. 1977. Demand and need. In *Foundations of social administration*, H. Heisler (ed.). London: Macmillan.

Parker, R. 1990. Elderly people and community care: the policy background. In *The kaleidoscope of care. A review of research on welfare provision for elderly people*, Ian Sinclair et al. (eds), 5–22. London: HMSO.

Pollitt, C. 1990. *Managerialism and the public services*. Oxford: Basil Blackwell.

Schorr, A. A. 1992. *The personal social services: an outside view*. York: Joseph Rowntree Foundation.

Smale, G. & F. Tuson and colleagues 1993. *Empowerment, assessment, care management and the skilled worker*. London: National Institute of Social Work.

Smith, G. 1980. *Social need, policy, practice and research*. London: Routledge & Kegan Paul.

Stevenson, O. & P. Parsloe 1993. *Community care and empowerment*. York: Joseph Rowntree Foundation and Community Care.

Social Services Committee 1990. *Sixth report of the Social Services Committee. Community care choice for service users*. HC 444. London: HMSO.

Social Services Committee 1990. *Eighth report of the Social Services Committee. Community care planning and cooperation*. HC 580–I. London: HMSO.

SSI & DH (Social Services Inspectorate and Department of Health). Letter, CI (92) 34 (14 December).

Titmuss, R. M. 1968. Community care: fact or fiction? Lecture delivered in 1961. In *Commitment to welfare*. London: Allen & Unwin.

Townsend, P. 1962. *The last refuge*. London: Routledge.

Ungerson, C. 1987. *Policy is personal. Sex, gender and informal care*. London: Tavistock.

Utting, Sir William 1993. Foreword. In *Squaring the circle. User and carer participation in needs assessment*. York: Joseph Rowntree. Foundation.

Walker, A. 1982. The meaning and social division of community care. In *Community care: the family the state and social policy*, A. Walker (ed.), 13–39. Oxford: Blackwell and Martin Robertson.

Walker, A. 1989. Community care. In *The new politics of welfare*, M. McCarthy (ed.), 203–24. London: Macmillan.

Walsh, K. 1989. Competition and service in local government. In *The future of local government*, J. Stewart and G. Stoker (eds), 30–54. London: Macmillan.

Webb, A. & G. Wistow 1986. *Planning, need and scarcity. Essays on the personal social services*. London: Allen & Unwin.

Webb, A. & G. Wistow 1987. *Social work, social care and social planning: the personal social services since Seebohm*. London: Longman.

Wicks, M. 1985. Enter right: the family patrol group. *New Society* (24 February).

Wilson, G. 1993. Conflicts in case management: the use of staff time in community care. *Social Policy and Administration* **27**, 109–23.

Wistow, G. 1990. *Community care implementation documents. Community care planning: a review of past experiences and future imperatives.* CCI 3. London: Department of Health.

Wistow, G. & M. Henwood 1990. Planning in a mixed economy: life after Griffiths. In *Privatisation*, R. Parry (ed.), 32–44. London: Jessica Kingsley.

Wistow, G. & M. Henwood 1991. Caring for People: elegant model or flawed design? In *Social Policy Review 1990–1*, N. Manning (ed.), 79–100. Harlow: Longman.

Wistow, G., B. Hardy, A. Turrell 1990. *Collaboration under financial constraint. Health authorities spending of joint finance.* Aldershot: Avebury and Centre for Research in Social Policy.

Wistow, G., M. Knapp, B. Hardy, C. Allen 1992. From providing to enabling: local authorities and the mixed economy of social care. *Public Administration* **70**, 25–45.

Wistow, G, I. Leedham, B. Hardy 1993. *Community care plans: a preliminary analysis of English community care plans*. London: Social Services Inspectorate.

8

Making sense of the new
politics of education[1]

Geoff Whitty, Sharon Gewirtz and Tony Edwards

In 1986, the British government announced a new education initiative which involved establishing a pilot network of up to 20 City Technology Colleges (CTCs) (DES 1986). CTCs were intended to be self-governing secondary schools for 11–18 year olds with a curriculum emphasis on science and technology, high levels of information technology and a licence to innovate in curriculum, pedagogy and school management. So far, 15 CTCs have been established. Most of them operate with an extended school day and a longer-than-average school year. They are funded directly by central government, with the assistance of business sponsorship, and represent a new "state independent" sector of schooling. The development of these particular schools represents a new direction for the English education service, but it also points to a number of significant changes in education policy as a whole – changes which are similar to those in other areas of state activity, particularly the housing, welfare and health services.

Jenny Ozga (1990) has argued that, while studies of individual policies can provide rich descriptive data, they can also obscure the "bigger picture" when trying to make sense of contemporary education policy as a whole. This chapter is based on data collected in a research project funded by the Economic and Social Research Council studying the government's CTC initiative (Whitty et al. 1993). It aims to provide an interpretation of the CTC initiative within the context of the overall development of government policy. It argues that CTCs need to be seen as part of a broader project on the part of the Conservative government in Britain in the 1980s and 1990s. In particular, they need to be seen alongside the 1988 Education Reform Act (Whitty 1989). This required local education authorities (LEAs) to introduce a policy of open enrolment to their schools and system of local management of schools (LMS), which has led to most schools operating with devolved budgets based largely upon the numbers of pupils they can enrol. The Act has also given some schools the opportunity to opt out of their local education authorities as self-governing grant-maintained (GM) schools. It is clear that the 15 prototype CTCs now need to be understood more generally in the context of a changing approach to the governance of schools. Indeed, as a result of the 1993 Education Act, many of their features are to be spread more widely – if also more thinly – throughout the education service.

Marketizing welfare?

Even if, in the past, education policy sometimes seemed to enjoy a degree of autonomy from other areas of policy-making, a strong commitment on the part of the Thatcher government to common policies – particularly those designed to enhance consumer choice – has also produced a closer articulation between education and other fields of policy. There are obvious parallels between recent developments in education and other market-oriented reforms. The announcement of the CTC initiative in October 1986 coincided with the inauguration of a more radical move towards a market-oriented welfare system than had been evident during the first two periods of Margaret Thatcher's administration. Some of the ideas informing CTCs, which became more clearly evident in the 1988 Education Reform Act (ERA), foreshadowed a more general thrust during Thatcher's third term of office towards the creation of what Le Grand (1991) has termed "quasi markets" in key areas of social welfare.

In the initial publicity accompanying the announcement of the CTC initiative, CTCs were presented as being a new choice of school for parents in the inner cities whose children were supposed to have suffered most from the consequences of monopoly LEA provision. These links with the rhetoric of "consumer choice" suggest that CTCs and subsequent education policies are part of a wider attempt to marketize welfare provision. The same principles underlie the "quasi-market" reforms that have been instituted in health and "community care", in the social services and in the housing sector. To take housing as an example, throughout the 1980s and into the 1990s, the council housing sector was being consistently eroded through the "right to buy" and "alternative land-lord" schemes, and the abolition of local authority subsidies for council rents. According to Le Grand (1992, 6), especially significant in this move to "quasi-markets" was "the gradual but accelerating phenomenon of the expansion of the housing association movement to supplant local authorities as the main new providers of social housing". A critical land-mark was the 1988 Housing Act, which allowed for the transfer of coun-cil housing to private landlords, housing associations or tenants' co-operatives. Housing associations can therefore be seen as the housing equivalent of CTCs or grant-maintained schools (even if such schools do not currently charge their clients the equivalent of rent). The 1988 Hous-ing Act also introduced Housing Action Trusts to take over run-down estates from local authorities, a housing version of the Education Asso-ciations which the 1992 White Paper envisages "rescuing" failing schools (DFE 1992). The effect of the new housing policies has undoubtedly been to create choice for some tenants, but it has equally clearly been to curtail choice for others. Ray Forrest and Alan Murie, writing in 1988, pre-dicted that "the public housing sector is well on the way to becoming an unambiguously residual, second-class form of housing provision, serving the poorest sections of the population" (Forrest & Murie 1988, 83); there are direct parallels with fears expressed by critics of the CTC policy and the Education Reform Act.

Depoliticizing education?

At one level this marketization and residualization of state welfare can be seen as part of a retrenchment in public expenditure. However, what has in fact changed has been the *pattern* rather than the *level* of public expenditure. This has particular relevance in the case of education, where privatization, in the strictly economic sense of the term, has been of lim-ited significance. What has been more in evidence has been a shift in the ways in which state-funded education has been provided and consumed. But equally significant has been the shift in the way education is *adminis-tered*. Alongside, and potentially in place of, collective provision by elected bodies with a responsibility to cater for the needs of the population, there are increasing numbers of quasi-autonomous institutions with devolved budgets competing for clients in the marketplace – CTCs, grant main-tained schools and LEA schools operating under open enrolment and LMS.

Along with changes in the way the state regulates other areas of social activity, such as housing and health, these administrative arrangements for managing education can be seen as new ways of resolving the problems of accumulation and legitimation facing the state in a situation where the traditional "welfare state" is no longer able to function effectively (Dale 1989). With the removal of tiers of government between the central state and individual institutions, conventional political and bureaucratic control by elected bodies is replaced by market accountability assisted by a series of directly appointed agencies, trusts and regulators. Such developments are a move in the direction of a market-based pluralism. The Americans, John Chubb and Terry Moe (1990, 1992), are among a growing number of commentators who argue that the combination of democratic control by elected bodies and the powerful bureaucracies they generate is a major cause of the poor performance of modern mass education systems. Under the new arrangements, education is given the appearance of having been removed from the political arena. Quasi-autonomous institutions, state-funded but with considerable private and voluntary involvement in their operation, blur the boundary between the state and civil society. Part of the reason for the intense opposition to these policies by those who currently run the education service, the so-called "liberal educational establishment", may be precisely *because* they constitute an attempt to reposition education in relation to the state and civil society; such policies are also an attempt to deny education's traditional claim that it is in some way a special case requiring a different form of administration from other services.

The political rhetoric accompanying the educational reforms certainly seeks to suggest that education has been taken out of politics as they are normally understood. This was made explicit by the Education Minister, John Patten, when he launched the 1992 White Paper (DFE 1992), and argued that one of its aims was to "depoliticize" education by removing it from the local political arena and giving power to parents and school governors. The special status of education was also to be reduced by the removal of the statutory requirement on local councils to administer education through a dedicated education committee. The changes brought about by the 1986 and 1988 Acts had already destroyed the quasi-corporatist approach to educational policy-making that had emerged in the postwar period. Teachers – one of central government's traditional partners in education policy-making – had been displaced from their role as partners in the initiation of educational policy, and

LEAs had been consigned to a distinctly subordinate rôle in its implementation. Charles Raab (1990) has observed that the new arrangements, in which policy is made by individuals making choices in a market, may constitute a form of dispersed pluralism.

In practice, recent education reforms are as much to do with transferring power from the local state to the central state as with giving autonomy to the schools. Indeed, Peter Riddell (1992) has suggested that the likely outcome is that criticism of education that has hitherto been directed conveniently at LEAs will now fall squarely on central government. Yet it is just as likely to fall on individual schools and their managers. In effect, it is a means of diverting attention/blame away from the state and towards individuals: central government can make cuts in education expenditure and blame the consequences on poor school management practices.

Another interpretation of current trends in education policy is that the government is pursuing the tradition of engaging in special interest group politics; new partners in the educational enterprise are being identified in the form of parents and industry (Raab 1990). These groups are more inchoate and hence more open to manipulation by central government than are the government's traditional partners in education policy-making – the LEAs and teacher trade unions. On the other hand, the reforms have also produced an increase in the number of potentially significant arenas for educational politics in its widest sense. Some of these may be highly susceptible to the influence of other vested interests – including, ironically, the liberal educational establishment. Indeed, some research has indicated that professionals and parents tend to act together on the newly powerful governing bodies of schools (Golby & Brigley 1989).

Nevertheless, at the level of policy formation and initiation in education, the rôle of central government has clearly been strengthened by recent legislation. To this extent, the new arrangements can be seen in terms of a reworking of the "dual polity" approach to contemporary politics (Saunders 1987), rather than as a straightforward abandonment of corporatist planning in favour of market forces. But this does not detract from the fact that, at least in terms of the rhetoric, the developments of which CTCs and grant-maintained schools are a part, are highly consistent with new ways of understanding and organizing public institutions that are fast becoming an orthodoxy in many parts of the world (Dale 1992; Rhodes 1991).

It can, then, be argued that CTCs and related reforms are part of a movement that is much broader and much deeper than the particular set of policies that have come to be termed "Thatcherism". In the rest of this chapter, we shall consider how far it is useful to draw upon contemporary social, economic and political theory to make sense of these reforms as part of Ozga's "bigger picture". We will look first at how far CTCs and related reforms can usefully be seen as paralleling similar changes taking place elsewhere in the world; secondly, at the extent to which they can be seen as a response to deeper shifts in patterns of production and consumption; and, thirdly, at the ways in which they may be an expression of that rather ill-defined constellation of changes that is sometimes taken to signal the existence of a "postmodern" age. While accepting that such concepts can provide some useful insights into the broader significance of the CTC policy, we shall conclude that it is important to recognize strong continuities between current policies and traditional patterns of educational inequality in Britain.

A global movement?

CTCs have a significance far beyond their numerical strength because of their similarities to reforms which have recently taken place elsewhere in the world. Not only is the rhetoric of the British government's "five great themes" – quality, diversity, parental choice, school autonomy, and accountability (DFE 1992) – echoed in other countries (Whitty & Edwards 1992); there are also specific policies with similarities to CTCs.

A symbolic link was forged between education policy in Britain and the USA with Kenneth Baker's much-publicized visit in 1987 as Secretary of State for Education and Science to a succession of "magnet" and other specialist schools in the USA (Cooper 1987). These schools had some similarities to CTCs but many of them were more selective; they offered a variety of curriculum specializations, rather than being limited to technology, and their main purpose was to make inner city schools more attractive to white parents. Then, in 1991, George Bush launched the New American Schools' Initiative, which seemed closer to the British CTC model. Five hundred and thirty-five New American Schools, one in each congressional district, were to be established by September 1996 through a unique collaboration between "communities, inventors, educators and entrepreneurs . . . a new partnership between the private sector and government". These schools would help "break the mould" of American education by challenging "assumptions commonly held about schooling" (New American Schools Development Corporation 1991). Such assumptions included the prevailing adherence to blackboards and chalk; a curriculum organized into subjects and class periods, the six-hour school day and the 180-day school year; technology located only in the computer lab and the principal's office; and policies that discouraged risk-taking and offered few rewards for improved learning. Breaking the school district monopoly in the provision of state education was also to be a key feature of the policy.

Despite these similarities, a White House official interviewed by the present authors during the Bush era denied any specific relationship between CTCs and the New American Schools Initiative, and judged CTCs to have been at most a very minor influence. Their relevance was recognized but, rather like magnet schools in relation to CTCs, as a source of confirmation rather than as a direct model. We concluded that policy-makers in both countries were working within similar frames of reference and producing parallel policy initiatives, rather than "borrow-ing" policies directly from each other. This process was no doubt facili-tated by the existence of a common policy community with a shared political philosophy (Whitty & Edwards 1992).

However, this network factor is less convincing as an explanation of developments in countries other than the USA. Support is being given to the diversification and specialization of educational provision and to site-based control of schools from a variety of political perspectives, as well as in countries with different political regimes. Indeed, although school choice policies in the USA received particular encouragement from Republican presidents Ronald Reagan and George Bush, the growth in site-based management policies, magnet schools, and other schools of choice, has been broadly supported by all political parties in the USA. Similar policies have been pursued by Labour as well as Liberal and National party governments in Australia. In New Zealand, where advo-cates of community empowerment united with exponents of consumer choice against the old bureaucratic order, the market-oriented policies now being pursued by a right-wing government are based on a Labour government's earlier moves in the direction of devolution and school autonomy (Gordon 1992; Grace 1991). In parts of Eastern Europe, the centrally planned education systems of Communist regimes are also being replaced by experiments in educational markets. International organizations are now encouraging the introduction of similar policies into some of the less developed countries.

Even though these directions in education policy have not penetrated all countries, and they have been mediated differently by the traditions of different nation states and different political parties, the similarity between British policies and those being introduced elsewhere suggests another reason why they may be more significant than they at first appear. Such policies may reflect deeper changes emerging within the world economy.

A facet of post-Fordism?

Some observers suggest that we are witnessing the transportation of changing modes of regulation from the sphere of production into other arenas, such as schooling and welfare services. They have pointed to a correspondence between the establishment of markets in welfare and a shift in the economy away from Fordism towards a post-Fordist mode of accumulation which "places a lower value on mass individual and collective consumption and creates pressures for a more differentiated production and distribution of health, education, transport and housing" (Jessop et al. 1987, 112).

Various observers have claimed to see in CTCs and other recent education policies a shift from the "Fordist" school of the era of mass production to what Stephen Ball has termed the "post-Fordist school" (Ball 1990). The emergence of new sorts of school may be the educational equivalent of the rise of flexible specialization driven by the imperatives of differentiated consumption, and taking the place of the old assembly-line world of mass production. According to Jane Kenway, "post-Fordist schools" are designed "not only to produce the post-Fordist, multi-skilled, innovative worker but to behave in post-Fordist ways themselves; moving away from mass production and mass markets to niche markets and 'flexible specialization' . . . a post-Fordist mind-set is currently having implications in schools for management styles, curriculum, pedagogy and assessment" (Kenway 1992, 14).

CTCs would appear to be in the vanguard of such a shift, with their shopping mall or business park architecture, their "flat" management structures and their emphasis on "niche marketing". Such features apparently offer support for an updated version of Samuel Bowles' and

Herb Gintis's "correspondence thesis" (Bowles & Gintis 1976), which pointed to parallels between the organization of the workplace and the organization of the school at the time of the development of mass schooling. There are now similar parallels to be drawn between the management strategies of post-Fordist industries and those of CTCs. So-called post-Fordist business entrepreneurs typically achieve maximum flexibility by abandoning the old industrial sites in favour of green-field locations, with planning deregulation and non-union labour. In a similar way, the CTC initiative, at least as initially conceived, facilitated flexibility for educational entrepreneurs. By virtue of direct state funding and green-field locations beyond the control of local authorities, CTC project directors and principals could avoid the "restrictive practices" of the teachers' unions and the LEAs. The early interest of CTCs in deregulated Urban Development Corporation sites is particularly significant here.

However, there are problems with the notion of post-Fordism as an entirely new regime of accumulation and there are similar problems with the argument as applied to education. We need to be cautious in concluding from any parallels that may exist between economic and social modes of organization that we are experiencing a wholesale move away from a mass-produced welfare system towards a flexible, individualized

Students at Harris CTC, South London (courtesy of City Technology Colleges Trust).

and customized post-Fordist one. In the field of education, it is difficult to establish a sharp distinction between mass and market systems. The so-called "comprehensive system" was never as homogeneous as the concept of mass-produced welfare suggests. Indeed, it was always a system differentiated by class and ability. We may, however, be witnessing an intensification of these differences and a celebration of them in a new rhetoric of legitimation. In this rhetoric, choice, specialization and diversity replace the previous language of common and comprehensive schooling.

A postmodern phenomenon?

Jane Kenway (1992) has brought together a number of theories underlying the idea of "new times" to argue that, in education as elsewhere, modern societies are now entering a qualitatively new era. She suggests that accounts which concentrate solely on institutional changes pay insufficient attention to other cultural shifts helping to explain why the notion of markets in education has found such a receptive audience. For Kenway, "the rapid rise of the market form in education is best understood as a postmodern phenomenon" (Kenway 1992, 12). In postmodernity, the significant nexus lies between the global and the local; the scope of the national state is thereby limited. Kenway sees the new technology as a key element in the development of new and commodified cultural forms. What she calls the "markets/education/technology triad" is a crucial feature of postmodernity, and it is a triad in which CTCs can clearly be located. Kenway's account of postmodernity is, as she readily admits, a pessimistic one in which "transnational corporations and their myriad subsidiaries . . . shape and reshape our individual and collective identities as we plug in . . . to their cultural and economic communications networks" (Kenway 1992, 19). The picture is one in which notions of "difference", far from being eradicated by the "globalization of culture", are assembled, displayed, celebrated, commodified and exploited (Robins 1991).

There are other accounts of postmodernity where the rhetoric of "new times" offers positive images of choice and diversity. In this context, CTCs and other current developments might be regarded as being part of a wider retreat from modern, bureaucratized state education systems (Chubb & Moe 1990; Glenn 1988). Such systems are perceived as having failed to fulfil their promise, and now seem inappropriate to the hetero-geneous societies of the late twentieth century. Thus, part of the appeal of current education policies lies in the claim that different types of school will be responsive to the needs of particular communities and interest groups brought into existence as a result of complex contemporary pat-terns of political, economic and cultural differentiation. These new pat-terns intersect the traditional class divisions upon which comprehensive education was predicated.

While the process of differentiation is partly about creating new mar-kets for new products, the multiplicity of lines of social fissure that are emerging may be associated with deeper changes in modes of social soli-darity. In so far as these divisions and associated identities are experi-enced as real, they are likely to generate aspirations that will differ from traditional ones. This has given rise to more optimistic readings of postmodernity than the one to which Kenway subscribes. Compared with the oppressive uniformity of much modernist thinking, it is possible to regard postmodernism as "a form of liberation, in which the fragmen-tation and plurality of cultures and social groups allow a hundred flowers to bloom" (Thompson 1992, 225–6). Many feminists, for example, have seen attractions in the shift towards the pluralist models of society and culture associated with postmodernism and postmodernity (Flax 1987). The real possibilities for community-based welfare, rather than bureau-cratically controlled welfare, are also viewed positively by some minority ethnic groups. In the USA, the recent reforms of the school system in Chi-cago were enacted as a result of an alliance between new right advocates of school choice, and black groups seeking to establish community con-trol of their local schools, together with disillusioned white liberals and some former student radicals of the 1960s (Hess 1990). In Britain, the Labour Party's traditional social democratic policies have been perceived as being unduly bureaucratic and alienating by many black parents, who (it is sometimes claimed) welcome the new opportunities offered by the Reform Act to be more involved with their children's schools (Phillips 1988). Some aspects of the Thatcherite dream seem to connect to the aspirations of groups who found little to identify with in the "grand mas-ter" narratives associated with class-based politics. Policies which seem to emphasize heterogeneity, fragmentation and difference may represent more than a passing fashion among neo-liberal politicians, as they resonate with changing notions of an open, democratic society as well as with a market ideology. Put in those terms, it is easy to understand why current policies have a potential appeal far beyond the coteries of the new right. Indeed, even in the Labour Party, there has been some support for more specialized and diverse forms of secondary schooling. While the idea of magnet schools has failed to gain backing from the Labour front bench, a commitment to cultural diversity within the comprehensive principle has gained official acceptance through support for the development of Muslim voluntary-aided schools.

Support for schools run on a variety of principles might, then, be seen as recognizing a widespread collapse of a commitment to modernity. Put another way, the reforms might be viewed as a rejection of totalizing narratives and their replacement by "a set of cultural projects united [only] by a self-proclaimed commitment to heterogeneity, fragmentation and difference". In this vision, social development is no longer "the fulfilment of some grand historical narrative", but "a pragmatic matter of inventing new rules whose validity will reside in their effectivity rather than in their compatibility with some legitimating discourse" (Boyne & Rattansi 1990). The notion of "unprincipled alliances", which at one time might have prevented such a political configuration as emerged in Chicago, is less appropriate in a context of postmodernity. A more appropriate way to see postmodernity may be as a pluralist, pragmatic and "restless" set of partially differentiated social orders (Lyotard 1986). One implication of this is that, if large-scale attempts at social engineering have been perceived as failing, less ambitious aspirations may now be in order.

Reworking old themes?

CTCs and policies associated with them may, then, seem to be part of a new politics of education. If we equate curriculum specialization with niche marketing, CTCs appear to display some of the characteristics of post-Fordism, while their relationship to government is more generally consistent with new forms of public administration. But there is another side to it. Notwithstanding conscious attempts to make CTCs look more like business organizations than schools (BBC Radio 4, 6 June 1989), they are still readily identifiable as secondary schools; there are more similarities than differences between CTCs and local comprehensive schools. These similarities do not suggest a radical break with the concerns of modernity. Rather, new institutional forms such as CTCs may merely be a different way of managing the modernist project. There are also serious problems in trying to see the sort of diversity sponsored by CTCs and other recent reforms as a postmodern phenomenon – as a sign of deep-seated changes in the nature of society.

Some aspects of CTCs are the very epitome of the modernist project. This was apparent in the way their "high tech" image was invoked in the early publicity. At least as much as comprehensive schools, CTCs appeared to express an underlying faith in technical rationality as the basis for solving social, economic and educational problems. Even in the White Paper devoted to "choice and diversity", this modernist project predominates: "specialization" rather than "diversity" is given prominence. And, although the subsequent legislation has been "drawn widely enough to encourage more schools to specialize in other fields too", the emphasis throughout has been on technology, which will help "to break down the divide between academic and vocational studies" and "equip young people with the technological skills essential to a successful economy" (DFE 1992, 45). Indeed, the justification for specialization is that "other leading industrialized nations combine the attainment of high standards with a degree of specialization" (DFE 1992, 43).

Although CTCs may have particular attractions for some members of the minority ethnic population, their ethos is often assimilationist, rather than actively fostering cultural pluralism. For example, some black pupils criticized Harris CTC in South London for "leaving out the black people – in Sylvan [the LEA school on which Harris was based] they taught us about Rastas, black history and culture" (*Daily Telegraph*, 4 July 1991). Despite the fact that Muslim leaders have interpreted clauses of the 1992 White Paper as heralding state-funded Islamic schools through the "opting in" of existing private schools (*Observer*, 2 August 1992), the message about this possibility in the White Paper is highly tentative and offers little real scope for significant state funding of minority schools.

The rhetoric of specialization and diversity in which CTCs and other educational reforms are embedded is given an added appeal by the suggestion that neither will entail selection and hierarchy. In the 1992 White Paper, the government stresses that it "wants to ensure that there are no tiers of schools within the maintained system [*sic*] but rather parity of esteem between different schools, in order to offer parents a wealth of choice" (DFE 1992, 10). There is no apparent commitment to parity of esteem between the public and private sectors. The emphasis is on encouraging parental choice rather than selection, but none of the government's rhetoric recognizes the reality of what happens, either overtly or covertly, when schools are massively over-subscribed. The impression is also given that each school is to be judged on its specific character and its merits, rather than as embodying the characteristics of a hierarchically arranged series of "types". However, our research found that parents choosing CTCs were more concerned with the extent to which this "new choice of school" was similar to independent and grammar schools and different from mainstream comprehensive schools, than with specialized excellence in technology.

Geoffrey Walford and Henry Miller claim that, while comprehensive schools attempted to overcome the historic links between diversity of provision and inequalities of class and gender, CTCs "have played a major part in re-legitimizing inequality of provision for different pupils". They argue that the "inevitable result" of the concept of CTCs, especially when coupled with grant-maintained schools and local management of LEA schools, is "a hierarchy of schools with the private sector at the head, the CTCs and grant maintained schools next, and the various locally managed LEA schools following" (Walford & Miller 1991, 165). While there are a few doubts about where exactly CTCs will eventually settle in this hierarchy, the idea that there will be *no* hierarchy of school types at all is difficult to sustain in the light of past experience. Grant-maintained schools have already sought to imply that they constitute a superior type of school by pointing out that, in the first tables of examination results published by the government, "60% of grant-maintained schools achieved above the national average scores for 5 GCSE A–C grades" (Grant-Maintained Schools Centre Press Release, 27 November 1992).

Even so, the White Paper rejects any idea that a new hierarchy of types of school will develop. It dismisses the relevance of the experience of the tripartite system of the 1950s and 1960s by arguing that we now live in "a different educational world" with the National Curriculum ensuring equality of opportunity (DFE 1992, 10). Yet the particular form of National Curriculum introduced by the Thatcher government, and the arrangements for testing the outcomes, are likely to arrange schools and pupils in a hierarchy through the combined effects of LMS, competition among schools for pupils, and the publication of assessment scores. This will leave the most disadvantaged and demotivated pupils concentrated in schools with low aggregate test scores, declining resources and low teacher morale.

There is little evidence yet that, taken as a whole, the education reforms of which CTCs are a part are helping to provide a structure that will encompass diversity and ensure equality of opportunity for all pupils. Rather, there is evidence that the emphasis on parental choice will further disadvantage those unable to compete in the market, by increasing the differences between more popular and less popular schools. This could have disastrous consequences for some sections of the predominantly working-class and black populations living in the inner cities. These groups never gained an equitable share of educational resources under social-democratic policies, but the abandonment of planning in favour of a quasi-market seems unlikely to provide a fairer outcome.

Stephen Ball suggests that a third tier of "'sink schools' – those which are unpopular and undersubscribed" (Ball 1990, 91) – is developing below the various types of schools of choice fostered by current policies. One of the results of the "deregulation" of schooling is that the onus increasingly is on parents to make separate applications to each school. The CTC policy also introduced a new mode of selection for schools, based on the criteria of motivation, commitment and aptitude – an approach which is now likely to be extended. These new modes of application and selection privilege those with the system know-how, and the time and energy to make applications, and to mount a good case (Gewirtz et al. 1992). At the same time, they discriminate against those who have more immediately pressing concerns than being an education "consumer", and who are less likely to have the appropriate cultural resources to exercise choice, whether it be in education, in housing or in the area of health care.

The distinction between those who are privileged and those who are disadvantaged by the CTC policy and parallel "market" initiatives is not, however, a straightforward middle class/working class or white/black one. Most of the housing reforms were aimed particularly at council house tenants; and the CTCs were to be established in inner city areas. While being detrimental to large sections of the working class, the reforms are likely to benefit some working-class families as well as some lower-middle-class ones. Similarly, the findings of our research suggest the CTC policy may have attracted particular fractions of the minority ethnic population in south-east London. But, while the new policies may reflect changes in the nature of class reproduction, they do not significantly interrupt it. Indeed, in some respects, they intensify it.

Thus, whatever the intentions of their sponsors, present policies are as likely to increase structural inequalities as to challenge them, while at the same time fostering the belief that the championing of choice provides

genuinely equal opportunities for all those individuals who wish to benefit from them. For those members of disadvantaged groups who are not
sponsored out of schools at the bottom of the status hierarchy, either on
grounds of exceptional academic ability or, as in CTCs, by using alternative definitions of merit, the new arrangements may just be a more
sophisticated way of reproducing traditional distinctions between different types of school and between the people who attend them. They certainly seem more likely to produce greater differentiation between
schools on a linear scale of quality and esteem than to create the positive
diversity hoped for by some of their supporters. If so, the recent reforms
will represent a continuity with a long history of inequality in English
education (Banks 1955).

Continuity and change

CTCs themselves lie at a point of tension between competing conceptions
of contemporary social policy. They embody many of the contradictions
more generally observable in education policy. Neo-conservative and
neo-liberal policies vie with each other and with the residue of traditional
social-democratic approaches to educational reform. This is symbolized
in ongoing debates within the CTC movement about the desirability of
the National Curriculum and of socially engineered catchment areas in
the context of markets and parental choice. Stephen Ball suggests that
CTCs may in fact go some way towards resolving the tensions between
the cultural restorationists and those who argue that education should be
more closely geared to the needs of industry (Ball 1990, 129). It is also
possible to read a degree of coherence into the various policies, and to
see them all as addressing core problems facing the modern state. Roger
Dale (1990) has argued that a policy of "conservative modernization",
which entails "freeing individuals for economic purposes while controlling them for social purposes", was a key feature of the Thatcher government's education policy under Kenneth Baker, and that it is a particularly useful concept for making sense of CTCs.

We would certainly argue that it is more helpful to see CTCs in these
terms than as a straightforward expression of postmodernity. Although
current education policies may seem to be a response to changing economic, political and cultural priorities in modern societies, it would be
difficult to argue, at least in the case of Britain, that they should be read

as indicating that we have entered into a qualitatively new phase of social development. Despite new forms of accumulation, and changes in the state's mode of regulation, together with some limited changes in patterns of social and cultural differentiation, the continuities seem just as striking as the discontinuities.

Visions of a move towards a postmodern education system in a postmodern society may thus be premature. To regard the current espousal of heterogeneity, pluralism and local narratives as indicative of a new social order may be to mistake phenomenal forms for structural relations. Marxist critics of theories of postmodernism and post-modernity, such as Callinicos (1989), who reassert the primacy of the class struggle, certainly take this view. Postmodernist cultural forms and more flexible modes of capital accumulation may be shifts in surface appearance, rather than signs of the emergence of some entirely new postcapitalist or even postindustrial society (Harvey 1989). At the very most, the current reforms in education would seem to relate to a version of postmodernity that emphasizes "distinction" and "hierarchy" within a fragmented social order, rather than one that celebrates positively "difference" and "heterogeneity" (Lash 1990).

Nevertheless, for whatever reason, CTCs and other new types of school are developing a significant market appeal. While much of this can be explained in terms of their perceived position in a developing "pecking order" of schools, it would be unwise to interpret it all in this way. Despite the absence of a clear postmodern break within either schooling or society, the recent reforms may have been more responsive than their critics usually concede to those subtle, but none the less tangible, social and cultural shifts that have been taking place in modern societies.

A straightforward return to the old order of things would be neither feasible nor sensible. Social democratic approaches to education which continue to favour the idea of a common school are now faced with the need to respond to increasing specialization and social diversity. Current discussions on the left about citizenship are seeking ways of creating unity without denying specificity (Mouffe 1992) and a similar challenge faces future education policy. James Donald (1990) calls for approaches based on "participation and distributive justice rather than simple egalitarianism and on cultural heterogeneity rather than a shared humanity". Donald himself wonders whether this puts a question mark against the very idea of comprehensive education, though others argue for a redefinition of that concept. Those who oppose the Education Reform Act and the 1993 Education Act certainly need to articulate alternatives capable of challenging the government's stereotyped view that its opponents all favour a "uniformity in educational provision", on the grounds that "children are all basically the same and that local communities have essentially the same educational needs" (DFE 1992, 3).

Notes

1. This chapter arose out of work on an ESRC Project, *City Technology Colleges: a new choice of school?* (Project C00232462) and is based on Chapter 7 of Whitty et al. (1993).

References

Ball, S. 1990. *Politics and policy making: explorations in policy sociology.* London: Routledge.

Banks, O. 1955. *Parity and prestige in English secondary education.* London: Routledge.

Bowles, S. & H. Gintis 1976. *Schooling in capitalist America.* New York: Basic Books.

Boyne, R. & A. Rattansi (eds) 1990. *Postmodernism and society.* London: Macmillan.

Callinicos, A. 1989. *Against postmodernism: a Marxist critique.* Cambridge: Polity.

Chubb, J. & T. Moe 1990. *Politics, markets and America's schools.* Washington: Brookings Institution.

Chubb, J. & T. Moe 1992. Classroom revolution. *Sunday Times* (19 February), pp. 18–36.

Cooper, B. 1987. *Magnet schools.* Warlingham: IEA Education Unit.

Dale, R. 1989. *The state and education policy.* Milton Keynes: Open University Press.

Dale, R. 1990. The Thatcherite project in education: the case of the city technology colleges. *Critical Social Policy* **9**(3), 4–19.

Dale, R. 1992. National reform, economic crisis and "new right" theory: a New Zealand perspective. Paper presented at the American Educational Research Association annual meeting, San Francisco, 20–24 April.

DES (Department of Education and Science) 1986. *A new choice of school.* London: DES.

DFE (Department for Education) 1992. *Choice and diversity: a new framework for schools.* London: HMSO.

Donald, J. 1990. Interesting times. *Critical Social Policy* **9**(3), 39–55.

Edwards, T., S. Gewirtz & G. Whitty 1992. Whose choice of schools? In *Voicing concerns: sociological perspectives on contemporary educational reforms*, M. Arnot & L. Barton (eds). Wallingford: Triangle Books.

Flax, J. 1987. Postmodernism and gender relations in feminist theory. *Signs* **12**(4), 621–43.

Forrest, R. & A. Murie 1988. The social division of housing subsidies. *Critical Social Policy* **8**(2), 83–93.

Gewirtz, S., S. Ball & R. Bowe 1992. Parents, privilege and the educational marketplace. Paper presented at the British Educational Research Association annual conference, Stirling University, 31 August.

Glenn, C. 1988. *The myth of the common school.* Amherst: University of Massachusetts Press.

Golby, M. & S. Brigley 1989. *Parents as school governors.* Tiverton: Fair Way Publications.

Gordon, L. 1992. The New Zealand state and educational reforms: "competing" interests. Paper presented at the American Educational Research Association annual meeting, San Francisco, 20–24 April.

Grace, G. 1991. Welfare labourism versus the new right. *International Studies in the Sociology of Education* **1**(1), 37–48.

Harvey, D. 1989. *The condition of postmodernity: an enquiry into the origins of cultural change.* Oxford: Basil Blackwell.

Hess, A. 1990. *Chicago school reform: how it is and how it came to be.* Chicago: Panel on Public School Policy and Finance.

Jessop, B., K. Bonnett S. Bromley & T. Ling 1987. Popular capitalism, flexible accumulation and left strategy. *New Left Review* **165**, 104–23.

Kenway, J. 1992. Marketing education in the postmodern age. Paper presented at the American Educational Research Association annual meeting, San Francisco, 20–24 April.

Lash, S. 1991. *Sociology of postmodernism.* London: Routledge.

Le Grand, J. 1991. Quasi-markets and social policy. *Economic Journal* **101**, 1256–67.

Le Grand, J. 1992. Paying for or providing welfare? Paper presented at the Social Policy Association annual conference, Nottingham University, July.

Lyotard, J. F. 1986. *The postmodern condition.* Manchester: Manchester University Press.

Mouffe C. (ed.) 1992. *Dimensions of radical democracy: pluralism, citizenship, democracy.* London: Verso.

New American Schools Development Corporation 1991. Publicity brochure.

Ozga, J. 1990. Policy research and political theory. *Journal of Education Policy* **5** (4), 359–63.

Phillips, M. 1988. Why black people are backing Baker. *Guardian* (9 September).

Raab, C. 1990. British education policy and its legitimation. Paper presented at the International Sociological Association, XII World Congress of Sociology, Madrid, 9–13 July.

Rhodes, R. (ed.) 1991. The new public management. Special issue of *Public Administration* **69**.

Riddell, P. 1992. Is it the end of politics? *The Times* (3 August).

Robins, K. 1991. Tradition and translation: national culture in its global context. In *Enterprise and heritage: crosscurrents of national culture*, J. Corner & S. Harvey (eds). London: Routledge.

Saunders, D. 1987. *Social theory and the urban question*. London: Hutchinson.

Thompson, K. 1992. Social pluralism and postmodernity. In *Modernity and its futures*, S. Hall, D. Held, T. McGrew (eds). Cambridge: Polity Press.

Walford, G. & H. Miller 1991. *City Technology College*. Milton Keynes: Open University Press.

Whitty, G. 1989. The politics of the Education Reform Act. In *Developments in British Politics, 3*, P. Dunleavy, A. Gamble, G. Peel (eds). London: Macmillan.

Whitty, G. & T. Edwards 1992. School choice in Britain and the USA: its origins and significance. Paper presented at the American Educational Research Association annual meeting, San Francisco 20–24 April.

Whitty, G., T. Edwards & S. Gewirtz 1993. *Specialisation and choice in urban education: the City Technology College experiment*. London: Routledge.

9

The relationship between research and policy: the case of unemployment and health

Mel Bartley

This chapter is based on a study of the ways in which the research and policy debates concerning the health effects of unemployment in Britain were related to each other over the period 1979–87. Its concern is not with the substantive content of the debate, but rather with the light its story can throw on the important, but poorly understood, relationship between research and policy. The chapter will argue that the question, "Does research affect policy debate, and if so, how?", is not an appropriate one; the two processes are thoroughly entwined. What the unemployment and health debate demonstrates is that it is not the mere existence of research findings, or even the opinion of the academic community as to their quality, which ensures the entry of the results of scientific studies into the public sphere, and from there into policy formation. Instead, the critical factors lie in the complex entrepreneurial process whereby certain research findings are first promoted as knowledge claims (Knorr-Cetina 1981), and then attract the assent of groups and of networks, which pick up and pass on the claim to a wider audience. Groups may do this for a variety of different reasons, and those forming a network around a given statement may have conflicting views and aims in other respects. Decisions as to what is "truth" or "fact" may result from strange coalitions, unholy alliances and historic compromises. Thus, while policy issues themselves give rise to a "demand for facts", how this demand is satisfied is a question concerning the organization of disciplines and professions, and of the relationship between these and the modern state.

The unemployment and health debate began when some work by an American social scientist, Professor M. H. Brenner, was published in the influential medical journal *The Lancet* (Brenner 1979). Brenner's paper indicated the existence of a positive relationship between unemployment rates and mortality: mortality rates rise with increases in unemployment. These findings were used to exert political pressure. This took a number of forms. First, Brenner's work was used as the basis for articles in the medical and epidemiological journals warning that the rapid increase in unemployment would lead to unanticipated costs in terms of ill-health and even death. Then Granada Television's "World in Action" series devoted a programme to the topic of the effect of unemployment upon health, giving Brenner a direct media platform. This was followed by questions and debates in Parliament sufficiently embarrassing for a new government seeking to justify tough monetary policies to commission some expert advice (Bartley 1992). The work of Brenner, which was already in use by social scientists teaching medical sociology and public health, was then subjected to extensive critique. First, several problems concerning his methods were pointed out (Gravelle et al. 1981). A British government study produced findings suggesting that unemployment has no effect on health (Ramsden & Smee 1981; Moylan et al. 1984). Several British research groups then entered the debate, using methods which were less open to the methodological criticisms aimed at the American research. However, when the largest and most sophisticated British study, which suggested that there is an independent effect of unemployment on mortality risk, was published in 1987 by Kath Moser and colleagues (Moser et al. 1987), there was hardly any response, either academic or political. While this finding has never been refuted explicitly, academic papers continue to appear which are written as if it had never been reported. Discussions of policy issues such as the level of unemployment benefits, or the availability of retraining, make no reference to health. Even more surprising is the fact that, in an era when unemployment is once again high in the UK, there has been no revival of the debate.

Understanding the relationship between research and policy is the same problem as understanding the construction of knowledge in general. The strength of taking such an approach is that *all* knowledge creation is seen as being linked *essentially* to policy debates in their widest sense. Barnes (1982, 168) has pointed out that:

knowledge does not have inherent implications . . . scientific theories do not arrive . . . with instruction books attached . . . Cognitively there is no fundamental distinction to be drawn between the creation of a scientific theory and its subsequent application.

The study on which this chapter draws treats the debate on the health effects of unemployment as a "social problem process". For the exponents of this idea, social problems are not in themselves self-evident states of affairs but rather the outcome of activities, which Malcolm Spector and John E. Kitsuse (1979, 72–3) term "claims-making". A primary task of the researcher in this field is therefore to examine how some situation or condition is defined and asserted to be a "social problem", and how collective activity is organized around these definitions and assertions: "The central problem of a theory of social problems is to account for the emergence, nature, and maintenance of claims-making and responding activities" (Spector and Kitsuse 1979, 76). The social problem analyst is not concerned with whether or not "condition x" even exists. Rather, s/he must analyze the discourse on the existence of the problem as "factual claims-making" and the moral discourse as "value claims-making". Factual and value claims are interwoven throughout the career of the problem. Spector and Kitsuse propose four "phases" in the career of a social problem. Stage 1 is when a group or groups point to the existence of some condition (a factual claim), indicate that it is undesirable in some way (a value claim), and attempt to promote it to a higher position on the agenda of public and political debate. In stage 2, some official organization or institution recognizes the "truth" of the knowledge-claim, or at least begins an official investigation to clarify the claim, and begins to formulate an official "policy response". In stage 3, the original groups declare themselves unsatisfied with official response, and the "policy failure" or "cover-up" becomes a new "problem claim". Finally, in stage 4, claims-making groups abandon their attempt to satisfy their grievances and/or to resolve the asserted problem through official channels and begin to develop "alternative, parallel, or counter-institutions".

The research procedure which Spector and Kitsuse advocate consists of investigating the claims-making strategies of all the groups engaged in a social problem process; these may include a wide variety of professions, pressure groups, "moral crusaders", official agencies and the media. A critical elaboration of this approach as it can be applied to the British policy process is offered by Manning (1985). Like Spector and Kitsuse, Manning takes a "developmental" approach, and focuses on the process of claims-making rather than on the question of "whether the problem really exists". To Spector and Kitsuse's stages, Manning adds a possible "loop" back from the third to the second stage (an example of this would be the setting up of a Royal Commission). He observes that "Group claims can get stuck in this loop and disappear" (Manning 1985, 9–10). He also adds the concept of "individualization" of social problems – "moral fragmentation"- and highlights the importance of the ways in which certain problem areas come to be defined as being exclusively the domain of "experts" (see Nelkin 1975) – "technical fragmentation". Both moral and technical fragmentation accompany the progress of problem-claims through the four stages elaborated by Spector and Kitsuse. However, "the state" as a "site of conflicts and struggle" over the allocation of goods and services is also involved. Claims upon the state for goods and services are made by pressure groups of various kinds, and here the analysis of J. J. Richardson and A. G. Jordan (1979) is a useful addition to the social problem model. Richardson and Jordan go so far as to argue that, in the course of social problem processes, "There is a breaking-down of conceptual distinctions between government, agencies and pressure groups; an interpenetration of departmental and client groups" (Richardson & Jordan 1979, 44). They contend that officials and pressure groups are to some extent symbiotic. An important reason for this was spoken of by participants in the unemployment and health debate described here: the need for an official wishing to carve out a "career" to be seen to initiate and/or promote a successful programme or innovation. Contact with pressure groups and "dissident" academics can be a good source of "bright ideas", and these, when used with skill and discretion, can benefit officials' careers.

Richardson and Jordan (1979, 90) offer their own version of the "stages model" of a social problem process. In this model, prominence is given to two additional "stages": first, the "dramatic event" which alerts the public to the issue; and, second, the "decline of public interest" which sets in once the high cost of "solving" the problem has been realized. They dismiss the idea that the policy agenda is set by pressure groups and interest groups openly lobbying the legislature: "Campaigns are the currency of unsuccessful groups; permanent relationships are the mode of the successful" (Richardson & Jordan 1979, 123).

"Social problem processes" are thus central to policy-making, and usually involve the making of both knowledge-claims and value-claims by various groups pursuing a range of interests. Each process may go on to give rise either to new facts or new policies, or both, or neither. But in many cases, it is the success of value claims in changing policy which leads to the acceptance of knowledge-claims as fact, rather than the other way round. The investigator needs therefore to keep an open mind about the direction of influence. Keeping such an open mind is one of the basic methodological principles of recent approaches to the social study of science. The difference between these approaches and the conventional model of the research-policy relationship can be illustrated by looking at two recent accounts provided by Timothy Booth (1988) and Barbara Tizard (1990).

Alternative models of the research–policy relationship

From the perspective of a distinguished research career, Tizard (1990) has written a comprehensive summary of opinions on how research influences policy. Drawing on the work of Carol Weiss (see, for example, Weiss 1979), Tizard lists four alternative models of the relationship: linear, problem-solving, political and enlightenment. The linear model, according to Weiss, best describes the relationship between basic research in the natural sciences and technological development. Most commentators agree that this is not an appropriate model for social research. The model which sees knowledge as being produced in response to policy-makers' specific needs is also dismissed: policy-makers do not, in fact, await the outcomes of studies before taking action (or deciding not to). The third model discussed by Tizard is the political model, which, she points out, may masquerade as a "problem-solving" one; here the policy-maker or customer commissions research which they know will support a decision to do what they had already decided upon. Under this heading falls the type of "cosmetic" research held to be commissioned by government departments when it is expedient to be able to say "research is being done" (as part of the "loop" phase in the social problem process). Lastly, Tizard chooses for discussion Weiss's notion of an "enlightenment" model: "That is, the new conceptualizations of an issue that emerge from research trickle and percolate through to both policy makers and the general public, challenging taken for granted assumptions and creating an 'agenda for concern'" (Tizard 1990, 437).

Finding none of these explanations to be fully satisfactory, Tizard moves on to discuss why it is that some studies have an impact on policy, in whatever way this impact might be conceptualized. One explanation that has been put forward is that new knowledge is more likely to be applied in policy areas where decision-making is more centralized. But Tizard feels this notion is thrown into serious doubt by the case of recent developments in British educational policy. Her experience also renders "very implausible" the idea that studies have impact because of their technical quality. She finally proposes a model in which, for every area of social policy, there are a series of crucial "gateways" through which research findings must go if they are to make an impact. Two important examples are the quality press and broadcasting. There are also "ideological gateways". Tizard concludes that there has to be some degree of match between the ideology of the researcher and the guardians of the gateways.

In Booth's account of the relationship between research and policy, the linear or, as he terms it, "purist" model is also contrasted with a "problem-solving" model. The first, in his view, "holds simply that research generates knowledge that impels action . . . [and is] firmly grounded in a rational view of the policy-making process," while in the second, "it is policy rather than theory that disciplines the research" (Booth 1988, 239).

Both Booth's and Tizard's definition of "problem-solving" models refer to the situation in which the customer devises the research needs, and the research practitioner carries out the necessary studies. Booth draws parallels with engineering research and development. Research and its applications are related in this model in a purely rational manner. In the case of social policy, such a model would lead us to expect that when policy failure leads to the demand for improvement, research is used to determine how best to proceed, and new policy is based upon the research findings. Booth goes on to list the standard criticisms of these rationalistic models: that research is often used to legitimate policies which would have been implemented in any case; that policy-makers use research selectively to vindicate existing states of affairs; that research is merely decorative; and that it is used to head off the need for action of any kind. He argues that the policy-making process is, in any case, not sufficiently clear-cut for anyone to be able to isolate an individual who makes a final decision. It is therefore futile to search for definitive signs of "the research influence".

Alongside the rationalist and problem-solving models of the research–policy relationship, Booth puts his own version of the *political model* in which:

> The policy process comprises different groups, with different interests, in pursuit of different ends [and] research becomes entangled in the political debate between these constituencies . . . For policy research to exert any influence it must inevitably be embedded in political struggle . . . In this process researchers act as *partisans for the value of their research* (Booth 1988, 244–5) (italics added).

In other words, researchers who influence policy debate are those who set out to do so.

Investigating "the politics of research" is potentially of great importance to social policy (Parker 1983). In the process of studying the interplay between social science and social policy, "utilization" cannot be seen as a one-way process (Rein 1980 & 1983). For example:

> there are no facts about unemployment . . . that are independent of the policy considerations that inform them . . . the analytic concepts are themselves policy concepts . . . the challenge is not linking research to policy but uncovering the latent policies which organize the empirical research (Rein 1980, 366–7).

It is important to add to this the shifting and negotiable nature of the "latent policies" themselves. According to commentators such as Charles Lindblom (1979), a form of dialogue may take place in which providers of information negotiate with policy-makers over the very definition of "policy needs" themselves. Eventually, the process may lead on to a mutually satisfactory account of "the facts", and a solution which will be implemented. Lindblom terms this process "partisan mutual adjustment". The interactive relationships discussed by Martin Rein and Lindblom, and the "partisan" approach recommended by both Booth and Tizard, have implications for understanding research itself as being tied-in with policy debates: the very "facts" themselves may be the outcome of the overall processes of mutual accommodation between all parties, scientists included. However, these approaches all somewhat underemphasize the micro-political activism undertaken by many scientists, regardless of their policy orientations at the macro level. Latour sums up the relationship between science and its applications in the following way:

Speaking about theories and then gaping at their "application" has no more sense than talking of clamps without ever saying what they fasten together . . . every time you hear about a successful application of science, look for the progressive extension of a network. Every time you hear about a failure of science, look for what part of which network has been punctured (Latour 1987, 242).

And furthermore:

We know that these networks are not built with homogeneous material but, on the contrary, necessitate the weaving together of a multitude of different elements which renders the question of whether they are "scientific" or "technical" or "economic" or "political" or "managerial" meaningless (Latour 1987, 232).

For sociologists of science, the networks in question include all the parties to what are thought of as the "issue communities" of a modern polity: political parties, professions, bureaucracies of both state and private industry. Latour gives us a graphic picture of the process "in action":

before the boss [of the laboratory] enters his office, the Minister of Health is still uncertain whether or not it is worth investing in neuroendocrinology; the boss is uncertain whether or not the minister will keep the promise . . . about funding a new laboratory; he is also uncertain as to whether or not . . . firm promises can be made . . . about [his newly invented substance] curing drug addicts . . . It is possible that the . . . drug addicts, the boss, the counsellors, the Minister and the Congressmen will all become aligned with one another so that, in the end, laboratory work has a bearing on health policy (Latour 1987, 176).

Which, according to Bartley, could be paraphrased as follows:

Before the Director of the Unemployment and Health Study enters his office, the Minister for Health is uncertain whether or not it is worth investing any more money in the study . . . The Director is uncertain whether any firm promises can be made that the study can reliably distinguish between those forms of health behaviour which are due to the social conditions of the unemployed and those which can safely be attributed to attitudes open to change by better targeted health education and therefore regarded as within the scope of politically feasible policy measures . . . It is possible that . . . the Director, the Minister, his Advisors, and the data from the Unemployment and health study and other studies will all become aligned with one another so that, in the end, the work of the study has a bearing on social policy (Bartley 1992).

Latour demonstrates by a rich collection of case studies that this possibility of alignment is a fragile one: it is an "accident prone process".

Studying the unemployment and health debate

In the study which forms the basis of this chapter, the objective was to "go behind" the public statements of the controversy on unemployment and health in order to look at the process of alignment (or non-alignment), whereby research findings either do or do not become relevant to social policy.

What was the "social map" which lay before potential participants in the early days of the unemployment and health debate? What were the aims and objectives of the most active participants? What kinds of alliance and enrolment could have appeared possible? Concentrating on the scientists rather more closely, we see them engaged in ongoing processes of knowledge construction, and can examine how "the health of the unemployed" fitted into these. Within this perspective, the debate can be re-examined as a series of attempts by the different individuals and groups involved to advance their own positions by creating and holding together networks of allies. It was the fate of these attempts that affected ideas about both "knowledge" and "policy". The aim of the study of the unemployment and health debate on which this chapter draws was not to make judgements about the "correctness" or "incorrectness" of the claims stated in the debate, but rather to trace the ways in which, as part of their own occupational and micro-political strategies, groups in the scientific and trans-scientific environment of the researchers adopted or opposed knowledge claims, or instead adopted a "wait and see" position.

In order to see how this process developed into the "UK unemployment and health debate", it is necessary to examine three sets of circumstances: the changes in the position of public health medicine, changes in the funding of research in social medicine, and the way in which government departments commissioned and carried out research on social questions in the UK in the late 1970s and the 1980s.

Professions, administrators and scientists

In the 1970s and 1980s a series of profound changes were taking place in what was called "community medicine" at the beginning of the period, and is now (once again) called public health medicine. Some of these changes were intended to rationalize public expenditure on health, and others produced a form of knowledge appropriate to this rationalization. During the early 1970s, there was an increasing emphasis on the need for planning, evaluation, efficiency and cost effectiveness, both in health and in other areas of public administration, in response to what had come to be seen as runaway growth in government expenditure. This emphasis on planning gave rise in turn to perceived needs for different kinds of information about the health and welfare of the population and about the provision of services, and for new types of expert to collect and analyze this information. In particular, there was increasing dissatisfaction with the clinical judgement of individual doctors being the determinant of spending on health care. This situation opened an opportunity for other professional or disciplinary groups to make claims to a different, non-clinical form of expertise in the health field. Practitioners of public health medicine could seek an important rôle by developing links with the planning and administration of health services, as part of the drive toward rationalization of the state sector which took place in the late 1960s and early 1970s. There was, however, another powerful group with ambitions to fill this position. This was health economics. Although not the same type of profession as medicine, and in some ways less powerful, the position of economics in the UK was, and is, strengthened by the dominance of economists as professional advisers to governments.

The first stage of the debate, in terms of the model of the social problem process, was initiated by "community medicine". The work of Brenner was brought to public notice by a group of "radicals" within this professional group. They were reacting to profound changes in the rôle of public health medicine following the 1970 reorganization of local authority health and social services, and the 1974 reorganization of the NHS. Effectively, these two changes stripped public health medicine of its "empire", and reduced its status considerably. Some regarded the work of community physicians as being in danger of becoming little more than administration, far removed from a concern with "the health of the community" in any real sense. Community physicians hoped to regain a position of greater importance by pointing out that policies adopted by governments could have hidden costs – health costs – which only public health doctors could understand and with which only they could deal. (At an international level, we can see a similar idea in the notion of "intersectoral" health work advocated by the World Health Organization (WHO).) The effect of unemployment on health was a good vehicle for this kind of argument.

Brenner's claims that unemployment levels affected health were promoted by a group of public health doctors, and picked up by the media. This gave rise to considerable political concern, and to a search for scientific backing for an opposite view. It is striking that in the debate on unemployment and health, all of the major papers which claimed that there was no danger to health were written by economists. In terms of the "social problem stages model" described above, the economists provided the "official response". It became clear that the economists were

Queuing to collect unemployment benefit (Crispin Hughes/Photofusion).

not interested centrally in community health issues; this debate was a "sideline" for them. But at the same time, they were making a series of advances into the territory of health planning, with some degree of success.

The major players in the debate were public health doctors and health economists. However, members of these groups were responsible for little original research on the question. This was done mainly by social scientists and statisticians working in independent research units funded by the UK Medical Research Council (MRC). The most rigorous research on unemployment and health was carried out by a group of demographers and social statisticians with close links to the government, using official government data taken from censuses and death registration records. These data were obtained from the Longitudinal Study based at the Office of Population Censuses and Surveys (OPCS). In order to see why this research group has become involved in the debate, it is necessary to take a step back and look briefly at what was happening to government research at this time.

Government and research in the 1980s

During the period of the unemployment and health debate, the position of statisticians within government departments appeared to many to be becoming weaker. This was partly due to the so-called Rayner Review of the Government Statistical Service (GSS). The atmosphere in 1979–80 can be contrasted to that of the mid- and late 1960s. In the earlier period, the prevailing assumption was that more information led to better planning, and there was considerable growth in the numbers of professional staff employed by the government. In contrast, the emphasis by 1980 was on the burden to businesses of having to collect so many statistics. Ministers were saying that businesses wasted too much time filling out forms rather than getting on with production. The Rayner Review concentrated on the cost of statistics, and the management of this work within individual government departments. As a result of the review, it was announced that the GSS was to be cut by some 25 per cent between May 1979 and April 1984. The subsequent efficiency reviews affected deeply the statisticians working inside government departments, particularly in OPCS (the government body which carries out censuses and registers births and deaths in England and Wales). There was a perceived need to demonstrate more vigorously the value of the kind of information-linkage studies made possible by a combination of the way the OPCS was organized, and new computing and information-handling technology. Examining links between employment and mortality was a perfect example of this. But why were the statisticians so happy to report findings which ran counter to government policy?

The answer to this lies in the value placed by professional statisticians on the integrity of their work. The Rayner Review had put the issue of "professional integrity" high on the agenda of debate both inside and outside Whitehall. As well as being civil servants, government statisticians have undergone specialist training which encompasses not only the transfer of skills, but also of values. Accuracy and objectivity are part of their professional ideology. In addition, there is a more general notion of "public service" which is common to many professions. In this way, the statisticians shared an ideology with medicine, rather than economics. Les Metcalfe and Sue Richards comment:

> members of the GSS felt the quality of statistics reflected on their professional integrity, that wider issues of the public interest were involved in the quality of statistical work undertaken and that statisticians were ultimately the only people qualified to judge this. (Metcalfe & Richards 1987, 127)

There were thus three groups seeking a more prominent rôle in the health planning process, at a time when health planning questions were high on government agendas. Those disciplines whose members claimed that unemployment *did* affect health were the more threatened ones (social/medical statistics), and the professional group with whom they allied (community medicine) was similarly threatened by successive rounds of NHS reorganization. Economists, in contrast, who tended to argue that unemployment *did not* affect health, had relatively well established alliances with policy-makers in government departments. Some were also quietly pursuing a long-term strategy of enrolling factions within the medical profession, by offering economics as the key discipline for management of the reorganized health service.

We come next to the question as to what accounts for the involvement of "pure researchers" in the debate. This was simply a matter of opportunity. Once again, we need to look at changes in the relationship between government and researchers. The late 1970s had also seen a reorientation towards efficiency and customer-relevance in research (the so-called "Rothschild principle"). Medical research units came under pressure to do work which was less dominated by internal criteria ("curiosity-driven research") and more influenced by the needs of customers, which included, increasingly, the government. It was therefore not too difficult to get funding for such a policy-relevant topic as the health of the unemployed. This did not mean that outside researchers, any more than the statisticians, produced answers which they thought the government wanted to hear: in fact, all the research carried out in independent units suggested that unemployment *did* affect health (particularly heart disease and suicidal behaviour). The customer–contractor principle did, however, mean that the research was done in a hurry, using data from studies which had not been designed to investigate this question.

Where independent researchers differed from economists and from government statisticians was in their relationship to pressure groups. Some researchers participated in pressure group activity, as did some public health professionals. It was especially the participation of the public health doctors in political pressure-group activity which placed the health of the unemployed on the political agenda, and thereby gave rise to a demand for research. For the public health professionals, the unemployment and health debate was far more important than an attempt to discover more facts about the determinants of community health. They intended to use the issue alongside others to show that wider social policies should not be decided without an input from medical experts. Only if this was done would policy-makers know the full impact of their decisions.

Fragile knowledge

During the long period of time needed to produce research results, the situation of the public health profession changed. Its status was increased by further reorganizations of the NHS, during which public health doctors began to develop a new empire based around health education and health promotion ("healthy cities"), and the measurement of health need and resource allocation. The appearance of AIDS may also have played a part in this. New posts of Director of Pubic Health became available, similar to the rôle of the Medical Officer in the interwar period. These changes made "unemployment and health" less interesting to public health doctors. As it had been public health doctors who had led the most determined of the pressure groups concerned with the issue, the activity of these groups soon flagged as well. And even if health promotion and health education officers had continued to press the case, the absence of "real doctors" as spokespersons on the issue would have greatly reduced its media impact. Once the pressure groups had lost interest in the question of the health of the unemployed, the impact of research commissioned during the period of high political activity was almost completely lost.

These considerations identify the fragility of many claims arising from research as the *consequence* of the strategic regrouping of those involved in the policy-related scientific debates. The claims made by the most prominent researchers were dropped by the rest of the policy community, but not because conclusive evidence against these claims had accumulated. The new ideas which emerged were not discredited; they were merely abandoned, left in the twilight world or "limbo" phase which some have regarded as being typical of the social problem process. Michael McCarthy (1986) has suggested that one reason why social problem processes enter the "fourth stage" of a "twilight world of lesser attention and spasmodic recurrences of interest" is to be found in the "dilettantism [of] those who simply become bored and disenchanted by the issue and passively await the arrival of a new . . . issue". Here, "those" include ministers, civil servants, academics and journalists, as well as "middle-class do-gooders" who "flippantly desert" issues, leaving them "largely unresolved" (McCarthy 1986, 100–104).

However, we can perhaps go beyond a concept of "dilettantism" in explaining why expert groups abandon social problems. Academics, for example, must enrol resource-holders if they wish to acquire the funds to do research of any kind. Secondly, questions about the degree of "pressure" applied to unruly experts have to be addressed. Only a fine line divides the ability to "see what the customer wants" from "government suppression of research", and some material in the unemployment and health debate case study did indicate that certain researchers felt under considerable pressure to abandon work on the effects of social inequality and unemployment on health. The spirit of routinely "moving on to the next thing" influenced some who decided to drop unemployment and health as a topic, but others were, by 1987, discouraged to the point of feeling a sense of "depression" and futility, which, they feared, was affecting their intellectual productivity. Thus, "dilettantism" would offer a rather simplified picture of the way in which unemployment and health faded as an issue of interest to researchers; any dilettantism or opportunism that was evident must be regarded as being institutional in nature.

The final question that might be asked is why labour movement organizations representing the unemployed, or the "poverty lobby", were so little concerned with the debate about the relationship between unemployment and health. One answer is provided by Jean Seaton (1986) in a study of the media reporting of unemployment issues. She found that as unemployment increased during the 1980s, its news value tended to fall. Her study of coverage in *The Times* showed an "inverse relationship between the percentage of the population out of work and the front page attention given to the subject" (Seaton 1986, 19). One journalist, commenting on the failure of the Labour Party to take up the policy implications of research on suicide and attempted suicide in unemployed men, remarked that, in addition to this, unemployment and suicidal behaviour was "too big" an issue for a political party. Opposition politicians look for issues over which they can demonstrate quickly the superiority of their own policies.

By late 1984, a government minister had admitted publicly that unemployment was probably bad for health. But the attitude of professional advisers to the government was to stand in terror, almost, at the enormity of what it entailed. This was reflected in a *Lancet* leading article of November 1984, which, perhaps unintentionally, highlighted the contrast between the (relatively) minute sums that could be spent on even the most expensive research, and what would be necessary to tackle the underlying problem of mass unemployment.

A second reason for the failure of labour groups to take up the unemployment and health debate might be something to do with "moral fragmentation". This term is used to refer to the process by which a problem facing a social group comes to be defined as a consequence of the personal characteristics of individual members of that group. To understand how this may have affected the unemployed requires knowledge of how the British labour market operates. There may be a concrete reason for the reduction of interest in unemployment. As the economists who took part in the debate (Stern 1979, for example) and some other social scientists who kept their distance (Sinfield 1981, Hakim 1982) were aware, the British labour market is "segmented". Low pay and the risk of unemployment are concentrated in certain sectors of industry and particular regions. By 1983–4, the pattern of unemployment was one of increasing

inequality of distribution: that is, the risk of unemployment was, if anything, more concentrated within social classes IV and V than it had been
in the mid-1970s (Sinfield 1987), and not even throughout these social
classes, but in certain segments within them. There were grounds for
thinking that this tendency had become even stronger as unemployment
rose and then stabilized at new heights. Long-term unemployment rose
far more than short-term, that is, it was not that a lot more people were
experiencing short periods of joblessness, but rather that a slightly larger
number than previously were experiencing much longer spells. As more
of the total amount of unemployment was experienced by the same people, either as long-term spells without work or as a life "in and out of
work", those in steady jobs had every reason to feel less personally preoc-
cupied by what unemployment might do to them if it struck. The concentration of unemployment made it easier for "the unemployed" to be
regarded as a certain type of person, different from the "ordinary" or
"normal", with personal characteristics which explained their plight.
When unemployment stabilized and then fell after 1986, this tendency
was strengthened. However, when unemployment began to rise again,
and to strike more at white-collar and professional workers in the early
1990s, there was no revival of the debate. This highlights the importance
of the rôle of entrepreneurial professions in the creation of "social problems" – economic trends in themselves do not seem to be decisive.

As labour market trends became clearer, it was less and less likely that
labour organizations would ever be included in a debate on the health of
the unemployed (although they did begin to take up the question of the
pay and conditions of workers in the "secondary labour market"). At the
same time, sociologists were showing that there was a growth in the proportion of the labour force employed in low-paid, part-time, and/or
intermittent forms of work (Fevre 1986, 1987; Harris 1987). Unions organizing unskilled and service-sector workers, as well as some industrial
and urban sociologists, could have been "enrolled" by those researchers
who believed there were important health consequences to recession,
and who wrote of "residualization", as did John Fox (1986; see also
Moser et al. 1987; Platt 1986). But there are notorious difficulties in sus-
taining any form of "enrolment" between reforming groups and the
"unskilled" working class, the unemployed, or other consumers of social
welfare services (Hall et al. 1978, 91; see also Ditch 1986).

Once the public health doctors, together with ancillary groups such as
health educators and health promoters, lost interest in the question of the

health of unemployed people, there were no other groups waiting to take it up. There was no-one to write press releases putting complex research into language more accessible to the popular media, or to explain them to government officials or parliamentarians. And once it was no longer a political hot potato, unemployment and health no longer motivated government departments to persuade scientifically respectable groups to devote resources to such a "mundane" topic.

Conclusion

The analysis provided in this chapter follows recent advances in the sociology of science and technology in Britain using the so-called "Strong programme" in the sociology of knowledge (Cameron & Edge 1979, Mackenzie 1981), and in France following the "translation" perspective in the social study of science and technology (Latour 1984, 1987). These perspectives stress the importance to the construction of knowledge of the macro- and micro-political contexts in which research is located. How are the agendas for scientists set, and by whom? What decides which projects will receive the backing of funding bodies and powerful groups? Adherents of the "Strong programme" claim that such influences go to the very heart of science. The "translation programme" stresses the intricacy of the interweaving interests involved, and sees scientists as entrepreneurial advocates of their own approaches and methods, searching constantly for possible customers. In the case study described here, the rise in unemployment created an opportunity for one professional group, the public health doctors, to advance a claim to a more important rôle. In turn, this created a new market for the skills of the demographers and social statisticians. The "government response" then created yet another opportunity, which was taken up by economists. A situation of rivalry between these groups of scientists then created a field of technical competition, using both data and methods in new ways. However, subsequent changes in both the macroeconomic climate and the institutional situation of public health meant that the "new knowledge" which emerged was very fragile and not universally accepted.

The evidence presented about the social processes behind the unemployment and health debate has some rather serious implications. In the first place, it draws attention to the ways in which political administration influences deeply the very questions which scientists are drawn to ask, and the data they have available to answer them. But, secondly, the type of process that characterized the unemployment and health debate does not only go on in cases where the topic of inquiry is so obviously "political". The extent to which unemployment may damage health and increase mortality risk has even now not been fully investigated, despite technical advances in medical and population statistics which the debate itself made possible. Many people had great sympathy with the move to make medical research in the UK more relevant to policy questions. But the central issue is: whose policy questions are they? If the scientific agenda is itself deeply affected by policy debate (and it would be surprising if it were not so), then this raises the question of the public involvement or "democratization" of science policy. A substantial amount of research in medical sociology shows the value to the understanding of disease processes of the "lay knowledge" of people who suffer from long-term chronic diseases. Epidemiology may be criticized for ignoring the possibility that communities may possess an understanding of their own conditions and situations which research ignores at its peril. In the UK, at least, it seems that the increased involvement of the government in the organization and funding of research may be closing off the possibilities for a more adequate understanding of the social determinants of health.

References

Barnes, B. 1982. The science–technology relationship: a model and a query. *Social Studies of Science* **12**, 166–72.

Bartley M. 1992. *Authorities and partisans: the debate on unemployment and health*. Edinburgh: Edinburgh University Press.

Booth, T. 1988. *Developing policy research*. Aldershot: Avebury.

Brenner, M. H. 1979. Mortality and the national economy: a review and the experience of England and Wales 1936–1976. *Lancet* **ii**, 568–73.

Cameron, I. & D. Edge 1979. *Scientific images and their social uses*. London: Butterworth.

Ditch, J. 1986. The undeserving poor: unemployed people, then and now. In *The state or the market*, M. Loney (ed.). London: Sage.

Fevre, R. 1986. Redundancy and the labour market. In *Redundancy, layoffs and plant closures*, R. M. Lee (ed.). London: Croom Helm.

Fevre, R. 1987. Subcontracting in steel. *Work, Employment and Society* **1**, 509–27.

Fox, A. J. 1986. *Socio-demographic origins and consequences of unemployment: a study of changes in individuals' characteristics between 1971 and 1981*. London: Social

Statistics Research Unit, City University, mimeo.

Gillespie, B., D. Eva, R. Johnson 1979. Carcinogenic risk assessment in the United States and Great Britain: the case of aldrin/dieldrin. *Social Studies of Science* **9**, 265–301.

Gravelle, H. S. E., J. Hutchinson, J. Stern. 1981. Mortality and unemployment: a critique of Brenner's time-series analysis. *Lancet* **ii**, 675–9.

Hakim, C. 1982. The social consequences of high unemployment. *Journal of Social Policy* **11**, 433–67.

Hall, P., H. Land, R. Parker, A. Webb 1978. *Change, choice and conflict in social policy*. London: Heinemann.

Harris, C. C. 1987. *Redundancy and recession in South Wales*. Oxford: Basil Blackwell.

Knorr-Cetina, K. 1981. *The manufacture of knowledge: an essay in the constructivist and contextual nature of science*. Oxford: Pergamon.

Latour, B. 1984. *Les microbes: guerre et paix*. Paris: Editions Metailie, Collection Pandore. Published in English as *The pasteurization of French society*. Harvard: Harvard University Press. 1987.

Latour, B. 1987. *Science in action*. Milton Keynes: Open University Press.

Lindblom, C. 1979. Still muddling, not yet through. *Public Administration Review* **39**, 517–26.

Mackenzie, D. 1981. *Statistics in Britain 1865–1930: the social construction of scientific knowledge*. Edinburgh: Edinburgh University Press.

Manning, N. 1985. *Social problems and welfare ideology*. London: Gower.

McCarthy, M. 1986. *Campaigning for the poor*. London: Croom Helm.

Metcalfe, L. & S. Richards 1987. *Improving public management*. London: Sage.

Moser, K. A., P. O. Goldblatt, A. J. Fox, D. R. Jones 1987. Unemployment and mortality 1981–83: follow-up of the 1981 Census sample. *British Medical Journal* **294**, 86–90.

Moylan, S., J. Millar, R. Davies 1984. *For richer, for poorer: DHSS cohort study of unemployed men*. London: HMSO.

Nelkin, D. 1975. The political impact of technical expertise. *Social Studies of Science* **5**, 35–54.

Parker, R. 1983. Research and the politics of comparison. In *Improving social intervention*, J. Gandy, A. Robertson, S. Sinclair (eds). Edinburgh: Edinburgh University Press.

Platt, S. 1986. Parasuicide and unemployment (annotation). *British Journal of Psychiatry* **149**, 401–5.

Ramsden, S. & C. Smee 1981. The health of unemployed men: DHSS cohort study. *Employment Gazette* **89**, 397–401.

Rein, M. 1980. Interplay between social science and social policy. *International Social Science Journal* **32**, 361–8.

Rein, M. 1983. *From policy to practice*. New York: M. E. Sharpe.

Richardson, J. J. & A. G. Jordan (1979) *Governing under pressure*. Oxford: Martin Robertson.

Seaton, J. 1986. The media and the politics of interpreting unemployment. In *The experience of unemployment*, S. Allen. A. Waton, K. Purcell, S. Wood (eds). London: Macmillan.

Sinfield, R. A. 1981. *What unemployment means*. Oxford: Martin Robertson.

Sinfield, R. A. 1987. Unemployment experience and policy response in overseas countries. Paper presented to Conference on income support and labour market change, Department of Social Security, Canberra, Australia.

Spector, M. & J. Kitsuse 1979. *Constructing social problems*. Menlo Park, California: Cummings.

Stern, J. 1979. Who bears the burden of unemployment? In *Slow growth in Britain*, W. Beckermann (ed.). Oxford: Clarendon Press.

Tizard, B. 1990. Research and policy: is there a link? *The Psychologist* **10**, 435–40.

Weiss, C. 1979. The many meanings of research utilization. *Public Administration Review* **39**, 426–32.

Index

223